D1738262

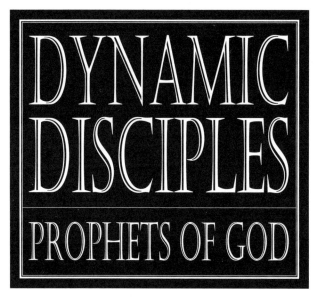

DYNAMIC DISCIPLES
PROPHETS OF GOD

LIFE STORIES OF THE PRESIDENTS
OF THE CHURCH OF JESUS CHRIST
OF LATTER-DAY SAINTS

FRANCIS M. GIBBONS

DESERET BOOK COMPANY
SALT LAKE CITY, UTAH

Library of Congress Cataloging-in-Publication Data

Gibbons, Francis M., 1921–
    Dynamic disciples, prophets of God: life stories of the presidents of The Church of Jesus Christ of Latter-day Saints / by Francis M. Gibbons.
        p.   cm.
    Includes bibliographical references and index.
    ISBN 1-57345-161-4 (hardcover)
    1. Church of Jesus Christ of Latter-day Saints—Presidents—Biography. 2. Mormon Church—United States—Presidents—Prophets. 3. Prophets (Mormon theology) I. Title.
    BX8693.G53   1996
    289.3'092'2—dc20
    [B]   96-19838
                                                              CIP

Printed in the United States of America

10   9   8   7   6   5   4   3   2   1

CONTENTS

CONTENTS

CHAPTER ONE

JOSEPH SMITH

Joseph Smith Jr., the fourth child and third son of Joseph Smith Sr. and Lucy Mack Smith, was born December 23, 1805, in Sharon, Windsor County, Vermont. Life was not easy for the Smith family. The marginal farm that Joseph Smith Sr. tilled was leased from his wife's father, Solomon Mack. Because his farming did not yield enough to support his family, he taught school in the off-season to cover the deficit.

What the Smiths lacked in material means was more than balanced by their spiritual wealth. Both parents were devout believers in the reality and the power of God. This was shown in the fervency of their prayers, the regularity of their Bible study, and the constancy of their Christian charities. Their religious convictions, based upon striking answers to prayers and, in the case of the father, remarkable visions, often were shared with the children as they matured. Such were the spiritual influences permeating the Smith household that young Joseph Smith later reported

1

that when he kneeled in prayer for answers to perplexing questions, he had no doubt God would hear and answer. His faith was firm and unyielding because of the teaching and the example of his parents.

In a futile search for economic security, Joseph Smith Sr. moved his family four times between 1805 and 1816. He operated leased farms at Tunbridge, Vermont; Royalton, Vermont; Lebanon, New Hampshire; and Norwich, Vermont. After three successive crop failures at Norwich, he decided to go to western New York, pursuing reports of fertile land available at affordable prices.

In New York the Smiths settled first in Palmyra. They remained there two years, living off the earnings of the father and the older sons, Alvin and Hyrum, who hired out as laborers. Their income was supplemented by the sale of painted oilcloth coverings Lucy made. By now there were eight living Smith children. A son, Ephraim, who was born in 1810, died in infancy. The family became active in the affairs of Palmyra, which was noted as a community of churches. Lucy and several of the children affiliated with the Presbyterian Church in Palmyra while young Joseph showed an interest in the local Methodist sect. He seems to have been attracted there by the preaching of a Reverend Lane, an articulate and charismatic man who was well schooled in the scriptures.

After two years, the father found a hundred-acre tract of wooded land near Manchester, New York, located about ten miles from Palmyra, which he was able to buy under contract. He and the older boys cleared thirty acres for farming and built a log cabin on the site. Later a substantial two-story home was constructed.

In the spring of 1820, a fervid religious revival came to the area. It was a recurring phenomenon, symptomatic of the times. This one was centered in Palmyra, and within an eight-mile radius were thirteen different religious congregations, including Quakers, Baptists, Presbyterians, and

Methodists. Caught up in the excitement, the Smith family traveled to Palmyra to attend some of the meetings. On one occasion young Joseph, who was confused by conflicting doctrines taught by the different sects, attended a revival meeting in the Methodist Church, where Reverend Lane addressed the subject "What church shall I join?" Among the scriptures the minister quoted was the first chapter of James, which admonishes those who lack wisdom to ask of God. Soon after, back home on the Smith farm, young Joseph, strongly impelled by the promise of James, decided to ask God for wisdom about which of the competing churches to join.

He retired to a grove of trees near the farmhouse where members of the family often went to pray. Kneeling, he began to pray vocally, the first time he had ever done so. Immediately he was seized by an evil power that temporarily bound his tongue and caused him to feel as if he were doomed. But by a powerful exertion of his will, Joseph held on, struggling in prayer, and the power was dispelled. At that moment, he saw a pillar of light over his head, "above the brightness of the sun," which descended until it fell upon him. He then saw two personages, "whose brightness and glory" defied all description, standing above him in the air. One addressed him by name and, pointing to the other, said, *"This is My Beloved Son. Hear Him!"* After regaining his composure, the boy asked which of the contending sects was right. He was told that none of them was right, that they were all wrong, and that he should join none of them. After telling him "many other things," the visitors ascended out of sight. When Joseph came to himself, he was lying on his back, completely drained of energy.

The boy shared this experience with his parents. They believed him implicitly. But when he told Reverend Lane about it, the minister scoffed, saying with contempt it was of the devil. The boy was hurt and humiliated because he had thought the preacher would be pleased to learn the

3

impact of his teaching and the truth of the scripture he had quoted from James.

The scornful attitude of Reverend Lane, and of others who learned about Joseph's experience, isolated young Joseph from the mainstream of the community. It was then he developed friendships with a group of boys his age. Typical of some teenagers, they were rowdy, sometimes impudent, and often insensitive to the feelings of others. After a while, Joseph felt condemned by this association, given the supernal nature of the experience he had enjoyed in the Sacred Grove. So on the evening of September 21, 1823, he knelt in prayer in his bedroom to acknowledge his "sins and follies" and to learn his status before God. As he prayed, a bright light filled the room, which became "lighter than at noonday." Immediately a personage appeared at his bedside, "standing in the air." After describing the general appearance of this personage arrayed in a robe of exquisite whiteness, Joseph added that the angel's "whole person was glorious beyond description, and his countenance truly like lightning."

After identifying himself as Moroni, the visitor told Joseph that God had a work for him to do, that there was a book written on gold plates giving an account of an ancient people who lived on the American continent, that with the book was an instrument called the Urim and Thummim to be used in translating it, and that the record would be given to him later to be translated. As the visitor spoke, a vision was opened to Joseph's mind and he could see the place where the plates were deposited. After quoting and explaining several scriptures from the Bible and giving other instructions, Moroni ascended from the room. To Joseph's surprise, the angel appeared two other times that night, rehearsing exactly what he had said before and then adding words of warning. The next day, he appeared to Joseph in the field, related all that was said before, and instructed him to tell his father what had happened. Later that day, following the advice of his father, Joseph went to the place shown him in a vision where the plates were buried. Prying up a large domed rock, he saw the plates and the Urim and Thummim in a stone box laid in cement. Moroni then appeared to him again, the fifth time in two days, and instructed him not to remove the plates but to return to the same place on the same day each year for four years.

Needing money for himself and his family, Joseph accepted employment with Josiah Stowel, a well-to-do farmer and entrepreneur of Chenango County, New York. At the time, Mr. Stowel was prospecting for an ancient mine in Susquehanna County, Pennsylvania, said to have been opened long ago by Spaniards. While engaged in this work, Joseph boarded at the home of Isaac Hale in Harmony, Pennsylvania. There he met the attractive Hale daughter, Emma, whom he later courted, then married on January 18, 1827, in nearby Bainbridge.

Word of Joseph's spiritual experiences followed him to Pennsylvania. Like Reverend Lane, most people rejected these stories as fabrications and regarded the young man as an impostor. Intense criticism of Joseph escalated when he would not recant but would persist in affirming the truth of his claims. This brought on a spiteful lawsuit in which Joseph was charged with being a disorderly person. It was dismissed for lack of evidence. Failing in this, Joseph's enemies sought to blacken his name by accusing him of being a "money digger" because of his employment with Mr. Stowel. This cruel lie followed Joseph throughout life.

At last Joseph received the gold plates, the Urim and Thummim, and the breastplate on September 22, 1827, from the angel Moroni. He was charged with responsibility to protect them and to show them to no one. Because of harrassing efforts to get the plates from him, Joseph took them and Emma to Harmony, Pennsylvania, in December, where the Hale family provided them with housing. By February 1828 he had copied and translated some inscriptions from the plates. These pages were given to Martin Harris, a prosperous farmer from Palmyra who, interested in Joseph's story, had offered help but wanted proof that Joseph was telling the truth. Mr. Harris took the inscriptions and the translation to Professor Charles Anthon of Columbia University. A statement from the professor satisfied Mr. Harris about the ancient character of the inscriptions and the accuracy of their translation. He therefore began to serve as Joseph's scribe.

Between April and June 1828, Joseph translated 116 pages of manuscript from the plates, with Martin Harris serving as scribe. Yielding to Martin's persistent nagging, Joseph allowed him to take the manuscript home so he could show it to his wife, who distrusted Joseph and objected to the help Martin had given him. She lost or destroyed the manuscript. Joseph was devastated. In a revelation he was rebuked for his lack of judgment, and the plates and the Urim and Thummim were taken from him. Although they were returned later in the summer, from then until April 1829 Joseph's translation work was at a standstill because he lacked a scribe. Through Joseph's fervent prayers, that lack was filled when Oliver Cowdery came to Harmony from Palmyra in early April. Oliver, a schoolteacher, had learned about the gold plates and Joseph's work in translating them. Moved by a spiritual impulse, he went to Harmony to visit Joseph and shortly after began to serve as his scribe.

With a reliable scribe, the Urim and Thummim, and Joseph's familiarity with inscriptions on the plates gained during nineteen months, the translation proceeded smoothly and was completed in less than ninety days. Separated from his scribe by a curtain, Joseph dictated while Oliver wrote in longhand. At the beginning of each day, Oliver read aloud the last words of the previous day's dictation. Joseph then picked up at that point and continued dictating, with no editing. Oliver's manuscript was unpunctuated. Therefore, except for added punctuation, spelling corrections, and division into chapters and books, the Book of Mormon as we now have it is essentially a first draft.

Written in reformed Egyptian, a hieroglyphic writing expressing Hebrew thought, the Book of Mormon is a record of three migrations of people from the Mideast to the American continent. It records God's dealings with these people, even as the Bible records God's dealings with people of the Eastern Hemisphere. The book relates, among other things, the appearance of Jesus Christ on the American continent and his ministry among some of the people there.

In the course of translation, Joseph and Oliver were intrigued by references to baptisms in the ancient record. Seeking additional understanding on the subject, they knelt and prayed to God. In response, John the Baptist, a resurrected being, appeared to them. The visitor conferred the Aaronic Priesthood upon them and instructed them to baptize each other, which they did. He also told them they would later be given authority to confer the Holy Ghost. This occurred weeks afterward when Peter, James, and John appeared and gave them the Melchizedek Priesthood.

During the course of translation, open opposition to Joseph at Harmony caused him to move to Fayette, New York, in company with Emma and Oliver. Here they lived with Peter Whitmer Sr., whose son David was Oliver Cowdery's friend. As the translation neared its end, John Whitmer replaced Oliver Cowdery as scribe while Oliver made a copy of the manuscript. The unhappy experience of the lost manuscript written by Martin Harris convinced Joseph Smith of the need to have a backup copy. Meanwhile, the truthfulness of Joseph's account of the origins and the appearance of the Book of Mormon plates was validated when three men—Oliver Cowdery, David Whitmer, and Martin Harris—were shown the gold plates by the angel

Moroni; and when eight men—Christian Whitmer, Jacob Whitmer, Peter Whitmer Jr., John Whitmer, Hiram Page, Joseph Smith Sr., Hyrum Smith, and Samuel H. Smith—were shown the plates by Joseph Smith Jr.

E. B. Grandin, a printer in Palmyra, was employed to publish the Book of Mormon. Martin Harris underwrote the cost. The first copies came off the press in March 1830.

Although Joseph and Oliver had performed a few baptisms, both in Harmony and near Fayette, they had never presumed to organize a church. Now, however, Joseph was instructed by revelation to do so (see Doctrine and Covenants 20). In obedience, a group gathered in the home of Peter Whitmer Sr. on April 6, 1830, at which time The Church of Jesus Christ of Latter-day Saints was officially organized. Of those present, six served as the legal organizers under the laws of New York: Joseph Smith Jr., Oliver Cowdery, Hyrum Smith, Peter Whitmer Jr., Samuel H. Smith, and David Whitmer. Afterward, those who had been baptized were confirmed members of the Church and were given the gift of the Holy Ghost. There followed a rich outpouring of the Spirit of God when "some prophesied, whilst [they] all praised the Lord, and rejoiced exceedingly."

Soon after the organization of the Church, Joseph went to Colesville, New York, not far from Harmony. There he stayed with his friend, Joseph Knight, while holding a series of meetings. By so doing, he was able to build up a branch there composed of his converts—the only time a Church unit was built up as the result of the direct teaching of the Prophet. The people in Colesville regarded this as such a distinction that they continued to identify themselves as the Colesville branch even when they later migrated to Missouri as a body. An outpouring of spiritual phenomena attended many of the meetings the Prophet held around Colesville. In one of them, the Prophet Joseph cast out an evil spirit from the body of his host's son, Newell Knight. This first miracle performed in the new Church created a great stir in the neighborhood and attracted many investigators who later became members.

The first general conference of the Church was held in Fayette, New York, in September 1830. During the conference the Prophet received a revelation instructing the Saints to gather together in one place (see Doctrine and Covenants 29:7–8). Later, in December 1830, Ohio was designated as the first gathering place (see Doctrine and Covenants 37). In another revelation received during the September general conference, Oliver Cowdery was instructed to preach the gospel to the Indians, called Lamanites (see Doctrine and Covenants 28:8). He left soon after in company with Peter Whitmer Jr., Parley P. Pratt, and Ziba Peterson. En route westward, the party stopped in Kirtland, Ohio, where Elder Pratt had once lived. Within three weeks, 127 converts were baptized. In a short time membership had swelled to several hundred.

Among the early converts were Sidney Rigdon and Edward Partridge, able and experienced men who were a generation older than Joseph Smith. Soon after their baptism, they traveled to Fayette to visit the young Prophet, the result being that Joseph and his family moved to Kirtland, Ohio, in January 1831. There Sidney Rigdon and Edward Partridge played key roles in the early development of the Church. Elder Rigdon served as Joseph Smith's scribe and associate in the translation of the Bible and later became his counselor in the First Presidency. Edward Partridge became the first bishop in the Church. They were typical of numerous other men who joined the Church in the early days— men who, though older and more experienced than Joseph, subordinated themselves to him and followed his direction.

The call of Edward Partridge as bishop in Kirtland was driven by the large influx of members from the eastern branches, many of whom were poor and in need of help. The bishop willingly left a thriving business to assume the immense task of caring for them. His call was the first step in the process of completing the administrative structure of the Church, accomplished through revelations given to the Prophet Joseph Smith. During 1832 and 1833, for instance, the Quorum of the First Presidency was organized and instructed (see Doctrine and Covenants 81; 90); and the Quorum of the Twelve and the First Quorum of Seventy were organized in February 1835 (see *History of the Church,* 2:180, 201–2).

Throughout the Kirtland period, Joseph Smith received numerous revelations that, along with others received before and afterward, were compiled and published as the Doctrine and Covenants of the Church. These revelations cover many matters of doctrine, procedure, instruction, prediction, warning, and explanation. Some were received through the Urim and Thummim or by vision, while others were dictated by Joseph as he received spiritual promptings or insights. Eyewitnesses reported that when a revelation was given by dictation, the Prophet spoke slowly enough that it could be recorded in longhand. The revelation stood as it was dictated, without editing. Some observers reported a subtle change in his appearance and facial expression while he dictated a revelation, denoting intense concentration and producing a kind of spiritual aura around him. During the Kirtland period, Joseph also translated an ancient Egyptian scroll pertaining to Abraham, which is now part of the Pearl of Great Price, the fourth of the standard works of the Church (Bible, Book of Mormon, Doctrine and Covenants, and Pearl of Great Price).

As Church membership escalated in and around Kirtland, many local residents became uneasy at the prospect of being dominated by the newcomers. Others were put off by Mormon beliefs in visions, revelations, and the appearance of heavenly beings. Still others, especially the ministerial class, were openly antagonistic as their flocks declined. These elements combined in the spring of 1832 to produce the first act of overt violence against Joseph Smith and the church he had organized. While he was a guest in the home of John Johnson at Hiram, Ohio, near Kirtland, he was dragged outside by a mob one Saturday night, stripped naked, beaten and scratched, then tarred and feathered. Helped by friends to clean up, he was able to speak at Sunday services the next day. But consequences to the family were tragic. One of the twins he and Emma had adopted after the death of their own twins became ill from exposure during the melee and died a few days later. It was a sad time for the Smiths, especially for Emma, who grieved over the loss of this adopted child and her own babies.

A sense of optimism came to the family and to the entire community a little more than a year later when construcution commenced on a temple in Kirtland. By revelation it was to be "a house of prayer, a house of fasting, a house of faith, a house of learning, a house of glory, a house of order, a house of God" (Doctrine and Covenants 88:119). Joseph Smith was the architect. His brother Hyrum was the chairman of the building committee. The master builder was Artemis Millett. Many skilled craftsmen found among the new converts helped in the construction. Brigham Young, for instance, supervised the inside plastering. The sandstone used in the walls, taken from a nearby quarry, was stuccoed. Sisters sacrificed some of their choice glassware, which was ground up and mixed with the stucco so that when the sun fell on the walls, they sparkled like jewels.

Great excitement stirred the community as preparations were completed for the dedication of the temple. It took place on March 27, 1836, as well as during several days thereafter, and was accompanied by spiritual outpourings likened to the Day of Pentecost. Heavenly beings appeared. Many of the members present spoke in tongues and prophesied. Later the Savior, Moses, Elias, and Elijah appeared in the temple. "I have accepted this house," said the Savior, "and my name shall be here; and I will manifest myself to my people in mercy in this house" (Doctrine and Covenants

11

110:7). Moses committed the keys of the gathering of Israel, Elias committed the dispensation of the gospel of Abraham, and Elijah committed the keys to turn the hearts of the fathers to the children and the children to the fathers.

Armed with these additional keys, Joseph Smith was in a position to make notable extensions to the work of the Church. A few months later, a significant step to that end was taken when, during a meeting in the temple, he called Heber C. Kimball to open missionary work abroad in England. Meanwhile, the upper rooms of the temple were used as a school to improve the knowledge and the skills of the elders who later would be added to the missionary corps.

Even while the Church exulted over the events connected with the dedication of the temple, seeds were being sown that would soon cause Joseph Smith to leave Kirtland in fear for his safety, or even for his life. In November 1836 Joseph and some of his associates organized the Kirtland Safety Society Bank. The timing was unfortunate; economic panic swept over the country in 1837. In May of that year, eight hundred banks failed. Underfunded, and overextended in real estate whose values were plummeting, the Kirtland Safety Society Bank never had a chance. It went under almost immediately, carrying with it the savings of many Latter-day Saint investors. Looking for a scapegoat, people laid blame for the collapse on the most prominent member of the bank organizers—Joseph Smith. Almost overnight, the beloved Prophet became the hated banker among many of those who had lost money. The speed of the change and the depth of the hatred were apparent in a meeting held soon after in the temple where disappointed investors bitterly attacked Joseph. "This order of things increased during the winter," wrote Heber C. Kimball, "to such an extent that a man's life was in danger the moment he spoke in defense of the Prophet of God." In these circumstances, Joseph left Kirtland in mid-January 1838 and traveled to Missouri in order to "escape mob violence, which was about to burst upon us."

The Prophet arrived at Far West, Missouri, in mid-March 1838 and began at once to counsel with the local leaders. The Church had had a presence in Missouri since early 1831 when Oliver Cowdery and his fellow missionaries had begun to work there. At a conference held in Kirtland in June of that year, Joseph received a revelation announcing the next conference of the Saints would be held in Missouri. It also said the land of their "inheritance" would be made known at the time, the land of Zion where the New Jerusalem would be built. Twenty-eight elders were named to go to Missouri, traveling in pairs and preaching along the way (see Doctrine and Covenants 52). Also, the Colesville branch was instructed to move to Missouri.

Arriving in late July, Joseph received a revelation that identified Missouri as the land the Lord had consecrated for the gathering of His people. It was called "the land of promise, and the place for the city of Zion." The site for a temple was designated, and the Saints were instructed to purchase as much land in the area as their resources would allow, so that they might "obtain it for an everlasting inheritance." (See Doctrine and Covenants 57:1–5.) During the first week in August, they began erecting a log house in Independence, Missouri; Sidney Rigdon dedicated the land of Zion for the gathering of God's people; and Joseph Smith dedicated the site where the temple was to be built. Soon after, the Colesville branch settled on a tract twelve miles west of Independence.

Before returning to Kirtland, Joseph appointed Sidney Gilbert as an agent for the Church to receive money and to purchase land; Bishop Edward Partridge was instructed to grant inheritances to the Saints as the lands were purchased; and W. W. Phelps was designated as the printer and publisher for the Church, assisted by Oliver Cowdery.

Later, the Church's first official organ, the *Evening and the Morning Star,* was published in Missouri.

Shortly after his return to Kirtland, the Prophet received two revelations that explained the present and future status of the land of Zion in Missouri. A few Saints were directed to go there to settle, but the general body of the Church was counseled to defer moving there until some future time (see Doctrine and Covenants 63; 64). These revelations convinced Joseph's followers of the subordinate role Missouri would play at the moment while underscoring the ultimate importance and the preeminent role of that land.

A few months after returning from Missouri, Joseph received a revelation, through vision, that described the three degrees of glory in the hereafter and prescribed the conditions for their attainment (see Doctrine and Covenants 76). The rich detail given and the elevated style of the language profoundly expanded the scope and the meaning of the doctrine of gradations in the hereafter first expounded by the Apostle Paul (see 1 Corinthians 15:40–44). The Prophet's reaction to this revelation shows a surprising detachment as if he were a spectator of the event, not a participant. "The sublimity of the ideas," he wrote, "the purity of the language; the scope for action; . . . the rewards for faithfulness, and the punishments for sins, are so much beyond the narrow-mindedness of men, that every honest man is constrained to exclaim: 'It came from God.'"

Meanwhile, a crisis had developed in Missouri. The influx of Latter-day Saints had raised concerns among the old settlers. It was a repetition of what had happened at Kirtland, but the situation was even worse because of the general coarseness of the people in this frontier area and also because of the revelation identifying Missouri as the place of the "inheritance" of the Mormon people. An added irritation was the false belief that the Church had encouraged the migration of free blacks into the state. These factors prompted a demand that the Church newsaper be discontinued and the store be closed. When the Saints refused, an angry mob destroyed the press and tarred and feathered several of the leading brethren. Hopelessly outnumbered and without legal recourse because most local officials were either members of the mob or sympathetic to it, Church leaders negotiated a "treaty" with the mob in July 1833. Under it the signers agreed to leave Jackson County by the following January and to use their influence to persuade others to do likewise. Unwilling to wait until the deadline, elements of the mob attacked three Mormon settlements in Jackson County on October 31 and November 1, 1833, stoning and ransacking houses, strewing furniture and other contents outside, and driving many of the Saints from their homes. Threats of further violence forced the Saints to leave Jackson County and to flee to counties to the north.

The news stunned Joseph Smith. He was concerned about the safety of the Missouri Saints and distressed that the sanguine plans for the temple and the gathering in Independence had been thwarted. He struggled in prayer to know what to do. In answer he received a revelation on February 24, 1834, part of which declared, "Behold, I say unto you, the redemption of Zion must needs come by power" (Doctrine and Covenants 103:15). Joseph was instructed to recruit a body of men and to "gather [them] together unto the land of Zion" (v. 22). There were no instructions about what to do when they arrived. By the first part of May two hundred men had been recruited, armed, and equipped. Known as Zion's Camp, they left soon after for Missouri, which was a thousand miles away.

It was a long, difficult march. The camp attracted widespread attention along the way. Questions about their destination and purpose were turned aside with nebulous answers. When they arrived in Missouri on June 16, 1834, things looked better for the Saints. Governor Daniel Dunklin had shown an inclination to assist them and had urged them not to use self-help in asserting their rights. Honoring that request, Joseph disbanded the camp on June 23 and soon after returned to Kirtland. Before doing that, however, he reorganized the leadership in Missouri that had been torn with controversy. Some of the high leaders had been caught up in this, including Oliver Cowdery. Sadly for the Prophet, Oliver later was cut off. Joseph grieved for the loss of this old friend who had endured so much for the Church and for him personally. After Joseph's martyrdom, Oliver returned to full fellowship. Throughout his disaffection, Oliver never denied the truth of his testimony about the translation and the validity of the Book of Mormon, nor about his participation in the heavenly appearances he shared with Joseph. His problems were caused by jealousy and by unfounded suspicion of the motives of others.

Some critics questioned the need and the value of Zion's Camp. To the contrary, Joseph and most members of it lauded its worth. For Joseph, it confirmed his leadership ability and his poise under pressure. The others acquired self-confidence and knowledge that would be important in the later expulsions of the Saints from Missouri and Illinois. Significantly, most of those who later were called to the Twelve and the Seventy were members of Zion's Camp.

During the four years between Zion's Camp and the arrival of Joseph Smith in Far West in mid-March 1838, the Latter-day Saints had settled in many Missouri communities in counties north of Independence. Joseph settled in Far West, the largest and the most prominent of those communities. Despite the upset caused by the disaffection of Oliver Cowdery and others, the Prophet moved forward confidently with major initiatives. It was at this time he began the immense task of preparing a history of his life and of the Church. He also laid plans for an expected influx of converts from England and elsewhere. On May 18, 1838, he traveled north of Far West to explore an area along the

Grand River and its tributaries, "for the purpose of . . . laying off a stake of Zion [Adam-ondi-Ahman]; making locations, and laying claims to lands to facilitate the gathering of the Saints, and for the benefit of the poor." A few weeks later he returned with Sidney Rigdon "to settle some Canadian brethren in that place, as they are emigrating rapidly to this land from all parts of the country."

The old settlers were alarmed, foreseeing that the Mormons, if unchecked, could soon dominate Missouri politics. They decided to take a stand at the ballot box. In August 1838 a group of them sought to prevent Mormons from voting at an election in Gallatin, Daviess County. A brawl ensued in which the Saints were greatly outnumbered. Learning of the incident, Joseph went there with several brethren to help protect their rights. Later a justice of the peace at Gallatin, Adam Black, signed a false affidavit alleging Joseph Smith and other Mormons had threatened his life over a dispute in a land transaction. This was followed by another false affidavit, this one signed by William Peniston, alleging the Mormons had raised an army of five hundred and had threatened his life and the lives of others. On the basis of these false affidavits, and ignoring contrary evidence, the local judge issued a warrant for the arrest of Joseph Smith. And the governor of Missouri, Lilburn W. Boggs, without inquiring into the validity of the charges, ordered the state militia to increase its forces.

In the following weeks, there were reports of sporadic mob attacks against Mormons in several northern Missouri counties. The main one was at DeWitt, located on the Grand River near its confluence with the Missouri River. A hundred mobbers invaded DeWitt, threatening to kill the Mormons if they did not leave by a certain day. The Mormons appealed to Governor Boggs for help. He answered that since the controversy was between local citizens, they would have to work it out among themselves. Under further threats from the mob, the Mormons left.

"After the evacuation of DeWitt," wrote Parley P. Pratt, "when our citizens were officially notified that they must protect themselves and expect no more protection from any department of the State Government, they assembled in Far West to the number of one thousand men, or thereabout, and resolved to defend their rights to the last."

The position of the Saints was weakened at this time by unfounded charges that Joseph Smith directed a murderous band called the Danites and that, like Mohammed, he intended to conquer by the sword. These charges were given weight by the false affidavits—based on misinformation—of Thomas B. Marsh and Orson Hyde of the Twelve. Later they acknowledged their error and returned to the Church in good standing.

The first armed conflict between the mob and the Saints occurred at Crooked River in early autumn 1838. Three Mormons were killed, including David W. Patten of the Twelve, and several others were wounded. The mob suffered similar casualties. Yet in a letter to Governor Boggs, Sashiel Woods, a sectarian preacher, reported the Mormons had "massacred" fifty to sixty men and had threatened to burn Richmond. "For God's sake, give us assistance as soon as possible," the letter pleaded. Without checking the facts, Governor Boggs ordered General John B. Clark to hasten to Richmond "with all possible speed. The 'Mormons' must be treated as enemies and must be exterminated or driven from the state, if necessary for the public good. Their outrages are beyond description."

A few days later, on October 30, 1838, a mob of more than two hundred attacked a small Mormon community at Haun's Mill, killing nineteen and wounding twelve. Joseph was crushed by the news. Foreseeing what would happen to his people under the governor's extermination order, he knew steps had to be taken to end the conflict. Before he could act, Colonel George Hinkle of the Caldwell County Militia, a member of the Church, acting without authorization from Joseph Smith, negotiated a pact with generals of the Missouri militia that surrounded Far West. Under it Joseph and other Church leaders were to be surrendered and tried; the property of the Saints was to be appropriated to pay their debts and to indemnify their enemies; and the Saints were to relinquish their arms and leave the state. Though annoyed by Colonel Hinkle's presumption and incensed by the sacrifice of the constitutional rights of the Saints, Joseph yielded in order to avoid further killing among his people. He and other Church leaders were taken into custody by the Missouri Militia.

The prisoners were moved first to Independence and then to Richmond, where they were imprisoned and shackled at night in a makeshift jail. During a fifteen-day preliminary hearing, a parade of prosecution witnesses gave inflammatory, mostly perjurious testimony against the Prophet and his codefendants. Deliberate efforts were made to prevent defense witnesses from testifying. The result was no surprise: Joseph, his brother Hyrum, Sidney Rigdon, and three others were bound over for trial on the charge of treason and sent to the jail in Liberty, Missouri. Parley P. Pratt and four others were bound over for trial on the charge of murder and were left in Richmond. All of the other defendants were released.

In the Richmond jail, Joseph rebuked his guards with striking effect. Revolted by their tales of degradation and rape of Mormon women, he stood erect and, in a loud, authoritative voice, commanded them to be silent else he or they would die immediately. There was such a tone of finality in his words, such an air of commanding authority in his bearing, that the guards instantly fell silent. Of the incident, Parley P. Pratt wrote, "Dignity and majesty have I seen but once, as it stood in chains, at midnight, in a dungeon in an obscure village in Missouri."

Liberty Jail was cramped, dark, rank, and oppressive. The beds were hard and dirty, the food barely edible. Yet from this sordid environment came some of Joseph Smith's most eloquent writings (see Doctrine and Covenants 121–23). To his family he wrote tender and loving letters devoid of complaint or self-pity. He also gave wise counsel to Brigham Young and other members of the Twelve about directing the exodus of the Saints from Missouri to Illinois. Joseph's conduct in the Liberty Jail is a convincing illustration of the conquest of mind and spirit over one's environment.

With the knowledge, if not the help, of certain Missouri officials, Joseph escaped from custody in April 1839. He arrived in Quincy, Illinois, on April 22, where he was reunited with his family and the Saints. The conditions in Quincy were deplorable. The Saints were living in makeshift shelters, sickness was rampant, and food was scarce. Many were discouraged. Something had to be done immediately to change attitudes and to provide hope. Eight days later, on May 1, Joseph contracted to purchase 182 acres of land from Isaac Galland and Hugh White at Commerce, Illinois, north of Quincy, on the east bank of the Mississippi River. Most of the land was undeveloped; some of it was swampy. Later, other lands were purchased, including tracts across the river at Montrose, Iowa. Soon the land was surveyed and divided into lots. The name Commerce was changed to Nauvoo, and the Saints began to gather there. Within two years twelve hundred homes and other buildings had been constructed. Joseph and his family first occupied a rough cabin on the Galland tract. Later he built a gracious, two-story, Federal-style home named the Mansion House.

In the summer of 1839, the Prophet spent many hours training the Twelve who were preparing for their missions to England. In addition to instructions about first principles, he gave valuable counsel about spiritual matters. "A person may profit by noticing the first intimation of the spirit of revelation," he told the Brethren. "For instance, when you feel pure intelligence flowing into you, it may give you sudden strokes of ideas, so that by noticing it, you may find it fulfilled the same day or soon; (i.e.) those things that were presented unto your minds by the Spirit of God, will come to pass; and thus by learning the Spirit of God and understanding it, you may grow into the principle of revelation, until you become perfect in Christ Jesus." He also warned them to guard against self-sufficiency, self-righteousness, and self-importance and admonished them to walk humbly and to observe charity toward all.

The Saints had suffered heavy losses in Missouri. The assets acquired during eight years were gone. They rightly felt entitled to reimbursement. Since Missouri's officialdom had callously denied their requests, the Prophet turned to the federal government for redress and decided to make the appeal in person. On October 29, 1839, Joseph, Sidney Rigdon, and two other companions left Nauvoo to go to Washington, D.C., for this purpose. They carried with them a sheath of protests, appeals, and memorials to support their contentions. Checking into a second-rate hotel at the corner of Missouri and Third Streets, they began to make the rounds of legislative and executive offices.

They might as well have left their papers at home, for no one would read them. The stock answer was that their remedy lay only in Missouri. This reflected the prevailing legal philosophy that the federal government possessed only limited, delegated authority that did not extend to local matters of this kind. That reasoning made no sense to the Prophet. Were they to seek justice from those who had mobbed, killed, and driven them? Joseph was especially incensed by the attitude of President Martin Van Buren, who treated him "very insolently" and who told him, "Your cause is just, but I can do nothing for you." The Prophet was convinced that with his vast authority and influence, the president could have found a way to help if he had wanted to despite the legal restrictions. "On my way home," the Prophet wrote later, "I did not fail to proclaim the iniquity and insolence of Martin Van Buren, toward myself and an injured people." Indeed, it seems the Prophet never failed ever after to berate President Van Buren on any fitting occasion when his name was mentioned. Perhaps this experience was an important factor in Joseph Smith's later decision to run for the presidency of the United States.

While Joseph's visit to the Capitol failed in its main purpose, there were beneficial side effects. For example, while there he accepted invitations to speak. His celebrity status guaranteed large and interested audiences. The general impression he created seems to have been favorable to him, the Church, and its doctrines. Congressman Mathew S. Davis, who attended one of these meetings, wrote about it in a letter to his wife: "I have taken some pains to explain the man's beliefs, as he himself explained it. I have done so because it might satisfy your curiosity, and might be interesting to you, and some of your friends. I have changed my opinion of the Mormons. They are an injured and much abused people."

Joseph Smith returned from Washington convinced that if the Saints were to receive civil justice, it would have to be under a government they devised. He began to work immediately on plans for a liberal charter for Nauvoo. He was assisted by many, but especially by a new convert, John C. Bennett, who had political influence in Springfield. It was an unusual document, likened by some to the charters that created the Greek city-states. The city courts were empowered to issue writs of habeus corpus, and the city council was authorized to raise and maintain an army and to organize a university. The city had almost complete autonomy. The act creating it was signed December 16, 1840. Joseph noted the event: "The City Charter of Nauvoo is of my own plan and device. I concocted it for the salvation of the Church, and on principles so broad, that every honest man might dwell secure under its protective influence without distinction of sect or party." Acting under the authority of the new charter, the Prophet and his associates soon organized a city militia and named the Nauvoo Legion and the University of Nauvoo.

While plans for the Nauvoo Charter were moving forward, an important new doctrine was introduced. At a funeral in the late summer of 1840, Joseph quoted 1 Corinthians 15:29 and explained that the Savior's disciples had taught the doctrine of baptism for the dead but that it had been abandoned during the Apostasy. This would be one of the basic vicarious ordinances to be performed in the Nauvoo Temple. Its cornerstones were laid at the general conference in April 1841. A revelation defining the procedure in recording vicarious temple ordinances was received September 6, 1842 (see Doctrine and Covenants 128).

About the time of the April 1841 conference, Joseph Smith married his first plural wife. The revelation explaining the doctrine of plural marriage was recorded on July 12, 1843 (see Doctrine and Covenants 132), though Joseph had received it more than ten years earlier while working on his translation of the Bible. He had memorized the revelation then and over the years had divulged parts of it to associates who subsequently leaked it to the public. These leaks had given rise to false charges in the 1830s that the Church taught and practiced plural marriage. Even in 1843, when it was put into writing, the revelation was not published and would not be published until years after the Prophet's death.

Because of his strict upbringing, Joseph Smith resisted entering into plural marriage. He did so only after being rebuked by the Lord. Afterward, he divulged the revelation to several members of his inner circle, including Brigham Young, Heber C. Kimball, John Taylor, and others, directing them to take plural wives. They too were reluctant but eventually obeyed. All this was done in secret. However, word of the practice leaked out, creating widespread rumors and gossip. Not being authorized to publicly discuss the revelation, yet under direction to teach and practice it privately, Joseph walked a narrow line. He adroitly avoided making direct denials while making ambiguous though true statements to try to silence the rumors. This dilemma created the controversies that led to his martyrdom.

While Joseph and Emma occupied the Mansion House in 1842, Julia, the adopted twin, was eleven; Joseph III was nearing ten; Frederick was six; and Alexander was four. It was a close-knit and loving family. To Joseph, Emma was the "elect lady" who had always stood loyally beside him in every crisis. Moreover, she was a woman of talent who compiled the first hymnal for the Church and who became the first president of the Relief Society, the women's auxiliary organization established in 1842. Most important, however, Joseph regarded Emma as an eternal companion with whom he would share an everlasting union, enjoying, if they proved faithful to the end, an association in the celestial kingdom with the Father and the Son, with their own children, and with a numerous progeny that would descend from them. Emma shared this vision with her husband, even as she had accepted the many other doctrines revealed through his prophetic ministry. However, Emma's acceptance of the doctrine of plural marriage did not come easily. Indeed, she rebelled at first. Later she accepted it grudgingly, even to the extent of approving those whom her husband took as plural wives. After Joseph's death, however, she reverted to her rebellion to the point of denying her husband ever had engaged in polygamy.

The whisperings in Nauvoo about plural marriages created an atmosphere of tension and suspicion. They became the subject of common gossip, spoken about guardedly at first and later erupting into topics of public conversation and condemnation, creating a furor. Meanwhile, a ring of enemies sought to revive the charge of treason leveled against the Prophet by the court in Richmond, Missouri. In the forefront of this scheme was John C. Bennett who, after losing his place as a counselor in the First Presidency because of adultery, turned against Joseph Smith. Through political influence, he persuaded the Missouri governor to seek the Prophet's extradition and the Illinois governor to issue a warrant for his arrest. The plot failed when, after his arrest, Joseph was released on a writ of habeus corpus. The same result followed when Bennett and his confederates attempted to have the Prophet extradited to Missouri as an accessory in the shooting of Governor Lilburn W. Boggs.

Yet another counselor turned traitor to Joseph Smith during this crucial period. William Law, called as a counselor in the First Presidency at age thirty-one, was a well-to-do entrepreneur convert from Canada. He had invested heavily in the growing Nauvoo economy. He became worried about his wealth upon learning of plural marriage, fearing it would cause the economy to crumble. Failing in his effort to persuade Joseph to abandon polygamy, he and several conspirators plotted the Prophet's death. Joseph became suspicious. "What can be the matter with these men?" he asked rhetorically in his journal on January 5, 1844. "Is it that the wicked flee when no man pursueth, that hit pigeons always flutter, that drowning men catch at straws, or that Presidents Law and Marks are absolutely traitors to the church, that my remarks should produce such an excitement in their minds? Can it be possible that the traitor whom Porter Rockwell reports to me as being in correspondence with my Missouri enemies is one of my quorum?" Within a few months, the mask would be ripped off the conspirators, causing them to change their strategy.

The Prophet's inclination to begin major initiatives during times of extreme stress surfaced again on January 29, 1844. A meeting with the Twelve that day focused on the qualifications of the presidential candidates and their attitudes toward the Saints. The men were dissatisfied with what they found, so it was decided that Joseph Smith would offer himself as a candidate for the presidency of the United States. No one believed he could win. The hope was that a vigorous campaign would present the plight of the Saints before the people, enhance the image of the Church, and introduce thoughtful issues into the national debate.

Plans for the campaign shaped up fast. Thirty-seven special conferences were scheduled throughout the country before the fall election. The final ones would be held in the nation's capital. Missionary-campaigners were to be sent into all twenty-six existing states to advance the Prophet's candidacy while expounding the gospel. These included all members of the Twelve except John Taylor and Willard Richards, who were to remain in Nauvoo to direct the campaign. A political tract was prepared that outlined Joseph's platform. It proposed a substantial decrease in the size of Congress and the compensation of its members; sweeping prison reforms, with emphasis on rehabilitative instead of punitive treatment of inmates; abolition of slavery by the purchase of slaves from their owners; development of a national banking system; annexation of Texas, Mexico, Oregon, and Canada; and power in the president to suppress mobs and to intervene in state affairs to protect the civil liberties of United States citizens. As the campaigners left Nauvoo, armed with the printed platform, Joseph wryly observed, "There is oratory enough in the Church to carry me into the presidential chair the first slide."

As Joseph's campaign gathered momentum throughout the nation, conditions in Nauvoo deteriorated rapidly. In March the Prophet learned from informants, A. B. Williams and M. G. Eaton, that William Law and Robert D. Foster had accused him of trying to seduce their wives and that, with others, they were plotting Joseph's death. The Prophet mounted the stand near the temple on March 24, 1844, and laid the entire matter before the public, accusing Law and Foster of plotting his death. On April 18 they were excommunicated from the Church for "unchristianlike conduct."

With the mask ripped away, the conspirators abandoned plans to kill Joseph Smith and launched a scheme to discredit and to humiliate him. William Law persuaded a grand jury in Carthage to indict Joseph for polygamy and adultery; Foster was able to get an indictment for false swearing; and Francis Higbee, another member of the ring, pressed a suit against him for alleged slander. They also pooled their resources to purchase a press and announced their plans to publish a newspaper in Nauvoo under the provocative name the *Nauvoo Expositor.*

The first and only issue of the *Expositor* appeared on June 7, 1844. It portrayed Joseph as a fallen prophet, ambitious and power hungry. A fictional story implied that the missionary effort abroad was a lure to trap unsuspecting women into polygamy. Joseph was characterized as "one of the blackest and basest scoundrels that has appeared upon the stage of human existence since the days of Nero and Caligula." The remedy proposed foreshadowed the bloody killings that would take place in less than three weeks: "Let us arise in the majesty of our strength," it intoned, "and sweep the influence of tyrants and miscreants from the face of the land, as with the breath of heaven."

Concerned that repeated attacks of this kind would create a mob spirit, Joseph recommended to the city council that the *Expositor* be abated as a public nuisance. There was common-law authority to support the action. His proposal prevailed, and on June 10, only an hour and a half after the council meeting ended, the *Expositor* press was destroyed and the type scattered.

The reactions were prompt and violent. Newspapers in nearby Quincy, LaHarpe, and Warsaw bitterly denounced the action. The most graphic was the *Warsaw Signal,* whose editor, Thomas C. Sharp, wrote: "We hold ourselves at all times in readiness to cooperate with our fellow citizens . . . to exterminate, utterly exterminate the wicked and abominable Mormon leaders." Two days later, the court in

Carthage indicted Joseph on a charge of inciting to riot. When Joseph avoided arrest through a writ of habeus corpus issued by the Nauvoo court, the mood of his enemies turned to rage. They appealed to Governor Thomas Ford to direct the state militia to take the Mormon prophet into custody. Meanwhile, they whipped up anti-Mormon sentiment among mobs throughout the area, even into Iowa across the river. Alarmed at the menacing tone of his enemies, Joseph declared martial law in Nauvoo and called on the Nauvoo Legion to defend the city against what he feared was imminent mob attack.

Governor Ford led the state militia to Carthage and invited Joseph to send emissaries to explain his actions. The hearing was held in public where the representatives from Nauvoo were surrounded by Joseph's bitter enemies, some of whom had called for his death. Their testimony was interrupted by frequent contradictions and angry outbursts from the audience. The governor, through ineptness or bias, was unable to control the proceedings, which degenerated into chaos. The result was embodied in a letter dated June 22. It ordered Joseph to submit to arrest by the Carthage constable and to stand trial on the charge of inciting to riot in the midst of those who had threatened to kill him. He was forbidden to invoke the writ of habeus corpus in Nauvoo and was told the state militia would enforce the order if he refused to obey.

Joseph was convinced he would be killed if he went to Carthage. To avoid that he considered fleeing west beyond the jurisdiction of the state of Illinois and the United States. Migrating west had been considered before, and tentative plans to do so had been made. Indeed, he had prophesied the Saints would migrate west and would become a mighty people in the Rocky Mountains. He had crossed the Mississippi River and was preparing to flee west when a delegation pleaded with him to return. He declined at first but changed his mind when he was accused of cowardice and of abandoning his flock. It was then he uttered the oft-quoted statement that if his life was of no value to his friends, it meant nothing to him.

In company with the others who had been charged with inciting to riot, Joseph went to Carthage on Monday, June 24, on horseback. It was while en route there he uttered the statement: "I am going like a lamb to the slaughter, but I am calm as a summer's morning. I have a conscience void of offense toward God and toward all men. If they take my life I shall die an innocent man, and my blood shall cry from the ground for vengeance, and it shall be said of me, 'He was murdered in cold blood.'"

There was a circus-like atmosphere in Carthage. Several companies of militia had been assembled. Many people had been drawn there by intimations of what would happen. Liquor flowed freely, and talk of assassination was whispered about. The legal proceedings were a charade. At the preliminary hearing on the charge of inciting to riot, Joseph and the other defendants were bound over for trial but were released on bail. However, Joseph's enemies had devised a spurious charge of treason against him and Hyrum based on the declaration of martial law in Nauvoo. Their imprisonment in the Carthage Jail on this charge of treason was illegal because the preliminary hearing had not been held at the time. The next day, on Wednesday the twenty-sixth, they were taken from the jail for the hearing, which was another mockery. Bail was denied, and they were returned to their cell Wednesday afternoon. Despite widespread rumors of assassination, Governor Ford left Carthage with most of the militia to go to Nauvoo to disarm the Nauvoo Legion. He left the Carthage Greys to guard the jail. Earlier, members of this company had made open threats against Joseph's life. The governor had dismissed these lightly with the statement, "The people [were] not that cruel."

Several friends were allowed to accompany Joseph and Hyrum to jail, including John Taylor and Willard Richards of the Twelve. They were housed in the debtors' cell upstairs, which did not have bars on the door or the windows. Joseph spent his last hours dictating letters to Willard Richards for his family and associates. Intermittently, he and the others read and discussed the scriptures and other literature brought with them to the jail. They also sang for diversion. John Taylor, who had a fine baritone voice, sang all fourteen verses of "A Poor Wayfaring Man of Grief," and then sang the hymn again at Joseph's request. During the day on Thursday, all the friends left the jail except Elders Taylor and Richards.

About 5:00 P.M. one of the guards served a light supper. Soon after a loud commotion was heard outside. Glancing out one of the windows, Elder Richards saw a large group of armed men with blackened faces. Some circled the building while others forced their way through the outside door and ran upstairs, firing as they came. Joseph and Hyrum reached for handguns that had been smuggled into the prison for their self-protection. Elders Taylor and Richards armed themselves with canes to try to ward off the attackers as they sought to enter the room. Hyrum was shot first by a ball on the left side of his nose, which snapped his head back violently and sent him crashing to the floor. In quick succession he was hit by three other balls—the first entering his left side, the second striking his throat, the third lodging in his left leg. Joseph reacted instinctively, thrusting his gun out through a crack in the door and firing it once without apparent effect. He then abandoned any further attempts at self-defense. As he sought to escape through one of the windows, he was hit almost simultaneously by three balls, two from inside the room and one from outside. He fell headlong out the window, landing on the ground near a well at the southeast corner of the jail. Joseph and Hyrum were dead. John Taylor was seriously wounded. Willard Richards escaped injury except for one ball that had slightly grazed his left earlobe.

The killers thought they had achieved victory over their victims and the Church they led. But they were mistaken. Actually, having died as martyrs for their religion, Joseph and Hyrum in death became even more powerful instruments for advancing the principles they had taught in life.

NOTE

This chapter is based on Francis M. Gibbons's book *Joseph Smith: Martyr, Prophet of God* (Salt Lake City: Deseret Book Company, 1977) and sources cited therein.

CHAPTER TWO

BRIGHAM YOUNG

The tenacious qualities of Brigham Young's character had their roots in his heritage and early environment. His father, John Young, was a veteran of the Revolutionary War, and his grandfather had fought in the French and Indian War. Both ancestors were frontier farmers whose livelihood depended on hard work, perseverance, and large families who could help share the load. Brigham, who was born on June 1, 1801, in Whitingham, Windsor County, Vermont, was the ninth child and fourth son of John Young and his wife, Abigail (Nabby) Howe Young. Two more children would be born into this family before the mother passed away in 1815. The family then lived in Aurelius, Cayuga County, New York.

The parents were staunch members of the Methodist Church and taught their children "to live a strictly moral life." Scripture study and family prayer were main features of their home. The children, who looked to the father for direction, looked to the mother for nurturing care. This seemed especially true of Brigham, who had a strong emotional attachment to his mother. Her death, therefore, was a grievous blow to him. However, two years later, when the father married Hannah Brown, Brigham, then in his seventeenth year, already had begun to chart his own course.

In addition to his training on the farm, Brigham had learned skills as a carpenter, joiner, painter, and glazier. He applied these while living as a young bachelor in Auburn and later in Port Byron, New York. In Port Byron he joined a debating society, which helped to develop his speaking skills and to broaden his interests. There he became active in the Methodist Church and was baptized at age twenty-two. He also courted and married Miriam Works in Port Byron. A year later their first child, Elizabeth, was born.

In 1829, when Elizabeth was four, Brigham and Miriam moved to Mendon, New York, where several members of the Young family had settled. The location was significant to Brigham Young's future. Nearby was Palmyra, where, during late 1829 and early 1830, a printer, E. B. Grandin, was busy setting in type a book named the Book of Mormon. It came off the press in March 1830. The following month a church, which came to be known as The Church of Jesus Christ of Latter-day Saints, was organized in nearby Fayette, New York. Its leader was Joseph Smith. According to the front pages of the Book of Mormon, Joseph Smith had translated it from gold plates delivered to him by an angel.

Phineas Young, Brigham's brother, acquired a copy of the book later in 1830. The Book of Mormon was circulated in the Young family, and its message and the teaching of missionaries caused most of the family to join the Mormon Church. Brigham was baptized on April 14, 1832, by one of the missionaries, Eleazer Miller. Years later he explained his conversion: "When I saw a man without eloquence, or talents for public speaking, who could only say, 'I know, by the power of the Holy Ghost, that the Book of Mormon is true, that Joseph Smith is a Prophet of the Lord,' the Holy Ghost proceeding from that individual illuminated my understanding, and light, glory, and immortality were before me. . . . I knew for myself that the testimony of the man was true."

Brigham Young's conversion soon was reflected in personal spiritual experiences. At a meeting shortly after his baptism, he spoke in tongues. "We thought only of the day of Pentecost," he reported later, "when the Apostles were clothed upon with cloven tongues of fire." He exercised this gift frequently. While holding meetings with Saints on his way to Kirtland a few months later, he spoke in tongues, as he did in a meeting with Joseph Smith when he arrived there. It was the first time the Prophet had witnessed the gift.

Miriam, who was seriously ill during the summer of 1832, passed away quietly on September 8. She left two daughters, Elizabeth and a baby, Vilate, named after her friend, Vilate Kimball, who, with her husband, Heber C., also had joined the Church in Mendon. Brigham grieved over the loss of Miriam, who not only was his wife and the mother of his children but also his friend. She had been baptized during the summer and had encouraged her husband in his desire to travel to Kirtland, Ohio, to meet the Prophet Joseph Smith. Knowing this, Vilate Kimball offered to care for Brigham's daughters so he could go there with Heber. Before leaving, Brigham performed a symbolic act fraught with significance. He gave away his earthly possessions so that he "might be free to go forth and proclaim the plan of salvation to the inhabitants of the earth. . . . I had not a coat in the world," he wrote. "Neither had I a shoe to my feet, and I had to borrow a pair of pants and a pair of boots."

In Kirtland, Brigham promptly sought Joseph Smith. He found the Prophet chopping trees in the woods. "Here my joy was full at the privilege of shaking the hand of the Prophet of God, and [I] received the sure testimony, by the

Spirit of Prophecy, that he was all that any man could believe him to be, as a true Prophet." At his residence that evening after he heard his visitor speak in tongues, Joseph prophesied that Brigham Young one day would preside over the Church.

A year after returning to Mendon, Brigham filled two missions to Canada, baptizing many and building up branches of the Church. He traveled more than twenty-four hundred miles, mostly on foot but also by boat and wagon. It was arduous work, but he gloried in it. After completing these missions, he moved to Kirtland with the Kimballs. There, realizing the need for a wife and mother in his home, he courted and married Mary Ann Angell.

With his varied skills as an artisan, Brigham had little difficulty finding work in Kirtland. Sometimes he had to wait to be paid, but he remained in Kirtland so as not to "build up the gentiles" by working elsewhere. In the end he prospered more than those who left town to work for immediate cash and for higher wages.

Shortly after his marriage to Mary Ann, Brigham was called by Joseph Smith to join Zion's Camp. This was a group of two hundred men who traveled to Missouri in May and June 1834 to assist the Missouri Saints, who were under mob attack. Because Brigham walked most of the way—a round trip of two thousand miles—sometimes he walked, as he later explained, with "blood in my boots." Because the camp was disbanded a week after arriving in Missouri, some critics questioned its purpose and value. Brigham had a ready answer: "I would not exchange the knowledge I have received this season for the whole of Geauga County; for property and mines of wealth are not to be compared to the worth of knowledge." The knowledge Brigham Young acquired by watching Joseph Smith lead Zion's Camp was important when he himself led the exodus of the Saints from Missouri and later from Illinois.

Elder Young was ordained an Apostle and set apart as a member of the Twelve on February 14, 1835. The blessing given him promised he would "do wonders in the name of Jesus; . . . cast out devils, heal the sick, raise the dead, open the eyes of the blind, go forth from land to land." Soon after, he went to the eastern states with members of his quorum on their first mission to proselytize and to organize local branches. Returning to Kirtland, he played a key role in building the Kirtland Temple, directing the crew that finished and painted the walls of the interior. He was buoyed up by the Pentecostal outpourings at the dedication of the temple in March and April 1836, when heavenly beings appeared and the Saints prophesied, saw visions, and spoke in tongues.

Within months after this supernal event, serious schisms appeared among the Saints. The cause was the failure of the Kirtland Safety Society Bank, which was caught in the economic panic of 1837 that swept the country. Many of the investors who lost money blamed Joseph Smith, president of the society. Blame soon turned to wrath and even to violent threats against the Prophet. At one meeting in the temple when angry calls were made for Joseph's removal as the head of the Church, his main defender was Brigham Young: "I rose up and in a plain and forcible manner told them that Joseph was a Prophet, and I knew it, and that they might rail and slander him as much as they pleased, they could not destroy the appointment of a Prophet of God, they could only destroy their own authority, cut the thread that bound them to the Prophet and to God, and sink themselves to hell." His defense of Joseph Smith brought the malice of these dissenters upon Brigham. It became so intense that he was forced to leave Kirtland three days before Christmas in 1837.

He arrived in Far West, Missouri, in mid-March 1838, built a snug cabin on Mill Creek, and sent for his family, which then consisted of Mary Ann and five children. The

Mormons in Missouri were under siege from mobs who feared political power would shift to the newcomers as their numbers increased. By lies and scare tactics, the mobs convinced Governor Lilburn W. Boggs that an army of Mormons had massacred numerous people during a battle at Crooked River and was advancing on Richmond, Missouri. Without confirming the charges, the governor directed the militia to guard Richmond and to surround Far West, where the Saints had assembled armed men for self-defense. He also ordered that the Mormons be driven from the state or exterminated. After nineteen Saints at Haun's Mill were massacred and more than twelve were wounded, Joseph Smith, concerned about the possibility of more killings among his people, surrendered to the militia. He was bound over on the charge of treason after a kangaroo court hearing in Richmond and was imprisoned in the jail at Liberty, Missouri. From the jail, Joseph gave instructions to the Twelve for the evacuation of the Saints from Missouri. Due to the apostasy of Thomas B. Marsh and the death of David W. Patten at Crooked River, Brigham Young then presided over the Twelve. He directed the exodus of the Saints from Missouri to Illinois. Arriving at Quincy, Illinois, in mid-March 1839, he arranged with a group called the Democratic Association for the temporary refuge of the Saints in Quincy.

Elder Young and other members of the Twelve traveled back to Missouri in late April. On April 26, in obedience to a revelation Joseph Smith had received a year before, they laid the cornerstones of the Far West Temple and made plans to go to England on a mission. Brigham spent the summer settling his family at Montrose, Iowa, across the river from Commerce City, Illinois, later renamed Nauvoo, where the Saints were gathering. In Montrose he renovated an apartment for Mary Ann and the children in an old army barrack. Still weak from fever that had afflicted him during the summer, and with limited money and little clothing,

Brigham, along with Heber C. Kimball, left for the East on September 18. Aided by members of the Church and generous strangers, and preaching along the way, they arrived in New York City on January 31, 1840. There they stayed in Parley P. Pratt's rented apartment until their departure for England.

By late March, Elder Young was ready to embark. With $19.50 donated by members of the Manhattan Branch, he purchased a steerage ticket for $18 and paid $1 as his share to hire the ship's cook, leaving 50 cents as his only cash surplus. On March 24, 1840, Brigham and his companions, Heber C. Kimball, Parley P. Pratt, Orson Pratt, George A. Smith, and Reuben Hedlock, boarded the *Patrick Henry*, a packet ship of the Black Ball Line. The passage was so rough that Brigham sampled but little of the cook's offerings. He spent much of the voyage in his bunk, deathly seasick. On stepping ashore in Liverpool on April 6, he was so emaciated that his cousin Willard Richards did not recognize him at first.

The brethren went immediately to nearby Preston, where Heber C. Kimball and his companions had opened the work in England three years earlier. Here they were joined by John Taylor and Wilford Woodruff, who had arrived in England in January. At a historic council meeting in Preston, Willard Richards was ordained to the apostleship, and plans were laid to publish the Book of Mormon and a hymnbook and to commence publication of a Church periodical called the *Millennial Star*. Also, work assignments were made. Brigham Young and Willard Richards accompanied Wilford Woodruff to Herefordshire, where Wilford had had extraordinary success laboring among a group called the United Brethren. With the three Apostles working together, the abundant harvest of converts continued. Their work was accompanied by unusual manifestations of spiritual power that healed the sick, cast out devils, and made the lame to walk. The most remarkable case of healing involved an eleven-year-old cripple, Mary Pitt. "Brigham Young being mouth," wrote Wilford Woodruff, "[he] rebuked her lameness in the name of the Lord, and commanded her to arise and walk. The lameness left her, and she never afterwards used a staff or crutch."

Converts John Benbow and Thomas Kington donated three hundred fifty pounds to advance the work. Elder Young returned to Preston with the money to arrange for the publication of the Book of Mormon and the hymn book and to help finance the *Millennial Star*. Meanwhile, steps were taken to help converts immigrate to the United States.

On April 6, 1841, a general conference assembled in the Carpenter's Hall in Manchester. Almost sixty-five hundred were in attendance, including six hundred priesthood bearers. Two weeks later, when Brigham Young and his brethren embarked for home, they could count the harvest of their mission in Great Britain: "We have gained many friends," wrote Elder Young, "established churches in almost every noted town and city in the kingdom of Great Britain, baptized between seven and eight thousand, printed 5,000 Books of Mormon, 3,000 hymn books, 2,500 volumes of the *Millennial Star*, and 50,000 tracts, and emigrated to Zion 1,000 souls, [and] established a permanent shipping agency."

With six other members of the Twelve and 123 converts, Elder Young embarked for the United States on April 20, 1841, on the sailing ship *Rochester*. It arrived in New York Harbor on May 20 after another turbulent passage. It was chaotic on the docks, where "a great crowd of draymen and pickpockets . . . stood ready to leap on board and devour all our baggage." Brigham had to threaten and to rap the fingers of some of the draymen to protect their belongings. After spending several weeks in the East working among the branches, Elder Young returned home via Philadelphia, Pittsburgh, and St. Louis, and then upriver by steamer to Nauvoo. He learned upon arrival that in his absence Mary

Ann and the children had moved from Montrose into a cabin in Nauvoo.

Other major changes soon faced Elder Young. A revelation received by Joseph Smith instructed him to remain home in the future and care for his family. Then at a public meeting on August 16, 1841, the Prophet announced the time had come for the Twelve to take their place next to the First Presidency. Later Joseph instructed the Apostles that full responsibility for the Church rested on the Twelve, subject only to his direction. Most notably, Joseph taught Elder Young and other members of the Twelve the principle of plural marriage. The doctrine had been revealed to Joseph in the early 1830s, but he had not begun to practice it until April 1841. Brigham had received hints about it while in England and so was not completely surprised. Yet, it was a startling development and difficult to accept, given his orthodox upbringing. At Joseph's direction and with Mary Ann's consent, Brigham Young married his first plural wife, Lucy Ann Decker, on June 15, 1842. She bore Brigham seven children and outlived him by thirteen years.

Elder Young engaged in business activities to maintain his families, became active in civic and political affairs, and continued to perform his apostolic duties. He also filled special assignments given him by the Prophet. The last one of these was to direct 344 men who were called to work for Joseph Smith in his campaign for the presidency of the United States. Brigham organized them so there were workers in all twenty-six states and instructed them to couple campaigning with missionary work. He also scheduled forty-seven conferences to be held throughout the country before the election, the last ones to be held in Washington, D.C.

Elder Young was in Massachusetts campaigning when Joseph was martyred in Carthage, Illinois, on June 27, 1844. He did not learn about the tragedy until July 16. He was overwhelmed by the news. After the first shock, however, he realized that the keys to govern the Church remained with the Twelve. He and his brethren returned to Nauvoo as soon as circumstances allowed to take charge of Church affairs at headquarters. He arrived in Nauvoo on August 6.

At a public meeting two days later, Sidney Rigdon presented his claim to serve as a "guardian" of the Church, representing Joseph Smith. "The Twelve are appointed by the finger of God," answered Brigham Young, President of the Twelve, "an independent body who have the keys of the priesthood—the keys of the kingdom of God to deliver to all the world: this is true, so help me God. They stand next to Joseph, and are as the First Presidency of the church." At the end of the meeting, those present, by hand vote, unanimously accepted the leadership of the Twelve. Many who were present attested that as Brigham Young spoke he appeared as Joseph Smith in voice and manner. Later there were a few dissenters, including Sidney Rigdon, who was excommunicated in September for insubordination.

Led by Brigham Young, the Twelve moved promptly to assert its leadership. The Saints were urged to follow a peaceful course, to improve their holdings, to complete the temple, and to live their religion. At a general conference in October, Wilford Woodruff was called to return to England to head the Church there, and eighty-five men were appointed to preside over mission districts in the United States. These actions frustrated the enemies who had murdered Joseph and Hyrum. They read into these actions an intention of the Saints to remain in Illinois permanently. This prompted pressure and threats for the Mormons to leave. Behind the scenes, Brigham and his brethren had been planning the exodus. Prayerful study had led to the decision to migrate west to the western slope of the Rocky Mountains. The original plan was to leave in the spring of 1846. Members were instructed what to take on the trek and how to maximize the return from the forced sale of their property. By December 1845 the temple was sufficiently completed to enable the Twelve to administer its sacred ordinances to the Saints. On February 15, 1846, Brigham Young and his family crossed the river with others to begin the Mormon exodus from Nauvoo.

It took three and a half arduous months to cross Iowa. Not all who started were cut out for pioneering. Some became discouraged and turned back. Of those who persevered, Brigham Young expected obedience and discipline. "I wish the brethren to stop running to Nauvoo, hunting, fishing, roasting their shins and idling away their time," he told the Saints at Sugar Creek, the first way station. Instead he expected them to "fix nosebaskets for their horses, and fix comfortable places for their wives and children to ride." After criticizing those who let their dogs run loose or kept horses with distemper, he added, "If any want to live in peace, . . . they must toe the mark." Yet with this sternness, Brigham showed the loving concern of a parent: "I would not go on until I saw all the teams up," he wrote at Sugar Creek. "I helped them up the hill with my own hands, . . . acting the part of a father to everybody."

Stopping periodically to care for the sick, to bury the dead, and then to rest and to regroup at Garden Grove and Mt. Pisgah, Brigham Young reached the Missouri River on June 14, 1846. Twelve days later Captain James Allen of the United States Army arrived from Fort Leavenworth seeking five hundred Mormon volunteers to serve in the war with Mexico. Influenced by loyalty to his country and by the benefits of army pay that would accrue to the families of the volunteers, Brigham aided the captain in recruiting what became known as the Mormon Battalion. However, the loss of these strong, young men caused Brigham to decide against going farther than the Missouri River in 1846.

Through negotiation with the Omaha Indian Chiefs and with government officials, the Saints acquired the right to settle temporarily on Indian lands west of the Missouri. By December 1 they had constructed 621 buildings in a community called Winter Quarters. With typical Mormon efficiency, it was divided into twenty-two wards, each with a bishop responsible to care for his flock. There, during a cold and bleak winter, the Twelve planned for the departure of a pioneer company the following spring, destined for an unidentified site on the western slope of the Rocky Mountains. The main body of the Saints would follow.

The Pioneer Company departed from a staging area several miles west of Winter Quarters in mid-April 1847. Comprising 143 men, three women, and two children, it included teamsters, blacksmiths, road and bridge builders, carpenters, masons, farmers, cattlemen, coopers, hunters, historians, musicians, a doctor, and a scientist—all with their wagons, equipment, and animals. President Young gave careful instructions about the behavior of the company, its objective, its historic importance, and its conduct toward Indians it might encounter. The company traveled on the north side of the Platte River as far as Fort Laramie, creating what became known as the Mormon Trail. This was done because of better grazing there and to avoid unnecessary contact with the thousands of immigrants traveling on the Oregon Trail south of the river.

The Pawnee Indians east of Fort Laramie were outwardly friendly while using veiled threats to enforce their requests for "contributions" of food and provisions. Brigham Young sought to minimize friction with the Indians by heeding their requests and by insisting the company kill only the number of buffalo needed for food. In some places "the face of the earth was alive" with these animals, "moving like the waves of the sea."

Frictions within the company were minimal. However, once near Chimney Rock, Brigham became annoyed by a spirit of levity and by profanity and idle games that had appeared among some members of the camp. Bluntly telling them he would not continue to travel under these circumstances, he delivered a pointed sermon, noting their failings and calling them to repentance. Commenting on the quieting effect of these remarks, William Clayton wrote, "It truly seemed as though we had emerged into a new element, a new atmosphere and a new society."

Seventeen Saints from Mississippi, who had wintered in Pueblo, Colorado, joined the Pioneer Company at Fort Laramie. Four brethren were sent toward Pueblo to lead the rest of this group westward. Also, at the crossing of the Platte near the present city of Casper, Wyoming, several brethren were left to operate a ferry to help later companies across and to hire out to non-Mormon caravans.

In barren Wyoming the pioneers were distressed by clouds of dust kicked up by the wagons and by hordes of crickets. At that point they also passed a number of trappers and mountain men, including Moses Harris, Thomas L. Smith, and Jim Bridger, all of whom were pessimistic about establishing a large settlement in the Salt Lake Valley. At the Green River, the Pioneer Company, which was augmented there by thirteen men of the Mormon Battalion, met Samuel Brannan, who had traveled east from San Francisco to encourage the Saints to settle in California. Little did he know that the rosy picture he painted of the wealth, the mild climate, and the expected explosive growth there were the very things Brigham Young sought to avoid. He welcomed the isolation the mountain valleys would offer the Saints, enabling them to live their religion in peace.

As the company neared the Salt Lake Valley, Brigham Young became ill with fever and transferred to Wilford Woodruff's carriage. When he saw the valley for the first time on July 24, 1847, he told Elder Woodruff, "This is the right place. Drive on."

Brigham Young remained in the valley a month and two days. At a meeting held soon after his arrival, the company approved the new gathering place, agreed on the layout of the city, and adopted general rules to govern its inhabitants. Later Brigham scouted the area, inspecting, among other places, the Great Salt Lake and a peak on the north end of the valley the pioneers had named Ensign Peak. This name suggested that the flag raised there would be an emblem, attracting people from all nations to gather to the new Zion. Before leaving the valley on August 26 to return to Winter Quarters, Brigham Young also designated the site for a temple and rebaptized the members of the Twelve in City Creek as a symbol of cleansing and rebirth.

En route to Winter Quarters, he passed four large companies of Saints on their way to the valley, led by Daniel Spencer, Parley P. Pratt, John Taylor, and Jedediah M. Grant. To these he gave instruction and encouragement. Soon after passing Elder Grant's company, a lapse in security resulted in the loss of twenty-eight of their best horses to a group of Sioux Indian rustlers. Putting the most optimistic light on this crucial loss, Brigham "called upon all the returning brethren, except the teamsters, to take a walk with me to Winter Quarters." This destination was seven hundred miles east. Exhausted and footsore, he and his companions arrived there on October 30, 1847.

During the winter months, devoted mainly to planning for three more major migrations of Saints the following summer, a significant historical event took place. On December 5 Brigham Young was ordained and set apart as the second President of the Church by the Twelve. He selected Heber C. Kimball and Willard Richards as his counselors. These actions were confirmed at a conference held on December 27. Also, an epistle was sent to the Saints everywhere, urging them to assemble at the new gathering place in the Rocky Mountains and to bring with them seeds, plants, and all kinds of implements and other resources needed to build a new civilization.

Brigham Young led one of the three migrations in 1848. The group left for the mountains on June 1 and arrived in the Salt Lake Valley on September 20. The presence of many women and children explains why the travel time was longer than that of the Pioneer Company. They arrived in time to witness the first harvest in the new home of the Latter-day Saints.

Brigham Young and his associates assigned "inheritances" of land to the Saints even though they lacked legal title, which at that time, 1847, was vested in the civil government of Mexico. But by provision of the treaty of Guadalupe Hidalgo in 1848, the underlying title passed to the United States. The Saints proceeded confidently on the assumption their squatters' rights would be confirmed later with legal title. Under President Young's leadership, they also devised their own local government, adopting building codes; prescribing rules of civic conduct; constructing roads, bridges, and irrigation systems; and erecting a council house. On the ecclesiastical side, a stake was organized in the Salt Lake Valley in February 1849, exploration parties were sent out to identify other places of settlement for the many immigrant converts who were expected, and missionaries, including members of the Twelve, were sent into the world to accelerate the conversion and migration process.

On September 9, 1850, the United States Congress passed an act creating the Utah Territory. Soon after, Brigham Young was appointed the first territorial governor. This merger of dominant civil and ecclesiastical authority in one man created little difficulty in the early days when the population was mostly Mormon. But when non-Mormons began to settle in larger numbers, the issue became a thorn in their side.

The first large influx of those of other faiths into Utah occurred during the gold rush to California that began in 1849. Salt Lake City was on the main path of the thousands who trekked to the coast to find fame and fortune. This proved to be both a boon and a bane to the Mormons. The benefit came from an unusual source: Many trekkers, facing the western desert and the rugged Sierra Nevada beyond, sought to lighten their loads at Salt Lake City. They gave away or sold at minimal prices a wide variety of food, clothing, furniture, and implements. The huge volume of these excess commodities sharply reduced prices, fulfilling a prediction made earlier by Heber C. Kimball that goods would sell as cheaply in Salt Lake City as in the eastern centers.

The main disadvantage of the flood of gold seekers through Salt Lake City was the enticement it created for some of the Saints to join them. The lure of instant wealth and an easier lifestyle in a mild climate was too tempting for some to resist. As President Young saw some members beginning to yield, he mounted an all-out campaign to head them. In many talks and private conversations, he pointedly reminded the Saints that God had led them to Utah and that the future success of the Church depended on strengthening their foothold in the mountains. Most of the Saints heeded his message and remained. A few left. Brigham Young seemed to take each departure as a personal affront and predicted that those who went would not prosper.

Following in the wake of the gold seekers came another invasion from the East in the person of federal employees who had been appointed to territorial offices. The first wave was led by Judge Perry E. Brocchus, whom the historian H. H. Bancroft called "a vain and ambitious" man. Soon after his arrival, the judge was granted permission to address the Saints. In a long, rambling speech, he justified the federal government's inaction in the mobbings in Missouri and Illinois, admonished the Saints to be more friendly and tractable, and questioned the morals of those who practiced plural marriage. In response Brigham said the judge was either profoundly ignorant or willfully wicked and expressed indignation "at such corrupt fellows as Judge Brocchus coming here to lecture us on morality and virtue." The judge and his friends left after only a few weeks. They carried with them false tales about alleged Mormon failings, and these reports added to the official misconceptions about the Latter-day Saints. Many other federal carpetbaggers would follow Judge Brocchus and his friends with similar results.

Indian difficulties claimed President Young's attention in 1853. At first the Mormons and Indians lived in peace. Indeed, Ute Indian chief Walker invited the Saints to colonize San Pete Valley in central Utah. Frictions developed, however, when Mormon fences interfered with Indian movements. Fighting erupted with killings on both sides. The conflict became known as the Walker War. Brigham, who always had followed a policy of friendliness toward the Indians, sought to end the conflict through negotiation. At a parley held at Chicken Creek, west of Nephi, Utah, an accord was reached. A breakthrough in the talks occurred when President Young, who had come to the conference bearing many gifts, healed the chief's ailing daughter by a priesthood blessing. This ended Mormon-Indian conflict until the late 1860s, when some hostilities broke out as part of the so-called Black Hawk War, which ended with the Indians being moved to reservations in eastern Utah.

The year of the Walker War saw President Young break ground and lay the cornerstones for the Salt Lake Temple. Forty long, laborious years would be required to complete it. The year also saw him complete the creation of a unified school system throughout the territory and build upon an ambitious public relations initiative. The latter, commenced in 1852, was deemed necessary because the public announcement that year that the Church taught and practiced plural marriage had created a powerful backlash. To counter this, President Young founded a newspaper, the *Seer*, in Washington, D.C., edited by Orson Pratt. Soon after, the *Mormon* was established in New York City, edited by John Taylor. Later the *St. Louis Luminary*, edited by Erastus Snow, and the *Western Standard* in San Francisco, edited by George Q. Cannon, were created. These papers, as well as the *Deseret News* in Salt Lake City, sought to change the harsh attitudes toward the Church and its members created by a hostile press and government. These papers presented the Latter-day Saints in a favorable light, something the mainline press had failed to do.

The Church faced a crisis in the mid-1850s. Its root cause was a change of focus. At first the Saints aimed to build a model society. Along the way, however, the focus of many changed to wealth, comfortable homes, and security, which appear to have become more important than creating an ensign to the nations. With that change among the Saints came a careless attitude toward their religion. Sabbath breaking, profanity, and sexual immorality crept in. Viewing this condition with alarm, President Young decided a strong antidote was necessary. His remedy was to launch what became known as "the Reformation." It was a call to repentance. For several months, President Young and his brethren conducted a vigorous speaking campaign throughout the Mormon communities. "If the people will not repent," President Young told one audience in a typical sermon, "let the sinners and hypocrites look out. . . . I shall not spare the wicked; I shall be like a flaming sword against them. . . . I cannot hold men and women in fellowship that serve the devil and themselves, and give no heed to the Almighty. . . . It cannot be suffered any longer. . . . You must part with your sins, or the righteous must be separated from the ungodly." This kind of straight talk had a bracing effect on most of the Saints who had strayed. They were rebaptized as a symbol of their repentance and returned to their obedient ways. However, a few left the territory, unwilling to live up to so strict a standard, while others remained to become sour dissidents, opposed to the Church and its leaders.

This reformation came in the midst of the tragedy of the handcart companies. Beginning in 1856, some of the poor Saints who lacked means to purchase wagons and teams walked across the plains, pulling handcarts loaded with their belongings. The first three of these companies arrived safely in Salt Lake City in late September. Two others led by James G. Willie and Edward Martin started late and were caught in early snowstorms on the plains. Almost a third of the nine hundred members of these companies died on the way or afterward because of their weakened condition. When word came of the peril these companies faced, rescue teams in wagons were sent out from Salt Lake. The last of these returned on November 30 while the Saints were assembled in the "Old Tabernacle." Speaking from the stand, President Young asked the Saints to "nurse and wait upon the newcomers and prudently administer medicine and food to them, . . . to wash them and nurse them up." He added, "I have sent word to Bishop Hunter that I will take in all that others will not take." Despite this tragedy, some Saints continued to cross the plains in handcart companies until 1860.

The home to which President Young invited the handcart company survivors consisted of two main buildings: the Beehive House, built in 1854, and the Lion House, built two years later. Connecting them was a structure that housed the offices of the First Presidency. Ordinarily, twelve of Brigham Young's wives and their children occupied the Lion House. Another family occupied the Beehive House. Later, other homes were built for different families, including the White House, in the block east of the Beehive House; Forest Farm, in the south-central part of the valley; and homes at Provo and St. George. Allowing for the conflict found in practically all families, the Brigham Young family was surprisingly peaceful. Each wife had her own apartment with a drawing account at the family store and at ZCMI. Household duties were shared and rotated. Meals were served in common. There were always ample babysitters if a mother had commitments out of the home. The older wives who were childless or whose children were raised had freedom to pursue private objectives. The numerous children, who were taught in the family school, never lacked for friends or playmates. While Brigham insisted on order and discipline in the home, he was kind and loving to his family. "He could be stern when occasion demanded," wrote daughter Clarissa H. Young, "but he was the wisest, kindest, and most loving of fathers. His constant thoughtfulness for our happiness and well-being endeared him to all of us. . . . I shall always be grateful that I was born his daughter."

Non-Mormon judges W. W. Drummond, George P. Stiles, and John F. Kinney created serious trouble for the Mormons in the spring of 1857. Returning to Washington, D.C., they falsely accused Brigham Young and others of destroying court records, sabotaging the government survey, and inciting the Indians to rebellion. Without consulting Governor Young to get his views, President James Buchanan ordered the muster of a large, well-equipped army. Its mission was to install a new territorial governor in Utah and, if necessary, to subdue the Mormons by force. The U.S. president's glaring negligence earned the mission the name "Buchanan's Blunder."

The army, under the command of General W. S. Harney, left Fort Leavenworth, Kansas in mid-July. Brigham Young learned about it on July 24. He promptly directed missionaries in the United States and abroad to come home; instructed Charles C. Rich and Orson Hyde to dissolve Mormon colonies in San Bernardino, California, and Carson City, Nevada; and instructed the Nauvoo Legion to defend against a threatened invasion. Hundreds of men were assigned to guard the mountain passes. Others conducted harassing attacks on the U. S. Army. All were instructed to avoid bloodshed if possible. President Young also prepared the minds of his people to follow a "scorched-earth" policy: "When these troops arrive," he told an army officer, "they will find Utah a desert; every house will be burned to the ground, every tree cut down, and every field laid to waste."

Through the mediation of Colonel Thomas L. Kane and others, a settlement was reached. Brigham Young willingly relinquished the office of governor to his successor, Alfred Cumming. The army was allowed to march through the city and camp west of the Jordan River. Later it moved to Camp Floyd, a permanent military post thirty miles southwest of Salt Lake City.

While the Saints awaited the invasion, a tragedy occurred in southern Utah during September 1857. An Arkansas wagon train of one hundred twenty en route to California was ambushed west of Cedar City. All except a few children were murdered. A federal judge in Provo, John Cradlebaugh, sought to implicate Brigham Young. Through collusion with officers at Camp Floyd, several hundred troops were sent to Provo as an obvious intimidation. Nothing came of it because there was no evidence President Young was responsible for the tragedy. Later events proved that some local members of the Church were involved with Indians in the ambush. But only one of them, John D. Lee, was tried, convicted, and executed for it.

After the Cradlebaugh affair, Salt Lake federal judge Charles E. Sinclair attempted to have President Young arrested on a false charge of counterfeiting and called on Camp Floyd troops to help make the arrest. The Nauvoo Legion was mustered to resist. Governor Cumming intervened to insist the troops be withdrawn. Later both Judges Cradlebaugh and Sinclair were reprimanded for exceeding their authority and were removed from office.

Brigham Young and the Saints were relieved when Camp Floyd was closed in the early 1860s before the Civil War began. The soldiers had been a disruptive force in the area with their drinking and brawling in the Mormon communities. In the first eighteen months after the camp was established, there were more murders on the streets of Salt Lake City than during the previous decade. The closure of the camp also benefited the Saints because the inventories on hand were sold at bargain prices. President Young purchased several thousand dollars' worth of these commodities and later sold them at a profit through his agent, H. B. Clawson.

The effects of the Civil War even reached into remote Utah. President Abraham Lincoln bypassed the territorial governor and, wiring Brigham Young directly, asked that he raise, arm, and equip a company of cavalry for ninety days' service "to protect the property of the telegraph and overland mail companies." The assignment was given to the Nauvoo Legion. After ninety days, Colonel Patrick Edward Connor was commissioned to enlist a corps of volunteers from California and move them to Utah, ostensibly to relieve the Nauvoo Legion. An ulterior motive was suspected when the colonel marched his troops through Salt Lake City with fixed bayonets and loaded rifles, camping on the east bench above the city. He later explained that his purpose was to bring "a large gentile" population to the area in order to dilute the influence of the Church, which he said was "disloyal and traitorous to the core."

Colonel Connor's attitude soon brought him into conflict with Brigham Young. The prophet thundered at the colonel from the pulpit and the Church's newspaper, the *Deseret News.* He urged Mormon merchants to up their prices for military personnel and admonished all the Saints to shun them socially. The colonel retaliated by establishing his own newspaper, the *Union Vedette,* in which he thundered back at Brigham. By way of insult, he required that all Mormons trading at the post exchange give an oath of allegiance to the United States. The Saints quit going there, completing the polarization of the community. Meanwhile, the colonel pursued his goal of diluting Mormon influence by encouraging his troops to prospect for minerals in the nearby mountains, hoping thereby to create another gold rush by a rich strike. It never happened. The dilution he hoped for had to await the completion of the transcontinental railroad in 1869. But this dilution did not achieve his goal of destroying Mormon influence, and especially the influence of his nemesis, Brigham Young.

Their enemies in Congress struck a blow at the Saints and the Church in 1862 by enacting an antibigamy law, the Morrill Act. It provided criminal penalties for those living in plural marriage. From the time of its passage, the Mormons contended the law was unconstitutional because it infringed on their religious freedom.

Since the constitutional question was not decided until two years after Brigham Young's death, he openly lived in polygamy the remainder of his life, confident his conduct was doctrinally, morally, and legally correct. He and other polygamists were able to avoid prosecution under the antibigamy act because jurisdiction in criminal matters lay with the territorial probate courts, whose jurists were elected by the popular vote of electors, who mostly were members of the Church.

As completion of the transcontinental railroad neared, President Young sought to prepare the Saints for the changes that event would bring. He added a spiritual dimension by reinstituting the School of the Prophets. At the temporal level, he urged increased production by mechanizing. He also suggested that costs and prices could be reduced if workers voluntarily accepted lower wages. These steps were thought necessary in order to compete with the expected influx of inexpensive goods from both coasts. Some Saints, including a few members of the School of the Prophets, opposed these policies, especially the reduction of wages. They also criticized President Young's refusal to encourage mineral development. These critics went public, airing their views in the *Utah Magazine,* whose name was later changed to the *Mormon Tribune.* When their rhetoric changed to slander and caricature, these dissidents were excommunicated. As a group they became known as Godbeites, named after one of their leaders, W. S. Godbe.

They presumed to organize a new church called the Church of Zion. Their voice of dissent was added to other groups, including several Christian sects who entered Utah hoping to "reclaim" the Mormons. And representatives of the Reorganized Church who came to Utah joined in the chorus. President Young's response to all this was to stay the course, expounding the gospel vigorously to his people and expanding the size and influence of the Church through colonization and missionary work.

Another activist federal judge, James B. McKean, arrived in the spring of 1871. He came to Utah with a mandate from President Ulysses S. Grant to "make the laws respected." He began by ignoring the law, decreeing that when the United States was a party to an action in a territorial court, it automatically became a federal court with federal officials in charge. Using this fictitious device, he entertained suits under the antibigamy law, using juries that systematically excluded Latter-day Saints. One was a suit against Brigham Young that included sixteen counts of "lewdly and lasciviously associating and cohabiting with women, not being married to them." In court, the judge said that while the suit was against Brigham Young, its real title was *Federal Authority versus Polygamic Theocracy.* While the aging prophet was in St. George seeking relief from severe arthritis, the judge set a hearing in the matter for January 9, 1872, which now included a spurious charge of murder. Without complaint, President Young made the long, painful trip home in the midst of a winter storm. In binding him over for trial, the judge denied bail but allowed the prophet to be incarcerated in his home. At this point, the judge's scheme began to unravel when the justice department disallowed court costs in the case totaling fifteen thousand dollars. This forced the judge to dismiss the jury because there was no money with which to pay the per diem charges. Soon after, the Supreme Court decided in another case coming up from Utah that a judgment was void because the jury had been impaneled contrary to law. This required the release of 138 defendants, including Brigham Young, in other cases in which juries had been illegally impaneled.

The prophet was not yet through with Judge McKean. Soon after, President Young's last wife, Ann Eliza Webb Young, sued for divorce. In the proceeding, the judge ordered the defendant to pay a living allowance of a thousand dollars a month. Defense counsel objected because under the court's rulings, polygamous marriages were void and therefore the plaintiff had no legal standing to sue. The judge ignored the legal precedents and went forward. When, on advice of counsel, Brigham Young refused to make the support payments, the judge charged him with contempt, imposed a fine, and ordered him jailed for twenty-four hours. Despite the ingrained anti-Mormon bias, leading papers across the country erupted with indignation. Five days later, Judge McKean was summarily dismissed from office.

President Young was harassed by this suit for several years through a series of other judges who succeeded Judge McKean. However, several months before the prophet died, a court decided in his favor, ruling that the marriage was void as a matter of law. Despite this, President Young retained love and respect for Ann Eliza, who had become an unwitting tool of the prophet's enemies. To the end, he was not unmindful of her needs.

Burdened with age, illness, and a heavy workload, President Young began to free himself of some responsibilities. In February 1873 he resigned as president of the Deseret National Bank and ZCMI. Later he relinquished his role as trustee-in-trust for the Church. To help carry the load, he called five additional counselors in the First Presidency: Lorenzo Snow, Brigham Young Jr., Albert Carrington, John W. Young, and George Q. Cannon. "For over forty years I have served my people," he explained, "laboring incessantly, and I am now nearly seventy-two years of age and I need relaxation." This did not affect his role as President of the Church. "In that capacity," he added, "I shall still exercise supervision over business, ecclesiastical and secular affairs, leaving the minutiae to younger men." With mingled pride and gratitude, he gave an account of his stewardship: "The result of my labors for the last 26 years, briefly summed up, are: The peopling of this Territory by the Latter-day Saints of about 100,000 souls; the founding of over 200 cities, towns and villages inhabited by our people, which extend to Idaho in the north, Wyoming in the east, Nevada in the west, and Arizona in the south, and the establishment of schools, factories, mills and other institutions calculated to improve and benefit our community."

The following year, President Young began his last major initiative, which was to establish the United Order of Enoch. His vision was embodied in this statement made at a meeting in Paris, Idaho: "I want you to be united. If we should build up and organize a community, we would have to do it on the principle of oneness, and it is one of the simplest things I know of. A city of one thousand or a million people could be united into a perfect family, and they could work together as beautifully as the different parts of a carding machine work together. Why, we could organize millions into a family under the order of Enoch." The key to him was not the pooling of material resources, but the pooling of talent and labor.

"We do not want your horses and cattle," he explained as he taught the United Order throughout the Church. "We do not want your gold and your silver. . . . We want the time of this people called Latter-day Saints, that we can organize this time systematically, and make this people the richest people on the face of the earth."

In June 1875 President Young took a painful action that had been considered for many years. At a meeting in San

Pete he announced a reordering of seniority in the Twelve due to gaps in the tenure of Orson Hyde and Orson Pratt caused by their brief disaffections during the hard days in Missouri and Illinois. The effect of this affirmed John Taylor as the senior member of the Twelve, in line to succeed Brigham Young at his death.

A crowning event of President Young's life was the dedication of the St. George Temple in 1877. In celebration, the annual general conference of the Church was held in St. George that year. On April 6 he delivered the last general conference sermon of his life. Wracked with arthritic pains, he slowly arose in the upper room of the temple to counsel his people. "This is the work of God," he testified, "that marvelous work and a wonder referred to by ancient men of God. . . . I never mean to be satisfied until the whole earth is yielded to Christ and his people. . . . I know not how soon the messenger will call for me, but I calculate to die in the harness."

He fulfilled that promise. On the way back to Salt Lake he dedicated the site for the Manti Temple. At home he counseled with his brethren, held meetings with the Saints, and set his personal affairs in order. His last major administrative action was to call home the members of the Twelve who had been living in outlying areas. He put in a full day at his office on Thursday, August 23. He rode out after dinner and later attended a bishops' meeting. During the night he became ill with severe abdominal pains. He suffered for six days, passing away Wednesday, August 29, 1877, at 4:00 P.M. In charge to the end, he had left detailed instructions for the funeral arrangements. He specified the size of the coffin which was to have the appearance "that if I wanted to turn a little to the right or to the left, I should have plenty of room to do so." He decreed that the females in the family were not to buy black bonnets or dresses, although he gave liberty to those who already had them to wear them. Remarks at the funeral services were to be by any of his friends who "really desire" to speak. By his direction he was to be buried in the family cemetery on the hill. His final injunction: "No crying or mourning with anyone as I have done my work faithfully and in good faith."

NOTE

This chapter is based on Francis M. Gibbons's book *Brigham Young: Modern Moses, Prophet of God* (Salt Lake City: Deseret Book Company, 1981) and authorities cited therein.

CHAPTER THREE

JOHN TAYLOR

John Taylor, third President of The Church of Jesus Christ of Latter-day Saints, was born on November 1, 1808, in Milnthorpe, England. To date (1996) he is the only Church President born outside the United States. His parents, James Taylor and Agnes Taylor Taylor, also were natives of England. John's father, who was proficient in Greek, Latin, and higher mathematics, mixed farming with government service. His parents had John baptized as an infant into the Church of England and saw that he was trained in its catechism and formal prayers.

As a boy, John showed unusual spiritual qualities. Often when alone, and sometimes in company, he "heard sweet, soft, melodious music, as if performed by angelic or supernatural beings." Finding the cold forms of the Church of England uncongenial with his temperament, John joined the Methodist Church at sixteen. Soon he became a Methodist exhorter, traveling about to instruct and to motivate others. Once while on assignment, he stopped in the road and, turning to his companion, said, "I have a strong impression on my mind, that I have to go to America to preach the gospel."

During the years of his spiritual growth, John also learned temporal skills, first on his father's farm, then as a cooper's apprentice, and finally as a turner. Financed by his father, he set up a turner's shop in Hale, Westmoreland, which he operated successfully for four years until 1832, when he liquidated his assets and migrated to Canada. During a terrible storm on his Atlantic crossing he went topside "and amidst the raging elements" felt total calmness and an assurance he would reach America and perform his life's work.

John settled in Toronto, Canada, opened a turner's shop, became active in the local Methodist Church, and soon was an exhorter. In the congregation was a charming English immigrant, Leonora Cannon, twelve years older than John, whom he courted and finally won over after she had a vivid dream confirming their relationship. They were married on January 28, 1833. Three years later, on May 9, 1836, they were baptized into the Mormon Church by Parley P. Pratt.

The next spring Elder Taylor traveled to Kirtland, Ohio, to meet the Prophet Joseph Smith. He found there the man whom, by spiritual means, he instantly recognized as a prophet of God. He also found turmoil and a spirit of apostasy there because of the failure of the Kirtland Safety Society Bank. Even Parley P. Pratt had become disaffected temporarily. John told him that if Joseph Smith was a prophet several months before, he was still a prophet. He also defended Joseph openly in the temple.

At a meeting with friends near Niagara Falls on the way home, John spoke in tongues and received the spiritual impression he would be called as an Apostle. A few months later he received a letter from Joseph Smith advising him he had been called to the Twelve. "I looked upon it as a life long labor and . . . for eternity also, and did not shrink now, although I felt my incompetency." Soon after, the Prophet instructed John and his family to move to Missouri. They arrived in the late summer of 1838. Staying briefly at DeWitt, where the Saints were under mob attack, they settled in Far West. There on October 6, 1838, he was sustained as an Apostle; and on December 19 he was ordained an Apostle and set apart as a member of the Twelve.

On the day of John Taylor's ordination, a report seeking redress for the losses suffered by the Saints through mob actions was submitted to the Missouri legislature. Elder Taylor was a chief author of this report and also of a similar report prepared later for the United States Congress. Neither report brought the relief requested. However, they demonstrated John's ability in research, analysis, and writing and foreshadowed his later role as an editor of Church publications.

The Taylors were uprooted again when the Saints were driven from Missouri under Governor Lilburn W. Boggs's extermination order. They arrived in Quincy, Illinois, on January 15, 1839. Three months later, Elder Taylor returned to Far West with other members of the Twelve. There on April 26 they relaid the cornerstone of the temple in obedience to a revelation received the previous year. They also ordained Wilford Woodruff and George A. Smith to the apostleship and made plans for their mission to England.

Returning to Illinois, Elder Taylor spent several months locating his family in an old military barracks in Montrose, Iowa, across the Mississippi River from Nauvoo. On August 8, 1839, he and Wilford Woodruff left Montrose on their mission. At the direction of the Prophet Joseph Smith, they traveled without purse or scrip. En route to New York City, Elder Taylor became seriously ill at Germantown, Indiana. He insisted that Elder Woodruff go on to New York alone, where Elder Taylor joined him on December 13. They stayed in an apartment in Manhattan rented by Parley P. Pratt while making arrangements to embark for Liverpool, England.

Upon arriving in New York, John had only a penny in his pocket. Yet when a member of the Manhattan Branch asked about his finances, Elder Taylor said he had "plenty of money." Being told about the remark, Elder Pratt asked for a loan to publish a pamphlet he had written. John told Parley he was welcome to all the money he had and produced the penny. When asked why he had said he had plenty of money, John answered: "I am well clothed, you furnish me plenty to eat and drink and good lodging; with all these things and a penny over, as I owe nothing, is not that plenty?"

Accompanied by Elder Woodruff and Theodore Turley, Elder Taylor embarked on the packet ship *Oxford* on December 19, 1839. Twenty-three days later, they docked at Liverpool. Leonora's brother, George Cannon, and his wife, Ann Quayle, lived there. This couple and three of their children, including twelve-year-old George Q. Cannon, were among the first converts John Taylor baptized in England. This nephew was ordained an Apostle later in life and was called as a counselor to John Taylor when he became the President of the Church.

Brigham Young and four other members of the Twelve arrived in England on April 6, 1840. At an organizational meeting held soon after in Preston, Willard Richards was ordained an Apostle. Also, Elder Taylor was appointed to continue his labors in Liverpool and to serve on a committee to publish the Book of Mormon and a hymnbook. Finding the doors of Protestant churches closed to him in Liverpool, Elder Taylor rented the Music Hall for his meetings. A delay in occupying it offered the chance to visit Ireland and Scotland. In Ireland he held meetings in Newry, Bellimacrat, and Lisburn. En route to Lisburn, a traveling companion named Tate asked to be baptized. John performed it in Loch Brickland, the first known Latter-day

Saint baptism in Ireland. In Scotland he held meetings in the Glasgow Branch, where the small cluster of Saints were in awe at the presence of an Apostle.

Back in Liverpool, Elder Taylor gave a successful series of lectures in the Music Hall. More conversions followed. When the lease on the Music Hall ended, he left the branch he had built up in charge of an associate and traveled to the Isle of Man. The work there, although contentious because of the strong opposition of Protestant ministers, was fruitful and was marked by another display of Elder Taylor's gift of tongues. He completed his mission by working again in Liverpool and in several other English cities, assisting with the publication of the Book of Mormon and a hymnbook and supervising the emigration of hundreds of converts. He returned to Nauvoo in 1841, arriving there on July 1.

Elder Taylor soon became involved in the life of the city. He was appointed an officer of the Nauvoo Legion, a member of both the city council and the board of regents of the university, and an editor of Church publications, the *Times and Seasons* and the *Nauvoo Neighbor*. He moved his family to a new frame home in Nauvoo and later into a large brick home adjacent to the office of the *Times and Seasons*.

A stressful decision faced Elder Taylor and his family when Joseph Smith revealed the principle of plural marriage to him. John struggled to accept it, doing so only after the Prophet gave him an ultimatum. With Leonora's consent, he married her cousin Elizabeth Kaighin on December 12, 1843. Later he was married to five other wives: Jane Ballantyne, Mary Ann Oakley, Sophia Whitaker, Harriet Whitaker, and Margaret Young. Despite the personal challenges plural marriage created, the Taylor family lived in harmony.

In January 1844 Joseph Smith, with the encouragement of his brethren, decided to run for the presidency of the United States. No one expected him to win; his purpose was to advocate sound principles for public debate and to advance the cause of the Church. John Taylor was appointed campaign manager, assisted by Willard Richards. The other members of the Twelve went on the stump to campaign.

Meanwhile, the apostasy and excommunication of two of Joseph Smith's counselors, John C. Bennett and William Law, created a serious schism in the Church. These men bitterly attacked the Prophet and even conspired to kill him. William Law and his associates also organized a paper, the *Nauvoo Expositor*, whose purpose was to defame Joseph Smith and to destroy his influence. The only issue of this paper was published on June 7, 1844. In it Joseph was depicted as a fallen prophet, grossly immoral and power hungry. Fearing that continued publication of the paper would produce civil chaos, the city council, John Taylor concurring, declared the *Expositor* to be a public nuisance and ordered it to be abated. Accordingly, on June 10 the press was destroyed and the type scattered. Newspapers in neighboring towns erupted in wild protest. One of them even called for the extermination of the Latter-day Saints. The mob spirit this aroused caused Joseph Smith to declare martial law in Nauvoo and to muster the Nauvoo Legion.

Meanwhile, an inciting-to-riot action was filed against Joseph Smith and others, including John Taylor. In a lame attempt to quiet things, Governor Thomas Ford went to Carthage with units of the state militia and invited Joseph Smith to send representatives there to explain his actions. The Prophet sent John Taylor and J. M. Bernhisel, whose explanations were interrupted and shouted down by a disorderly crowd the governor allowed to be present but failed to control. The result was an order for Joseph Smith and the others charged to appear for arraignment before the court in Carthage. Although the Prophet was convinced he would be killed in Carthage, despite the governor's promise of protection, he eventually went there with John and his other codefendants.

At the arraignment, all the defendants were bound over for trial and released on bail except Joseph and Hyrum Smith, who later had been charged with treason. The brothers were ordered jailed on the treason charge. John Taylor and Willard Richards voluntarily entered the Carthage Jail with them.

On the evening of June 27, the four friends were preparing to eat dinner in the upstairs debtors' cell, which had no bars on the door or windows. Suddenly a mob with blackened faces, which included militiamen appointed to protect the prisoners, ran upstairs shouting and swearing, forced the door, killed Joseph and Hyrum, and wounded John Taylor with five balls. One of the balls, which otherwise might have proved fatal, luckily was stopped by the watch in Elder Taylor's vest pocket. Willard was unharmed except for one earlobe that had been grazed by a ball.

Stifling their sorrow, anger, and fear, the two Apostles sent conciliatory messages to the Saints in Nauvoo, urging calmness and counseling against retaliation. After several days, Elder Taylor was moved to Nauvoo to convalesce. Although confined to bed, he continued to direct the *Times and Seasons,* writing editorials to compose the feelings of the Saints and to urge patience until the other members of the Twelve had returned from the East. At a public meeting on August 8 in which Sidney Rigdon sought to be appointed "guardian" of the Church, the Saints, moved by an eloquent speech of Brigham Young, unanimously accepted the leadership of the Twelve.

After a brief lull, the enemies of the Church resumed their attacks, falsely accusing the Saints of illegal acts and demanding that they leave Illinois. Incensed by an officer of the Illinois militia who came to admonish the Saints to observe the law, John Taylor had had enough. "You talk about the majesty of the law! What has become of those murderers? Have they been hung or shot, or in any way punished? No, sir, you know they have not."

Meanwhile the Mormon leaders were quietly preparing for the exodus, instructing the Saints what to take with them and how to maximize the return from the sale of their property on a depressed market. John Taylor and his family were ready to leave by mid-February. Before leaving, he published the last issue of the *Times and Seasons,* dated February 15, 1846, which carried its usual masthead: "Truth Will Prevail."

Elder Taylor and his family crossed the river on February 16, 1846. Their belongings were stowed in eight freight wagons. They also had a carriage with springs that afforded occasional relief from the jarring ride of the wagons. In a letter to the *Millennial Star,* Elder Taylor sought to minimize the discomforts and trials of their four-month trip across Iowa. "Our health and our lives were preserved," he wrote, adding that "we outlived the trying scene, we felt contented and happy and the songs of Zion resounded from wagon to wagon." He also minimized the fact that his Nauvoo holdings sold for only a third of market value. Noting the rapid inflation that had occurred during the Nauvoo years, he reasoned that the Saints had been "well paid" for their labor. Persistent optimism was at the core of John Taylor's character.

Soon after Elder Taylor arrived at the Missouri River on June 17, 1846, word came there was serious trouble in the Church in England. He and Elders Parley P. Pratt and Orson Hyde were assigned to investigate. Traveling by river scow, boat, and then sailing ship, they arrived at Liverpool on October 3. Sadly, they found that the brother in charge was guilty of theft and adultery. He was excommunicated. Others implicated with him were disfellowshipped. While in Great Britain, Elder Taylor visited branches throughout England and in Scotland, Wales, and the Isle of Man. He also made an unsuccessful attempt in London to obtain subsidies for British Saints to migrate to Vancouver. Leaving Elder Hyde in charge, he and Elder Pratt returned to

America. Elder Taylor arrived at Winter Quarters in April 1847, in time to deliver to Brigham Young valuable scientific equipment needed by the Pioneer Company—two sextants, two barometers, two artificial horizons, a circular reflector, seven thermometers, and a telescope.

Elders Taylor and Pratt had only two months to organize a large group of Saints—men, women, and children—for the trek west, following the trail blazed by the Pioneer Company. Divided into four units, they departed in June. Elder Taylor's unit arrived in the Salt Lake Valley on October 3, 1847. For him it was a repetition of the trek across Iowa. The dust, wind, rain, insects, tedium, and uncertainty were submerged in the marvel of the exodus of God's people to another promised land. "I might talk of trials, afflictions, and so forth," he wrote in another letter to the *Millennial Star*, "but what avails it? They are the common lot of man—they are momentary and pass away, and are not to be compared to the glory that is and shall be revealed, and I have not time to think, speak, or write about them."

Neither did Elder Taylor have much time for reflection after he arrived in the Salt Lake Valley. There was too much to be done. "About Christmas," he wrote, "I had put up, enclosed and covered about ninety feet of building made of split logs, out of which was taken a four inch plank. The plank was used for partitions, etc. . . . In addition to this, I had built corrals and stables behind, and enclosed a garden spot in front, with a board-rail fence. I assisted in all this labor of sawing, building, hawling, etc.—enough for one fall."

During 1848 and until October 1849, most of Elder Taylor's energies were devoted to developing the new gathering place. He was active in helping to build roads and bridges, to develop an irrigation system, and to explore the area for new sites for settling the immigrating Saints. At the October 1849 general conference, it was announced that four members of the Twelve had been called to serve missions abroad: Franklin D. Richards to England, Erastus Snow to Scandinavia, Lorenzo Snow to Italy, and John Taylor to France. Traveling light, Elder Taylor left the valley on October 19 with a group of missionaries headed east. With his gear were books on the French language and French history that he studied avidly on the way to his field of labor. En route he stopped intermittently to hold meetings, to counsel the Saints, and to transact personal business. At St. Louis, for instance, he purchased a wagon load of supplies that he sent home with a friend to be sold to help sustain his family. He embarked for England at New York City on the packet ship *Westwelt,* arriving at Liverpool on May 27, 1850. After conferring with associates and friends in England and obtaining necessary government clearances, Elder Taylor crossed the English Channel with several companions. They worked for a while at Jersey in the Channel Islands, then moved up the channel to Boulogne sur Mer, France. There on a secluded beach the missionaries sang, prayed, and shared testimonies, after which Elder Taylor dedicated France for the preaching of the gospel.

After obtaining permission from the mayor, Elder Taylor rented a hall and announced a series of public lectures. Several ministers attended, interrupting to ask devious questions. Elder Taylor tried to ignore them or to put them off, knowing that argument and debate were the least effective means of teaching. However, they persisted; and when three of them openly challenged him to a debate, he could not gracefully decline. The debate was held over three nights and focused on the issues of Joseph Smith, the Book of Mormon, and the authority of the elders compared with that of the ministers. The strategy of the ministers was to blacken Joseph Smith by quoting the apostate John C. Bennett and a bitter Protestant enemy of the Church, the Reverend Henry Caswell. While Elder Taylor made an able defense, the slashing attacks of his opponents and the bias of the audience turned the tide against him. When on the night after the debate only two people showed up, Elder Taylor relinquished the hall. Soon after, the missionaries traveled to Paris.

The unsatisfactory experience at Boulogne sur Mer and government restrictions in Paris convinced Elder Taylor that success in France would not come from large public meetings as in England. He therefore began to concentrate on translating and publishing the Book of Mormon in French. He also established a French language Church publication, *L'Etoile du Deseret* (The Star of Deseret), in which the history and doctrines of the Church were explained. During this period, he also began to write his distinguished literary work, *The Government of God*, which was published in England in 1852. Of this work the historian H. H. Bancroft wrote, "As a dissertation on a general and abstract subject, it probably has not its equal in point of ability within the range of Mormon literature." Slowly the Church began to take hold in France. Elder Taylor and his associates were able to build up branches in Paris, Calais, and Le Havre.

Near the end of summer 1851, believing his work in France had been completed, Elder Taylor prepared to return home. He was deterred, however, by a letter from Salt Lake City asking that he remain in Europe for a few more months. He then went into Germany, repeating the kind of work he had performed in France. He organized a German language Church publication called *Zions Panier* (Zion's Banner) and arranged to have the Book of Mormon translated and published in the German language. Returning to France in December, he found Paris in chaos. Three weeks before, Louis Napoleon had overthrown the first republic in a bloody coup d'etat. Despite the upset, Elder Taylor went forward with a conference that had been scheduled previously. Four hundred Saints from the branches in France assembled in Paris on the same day the French people were going through the charade of voting for Louis Napoleon. Commenting on the event, Elder Taylor said the Church would stand "when their [cause] is crushed to pieces; and the kingdom of God will roll on and spread from nation to nation, and from kingdom to kingdom."

Unknown to Elder Taylor, the French authorities had compiled a dossier on him as a suspected subversive. Unaware of their intention to question him, he left Paris without hindrance and traveled to a quiet seaside town to work on a plan he had conceived some time before. The plan was to organize a company to manufacture sugar from sugar beets in Utah. The company was named the Deseret Manufacturing Company. Well-to-do members had purchased stock, a management team and a team to construct the facility in Utah had been assembled, blueprints for the plant had been obtained from a refinery in France, twelve hundred pounds of choice beet seed had been purchased, and Fawcett-Preston & Co. in Liverpool had contracted to manufacture the machinery.

On March 6, 1852, the freighter *Rockaway* left Liverpool destined for New Orleans. On board was the machinery for the sugar plant. On the same day, Elder Taylor, along with a company of twenty Latter-day Saints aboard, departed on the steamer *Niagara* destined for Boston. John was to rendezvous at St. Louis with those who were to accompany the machinery upriver. At New Orleans the carefully laid plans began to unravel. Customs officials at New Orleans levied a four-thousand-dollar duty on the machinery, 40 percent of its cost. Then the steamer carrying the machinery upriver exploded and sank. After the machinery had been salvaged and transported to Fort Leavenworth, differences developed between Elder Taylor and the chief stockholder of the company about the wagons being constructed to carry the machinery to Salt Lake City. Then, in Salt Lake City, differences arose about the location of the plant; and because of complaints by the chief stockholder, President Young replaced Elder Taylor with Orson Hyde. The plant never produced sugar. Ultimately it was moved to a site southeast of town, a site appropriately called Sugarhouse. This enterprise, begun with such promise and careful planning, was the chief failure and disappointment of John Taylor's career.

Elder Taylor put the painful experience behind him as he took up his duties again at Church headquarters. In 1853 he became involved with his brethren in preaching repentance to the Saints during the so-called "reformation." The following year he moved to New York City to establish a Church publication named the *Mormon*. This was part of an elaborate plan of the Church to change its public image. Other Church publications were established at the time in Washington, D.C., St. Louis, and San Francisco. Their purpose was to present the history and the message of the Church accurately and to try to influence public opinion.

Elder Taylor boldly rented space on the corner of Nassau and Ann Streets, between the offices of the New York City's largest newspapers, the *Herald* and the *Tribune*. A message in the first issue of the *Mormon* set the tone of its editorial policy: "We have said before, and say now, that we defy all the editors and writers in the United States to prove that 'Mormonism' is less moral, scriptural, philosophical; or that there is less patriotism in Utah than in any other part of the United States. We call for proof; bring on your reasons, gentlemen, if you have any." The big newspapers responded with more bitter, unfounded attacks on the Church and its members. But Elder Taylor gave as good as he received, ably defending the Church while including in the *Mormon* well-written sketches of Church history and doctrine. He also commented on current issues of national interest, including plans to construct a transcontinental railway, a project he warmly endorsed.

Elder Taylor closed out the *Mormon* and returned to Utah in 1857 at the time of the so-called Mormon War. He joined President Young and others to prepare for the threatened invasion by U.S. Army troops sent to Utah through the blundering of President James Buchanan. Indeed, the operation became known as "Buchanan's Blunder." Without checking, President Buchanan accepted as the truth false reports about the Saints and sent the army to quell an uprising that never existed. The Mormon strategy was to burn their own homes and withdraw from the Salt Lake Valley should the army invade, leaving nothing but scorched earth behind. To that end, Elder Taylor gathered his family and belongings and moved south to Provo, determined to torch his homes if necessary. Seeing the resolve of the Mormons, and realizing its error, the government eagerly sought a compromise. "I do not remember having read in history," Elder Taylor said later in the Old Tabernacle, "where an army has been subjugated so easily, and their power wasted away so effectually without bloodshed, as this in our borders." He attributed it to the power of God shown in behalf of the Saints.

Soon after, Elder Taylor became immersed in the spiritual and temporal affairs of the territory. While continuing his service in the Twelve, he became the speaker of the territorial house of representatives, the superintendent of public schools, and a probate judge in Provo for a time. Meanwhile, he retained a keen interest in events back East as they affected the Church. He and the other leaders were alarmed by politicians in Washington, D.C., who had been elected on a platform of abolishing what were called the "twin relics of barbarism"—slavery and polygamy. Despite the efforts of friends of the Church to prevent it, this faction was able to enact an antibigamy law in 1862. It imposed criminal penalties on those who engaged in plural marriage. The Church contended the law was unconstitutional as applied to its members because it infringed on their freedom of religion. Thus John Taylor and others like him continued to live openly in plural marriage, ignoring the law. They did not fear prosecution as the Utah probate courts, which had original jurisdiction in criminal matters, were administered by elected officials who were members of the Church.

This condition angered the Church's enemies, who sought to change it. An army officer, Colonel Patrick Edward Connor, who commanded troops stationed at Fort Douglas near Salt Lake City, tried to dilute Church influence by encouraging non-Mormons to settle in Utah. He did this by promoting efforts to find and develop mineral deposits, hoping thereby to create another gold rush. He failed. Legislators in Washington, D.C., tried to pass laws to give federal courts in Utah original jurisdiction in criminal matters. These efforts failed until the mid-1870s. A federal judge, James B. McKean, tried to solve the problem by the simple expedient of declaring that a court became a federal court with original jurisdiction when the United States was a party to an action. Using this illegal device, he impanelled in bigamy cases juries from which Mormons were systematically excluded. One of these was a suit against Brigham Young. While the prophet was under house arrest, the Supreme Court, in a parallel case, held that Judge McKean's actions were unconstitutional. This required that President Young, and others similarly affected, be freed. Later Judge McKean was summarily dismissed when he jailed the prophet for twenty-four hours in a civil matter.

During this period, Elder Taylor wrote astute editorials in the *Deseret News,* criticizing official misconduct and promoting the cause of the Church. Later he became involved in a celebrated debate with the vice president of the United States, Schuyler Colfax. Mr. Colfax, a former newspaper editor, spoke in Salt Lake City, severely censuring the Church for its stand on polygamy. Elder Taylor responded in a skillful editorial. In a rejoinder, the vice president expanded his attack to demean Mormon colonizing achievements and to blame them for the difficulties in Ohio, Missouri, and Illinois. In rebuttal, Elder Taylor adroitly answered Mr. Colfax, bringing to bear the full weight of his experience, intellect, and writing ability. Compiled in a set, these writings represent perhaps the best public debate on key issues then facing the Church. And they demonstrate the competence of John Taylor as a defender and advocate of the Church against a man of intelligence, ability, and public stature. This incident marked Elder Taylor as the public spokesman for the Church on the issue of plural marriage. When John Taylor later became President of the Church, that issue dominated his administration, because Mormon leaders ultimately were forced underground by the pressures of anti-Mormon legislation.

Some of that legislation appeared in 1874 when Congress passed the Poland Act. This gave federal courts in Utah original jurisdiction in criminal cases and abolished the offices of territorial marshal and attorney general. This put teeth in the 1862 antibigamy law and, without the shield of the sympathetic probate courts, exposed Mormon polygamists to criminal prosecution. Aware of the critical effect of such legislation, the Church opposed it vigorously. In Utah Elder Taylor wrote telling editorials and compiled statistics showing the inefficiency and the anti-Mormon bias of the Utah federal courts. In Washington, D.C., George Q. Cannon, then a member of Congress, opposed the legislation with the tools of persuasion and influence. All this availed nothing, and the bill passed by a wide margin. The Church continued to assert that the antibigamy law was unconstitutional and to teach and live the principle of plural marriage, although with more caution than before.

Elder Taylor's status in the Church was radically altered the following year. In June 1875, at a meeting in San Pete County, President Young changed the order of seniority in the Twelve. This action, which had been discussed intermittently for years, made John Taylor the senior Apostle in the Twelve, positioned to succeed President Young at his death. The action also confirmed the policy that seniority dates from the ordination and induction into the quorum and took into account the gaps in service of Orson Hyde and Orson Pratt that occurred in the early years. It was a very sensitive move because Elder Hyde had served as President of the Twelve for twenty years. This fact dictated the location of the meeting, as Elder Hyde had lived and presided in San Pete for many years. Every effort was made to soften the blow for him, his family, and friends. The quiet way this drastic change was accepted by all underscores the selfless nature of apostolic service.

President Brigham Young passed away on August 29, 1877, and was buried four days later. At the moment of death, the First Presidency was automatically dissolved and Elder Taylor became the de facto head of the Church in his role as the President of the Twelve. In consultation, the Twelve decided to defer reorganization of the First Presidency. At a meeting held in connection with the October general conference, Elder Taylor was sustained as the President of the Twelve, confirming his status as the head of the Church. In remarks made during the conference, he stressed the need for humility in Church service, quoting extensively from section 121 of the Doctrine and Covenants. He also emphasized the importance of the priesthood and admonished the brethren to be more diligent in their duties. "Some of our brethren feel sometimes that these things draw heavily upon them," he said. "Of course they do; and God expects to try us, to see what we are made of, and see whether the right ring of metal is in us or not, and whether we are prepared to stand up to the rack and walk forth in the name of Israel's God." Talk of this kind dispelled any question whether John Taylor, the learned writer, editor, and philosopher, was mentally and spiritually prepared to lead the Church in the troubled days ahead.

Following the death of President Brigham Young, President Taylor became the Trustee-in-Trust of the Church, which enabled him to oversee the Church's temporal affairs. The ecclesiastical duties were administered by the Twelve through task committees; so as chairman of the Church's Executive Committee, President Taylor could direct the priesthood functions of the Church almost as efficiently as if the First Presidency were in place.

His leadership style soon emerged. He resolved a dispute between two brethren merely by singing several hymns at the beginning of their meeting. They were so touched that they left afterward without explaining their difficulty. He resisted a recommendation to release a stake president because of discord in the stake until members of the Twelve had visited the stake and in a meeting with the local leaders had elicited positive comments about the stake president. Then months later, when there was unity again in the stake, he authorized the reorganization of the stake presidency. And he refused to release a stake president who had said in an open meeting that he did not know the gospel to be true but that he merely believed it. President Taylor told the Apostle with him the young stake president had a testimony but didn't know it yet. That stake president, Heber J. Grant, later became the President of the Church.

At the October 1877 general conference, President Taylor followed up his comments about priesthood responsibilities by convening a special meeting of the General Authorities and stake presidents. There the principles of delegation and personal initiative in priesthood service were emphasized. Soon after, he laid the cornerstones of the Logan and Manti Temples and encouraged increased use of the St. George Temple. With that came instructions about genealogical research. Meanwhile, he attended and gave counsel at ward and stake meetings as his schedule allowed.

In 1879 the Supreme Court upheld the antibigamy act of 1862. This undercut the Church's claim that the act was unconstitutional. Thereafter, those practicing plural marriage clearly were in violation of the law. Yet President Taylor continued to teach and to practice the principle. His stand, differing from the concept of civil disobedience as taught by Leo Tolstoy and Henry David Thoreau, embodied these ideas: First, because the antibigamy act was directed solely at the Saints and was passed more than twenty years after they began to practice plural marriage, the law should be administered with equity and a benign tolerance. Second, to help bring about an equitable solution, the Saints should pray for Congress. Third, while the Church did not intend to rebel openly, the Saints would not cooperate with the government or do things they were not specifically required to do. Fourth, in appropriate cases, some new polygamous sealings would be allowed. In the end, the brethren who had more than one wife simply disappeared into the underground to avoid prosecution under what they considered to be an unjust and inequitable law.

At a solemn assembly held on October 10, 1880, John Taylor was sustained as the third President of the Church. He selected George Q. Cannon and Joseph F. Smith as his counselors. In the same year he declared a jubilee to celebrate the fiftieth anniversary of the organization of the Church. In the spirit of the jubilee, the Church forgave many of the debts owed to it and encouraged members of the Church to do likewise with their debtors.

In December 1881, President Taylor moved from "Taylor Row" into the Gardo House, across the street south from the Beehive House. Called "Amelia's Palace," this ornate, Church-owned building once was occupied by one of Brigham Young's families. President Taylor had resisted moving there because he thought it was too fancy. He finally yielded because of its convenient location. A few days later, on January 2, 1882, the Taylors hosted a public reception in the home, and streams of guests, both members and nonmembers, were shown the house and served refreshments.

The pleasant mood created by this occasion was ruined on March 14, when the Edmunds Act became law. This statute expanded the criminal sanctions of the 1862 antibigamy law and excluded polygamists and those who believed in polygamy from jury service. It also placed the elective process in the hands of enemies of the Church. President Taylor commented on the act at the April general conference: "Let us treat it the same as we did this morning in coming through the snow storm—put up our coat collars and wait till the storm subsides. . . . While the storm lasts it is useless to reason with the world; when it subsides we can talk to them."

The prophet followed his own advice and went about his work, counseling with the Brethren, speaking at meetings, greeting new immigrants, sending out missionaries, and planning new settlements. A special revelation later in the year called George Teasdale and Heber J. Grant to the Twelve. Meanwhile, as time allowed, President Taylor worked on his other literary masterpiece, *The Mediation and Atonement*.

The first case under the Edmunds Act came to trial in 1884. The defendant was twenty-seven-year-old Rudger Clawson, a son of Hiram B. Clawson, who had been one of Brigham Young's business agents. President Taylor was subpoenaed as a witness, not because he was in possession of any relevant facts but because of the desire of government attorneys to heighten publicity in the case. The packed jury guaranteed a conviction of the defendant. At a meeting held in Ogden, the prophet openly condemned the decision. He told the audience that all that would have been necessary for Rudger Clawson and his plural wife to avoid prosecution would have been "to walk in the way of the world today, unite with our modern Christian civilization, and if passion guide their actions, why call each other husband

and wife, why hallow their association by any sacred cere-mony—was there any need of such?" However much this scathing irony may have troubled the conscience of the offi-cials, it did not deter them from pressing aggressively for other convictions.

President Taylor saw clearly how this would disrupt the lives of all Mormon polygamists and their families. He sought some relief from the pressure by establishing Mormon communities beyond the jurisdiction of the United States. He traveled to Mexico in January 1885, where arrangements were made to purchase property in northern Chihuahua. Later the Mormon communities of Colonia Juarez, Colonia Diaz, Colonia Pacheco, and Dublán were established there. President Taylor also visited the governor of Sonora, who assured him the Latter-day Saints would be welcome. When President Taylor returned to Salt Lake City in late January, he found that President Cannon had been arrested and was free on bail and that warrants for his own arrest and the arrest of President Joseph F. Smith had been issued. The strategy of the federal officials was to prosecute the high leaders of the Church in the hope this would cause others to yield. These circumstances prompted President Taylor to go underground to avoid arrest.

The prophet delivered his last address in the Salt Lake Tabernacle on February 1, 1885. In it he denounced the gov-ernment for its double standard of justice. He contrasted the vigorous enforcement of the antibigamy laws against a peaceful, industrious people with the negligent enforce-ment of the law when Mormon rights were infringed upon. "I want to know if any one of you can tell me of any indi-vidual that was ever punished according to law for killing a Mormon," he asked the audience. Convinced there was no justice for the Latter-day Saints in the current environment, he said, "We must take care of ourselves as best we may and avoid being caught in their snares." Leaving the meet-ing early, President Taylor was accompanied by his two bodyguards, Charles Wilcken, a veteran of the Prussian Army, and Samuel Bateman, a convert from Manchester, England. These two faithful men would be the almost constant companions of the prophet until the time of his death.

President Taylor's first place of refuge was at the home of Samuel Bennion, bishop of the North Jordan Ward in Taylorsville, Utah. He remained there for nine days and was then moved to another safe place. During the first year, the prophet lived in eleven different homes. Although his hosts did everything possible to make him comfortable, it was a difficult life for a seventy-seven-year-old man. The cramped quarters, changes in diet, lack of adequate exercise, absence from his family, concern about the Saints, and the constant emotional strain took their toll on the aging prophet. He received frequent reports from some of the Brethren not on the underground; and he and his counselors sent messages to the Saints, published in the *Deseret News* and read in stake and ward meetings. The last of these, dated April 8, 1887, which covered a wide range of subjects, gave special attention to the Edmunds-Tucker Act, which had been passed a few weeks before. This act contained stringent new provisions to penalize the Church and those practicing polygamy. The message said the Church was passing through a period of "transition and evolution" such as appeared "to be necessary in the progress and perfecting of all created things." It concluded with this optimistic forecast: "The result will be that we shall be stronger, wiser, purer, happier, for the experience gained, and the work of the Lord . . . will yet triumph gloriously over all its foes."

On November 22, 1886, President Taylor moved to his last place of refuge. It was the farmhouse of Thomas F. Roueche, located on the flatlands west of the peaceful community of Kaysville, Utah. There President Taylor continued to receive reports and to send messages to the Saints. He also kept in touch with his family through regular letters that breathed a spirit of optimism despite the tragic circumstances of his life. "Some people suppose that persecution and trials are afflictions," he wrote in one letter. "But sometimes, and generally, if we are doing the will of the Lord and keeping His commandments, they may be truly said to be blessings in disguise." There followed comments on the law of compensation and on his conviction that life's battles are intended by a loving heavenly parent to assist in honing character and to help one to prepare for celestial glory. "I must fight, if I would reign," he quoted approvingly from John Wesley. "Increase my courage, Lord; I'll bear the toil, endure the pain, supported by thy word."

In February 1887 Congress passed the Edmunds-Tucker Act, the last and most stringent of the antipolygamy laws. It disincorporated the Church as a legal entity, forfeited all Church property in excess of fifty thousand dollars, and dissolved the Perpetual Emigrating Fund Company. It decreed the legality of testimony by a wife against her husband and empowered the president of the United States to appoint county probate judges. It also abolished women's suffrage in Utah, provided a new voting test oath, redefined voting districts, and abolished the office of territorial superintendent of schools.

The effect of this law was devastating. It practically guaranteed that in time the Church would be destroyed as an earthly organization with its leaders imprisoned, its temples and other properties in the hands of the government, and its missionary system in disarray. While President Taylor was prepared to accept this result, it had to be measured against the apostolic mandate given to him and his brethren to preach the gospel to *every creature* and to prepare a people ready to receive the Savior at his Second Coming. While he knew the law of plural marriage is an eternal principle and was given by inspiration through the Prophet Joseph Smith, he also knew that Joseph waited almost ten years after receiving the revelation before he lived it; and he knew from the Book of Mormon (see Jacob 2:23–30) that plural marriage on earth is allowed or disallowed intermittently as God decrees through his prophets. President Taylor never felt impressed to direct a cessation of plural marriage; yet a few weeks before he died, he approved the draft of a proposed constitution for Utah that contained a provision prohibiting plural marriage. He was prepared to leave the matter in the hands of the Lord and of the prophet or prophets who would succeed him.

Life on the underground took a heavy physical toll on President Taylor. As he was deprived of regular exercise, his health declined rapidly. In the summer of 1887 he became bedridden. Seeing the end approaching, President George Q. Cannon urged President Joseph F. Smith to return from his exile in Hawaii, which he did on July 18. When the two counselors entered the prophet's room, President Cannon mentioned it was the first time the First Presidency had been together since December 1884. In response, President John Taylor uttered the last recorded words of his mortal life. "I feel to thank the Lord," he said quietly, almost inaudibly.

The prophet passed away on July 25, 1887. After the body was prepared, it was moved to the Gardo House, where family and friends gathered to pay their last respects. The funeral was held in the Tabernacle on July 29. Before the services commenced, there was a public viewing. After appropriate eulogies were spoken, President Taylor was lovingly interred in the Salt Lake City Cemetery. Nearby were the graves of members of his family and of many of his brethren with whom he had fought the good fight.

NOTE

This chapter is based on Francis M. Gibbons's book *John Taylor: Mormon Philosopher, Prophet of God* (Salt Lake City: Deseret Book Company, 1985) and sources cited therein.

CHAPTER FOUR

WILFORD WOODRUFF

Wilford Woodruff, born March 1, 1807, in Farmington, Hartford County, Connecticut, descended from long-lived and hard-working British ancestors. His parents, Aphek and Beulah Thompson Woodruff, were strict Presbyterians who trained their children in their church's catechism but disbelieved in modern revelation and other spiritual gifts. For Wilford, that lack was filled by a neighbor called Father Mason, a spiritual man who shared with Wilford a vision he had received years before in which he saw a restoration of the church and kingdom of God on the earth "with all its gifts and blessings." He predicted Wilford would become "a conspicuous actor in that kingdom." This and an inborn sense caused Wilford to retire frequently to a secluded place where he "offered up [his] soul in prayer to the Lord."

On December 29, 1833, Wilford and his brother, Azmon, attended a meeting conducted by two Mormon missionaries, Zera Pulsipher and Elijah Cheney. On an impulse, Wilford arose in the meeting and bore witness of the truth of what had been said. Two days later, the Woodruff brothers were baptized into The Church of Jesus Christ of Latter-day Saints. Soon after, Wilford began to keep a journal. With only a few gaps, he kept it faithfully the rest of his life. It became one of the most important historical records of the early years of the Church.

In April 1834 Parley P. Pratt recruited Wilford as a member of Zion's Camp, a group organized to assist members of the Church in Missouri who were under mob attack. After arranging his affairs, Wilford went to Kirtland, Ohio, where he met Joseph Smith, who, in Wilford's words of certitude, was "the Prophet & Seer which God hath raised up in these last days." He stayed in the Prophet's home until the camp departed on May 1. The seven-week trek was one of the key experiences of Wilford Woodruff's life. It trained him in leadership and revealed his dependable character to Joseph Smith.

When Zion's Camp was disbanded in June, Wilford remained in Missouri. He worked for Lyman Wight and lived in his home. Soon after, he was ordained a priest by Simeon Carter. This imbued him with a desire to fill a mission. He prayed fervently in secret to this end. His prayers were answered, and in January 1835 he was called and left on a mission to the Southern states with his companion, Henry Brown. Before leaving, he inventoried all his possessions and consecrated them to the Lord, "that I may be a lawful heir to the Kingdom of God even the Celestial Kingdom."

Wilford labored for twenty months in the states of Missouri, Arkansas, Tennessee, and Kentucky. He traveled mostly by foot, often in rain and mud, through rural areas where wild animals were common. After Elder Brown gave up and returned home, Wilford worked alone for a while. What he lacked in polish and poise he made up in fervor and spirituality, for he possessed the gifts of tongues and prophecy. His diligence was rewarded when he was ordained an elder on June 28, 1835, by Warren Parrish and then a seventy on May 31, 1836, by David W. Patten of the Twelve. When he left the mission field in September 1836, he sent twenty-two of his converts to Missouri in obedience to directions he had received. He was told to return to Kirtland.

In Wilford's absence, the Kirtland Temple had been completed and dedicated. He soon received special blessings in that sacred building, where "the Lord poured out his spirit" upon him. On January 3, 1837, he was set apart as a member of the First Quorum of Seventy by Zebedee Coltrin, who promised that the Lord would give him "great power, knowledge & wisdom & faith" and that he would "preach to the nations of the earth & to the inhabitants upon the islands of the sea." Three months later when Wilford received his endowment in the temple, Elder Coltrin promised him he would "have long life & bring many into the Kingdom of God." And on April 15, 1837, when he received a patriarchal blessing from Joseph Smith Sr., he was told that God had looked on him "from all eternity." Meanwhile, Wilford became a member of the School of the Prophets, where he studied history and languages and was inspired by the doctrinal teachings of Joseph Smith.

After a short courtship, Wilford married Phoebe W. Carter on April 13, 1837. The following month he left for a mission to the Fox Islands, off the coast of Maine. Visiting members of his family in Richland, New York, and in Farmington, Connecticut, along the way, he arrived at the home of his wife's parents in Scarborough, Maine, in early August. Phoebe joined him there.

Elder Woodruff and Jonathon Hale sailed from Portland, Maine, to the Fox Islands on August 19, 1837. The elders began their ministry by finding a place of seclusion where they prayed fervently for guidance in this the first missionary work of the restored Church on the "Isles of the Sea."

Their first conversions occurred on September 3, when Captain Justus Eames and his wife were baptized. Ebenezer Eames was baptized a week later. "I truly felt to rejoice to behold the mighty captains of the sea enter the new and everlasting covenant," Wilford exulted. By the end of December he was "preaching and baptizing almost daily." Great spiritual fervor accompanied his efforts. "I spoke in tongues and interpreted and prophesied and we rejoiced," he wrote on December 17.

The success of the missionaries was accompanied by increasing opposition from the clergy. Hecklers began to attend their meetings, and an ugly spirit of mobocracy appeared. Yet the number of converts grew. In the spring of 1838, Wilford was instructed to encourage the converts to move to Missouri. By October, fifty-three of them had liquidated their holdings and were prepared to leave.

On August 9, 1838, Elder Woodruff received a letter from Thomas B. Marsh advising that he had been called to the Twelve and instructing him to go to Far West, Missouri, to meet with his quorum and to leave from thence on a mission overseas. Settling his family (which now included a daughter, Sarah Emma) temporarily in Rochester, Illinois, Wilford went to Far West as directed. There on April 26, 1839, he was ordained an Apostle by Brigham Young and helped to re-lay the cornerstone of the Far West Temple. Later in the summer, he settled his family in an old army barracks in Montrose, Iowa, across from Nauvoo; and on August 8 he and John Taylor left Nauvoo on their mission. Making their way to New York without purse or scrip, they boarded the packet ship *Oxford* on December 19, 1839, in company with Theodore Turley. They arrived in Liverpool on January 11, 1840.

Accompanied by Elder Turley, Wilford Woodruff began his missionary work in the Potteries, small market towns where china and stoneware were manufactured. There they had success and baptized many. Yet, during a sermon at a

Sunday service on March 1, he cancelled meetings he had scheduled and announced he was leaving. "The Lord warned me to go south," he reported later. With William Benbow, he traveled to the Hill Farm of John Benbow in Castle Frome, Ledbury, Herefordshire. There he found six hundred former members of the Wesleyan Methodist Church who called themselves the United Brethren. The day after his arrival, Elder Woodruff spoke to a large group of them. He was impressed that "many present would be Saints." The next day he baptized six converts, including John Benbow and his wife. Foreseeing what was ahead, he prepared a baptismal pool. During the month that followed, Elder Woodruff's pool was in almost daily use. "Glory hallelujah!" he exclaimed following baptisms at the pool on March 21, "the work of God rolls on." The baptisms continued amid ever increasing opposition from mobs. Once he was stoned as he baptized in his pool.

In early April he traveled to Preston to meet with Brigham Young and several other members of the Twelve who had arrived in England later. Learning of Wilford's success in Herefordshire, Brigham Young and Willard Richards accompanied him there after the Preston meetings. With the three Apostles working together, the process of teaching and baptizing accelerated. When John Benbow donated two hundred pounds and Thomas Kington one hundred pounds to the Church, Brigham Young went to Manchester with the money to arrange for the publication of the Book of Mormon and a hymnbook. When Elders Woodruff and Richards left for Manchester to attend a conference in late June, there were 541 members of the Church in Herefordshire who were organized into thirty-three branches. "I never before left a field of labor with as much satisfaction as on this occasion," Wilford reported.

By July 26 the first group of converts from among the United Brethren, fifty in number, was prepared to migrate to the United States. Many others followed. Later Wilford worked for a while in London but with much less success and much more trauma. There on October 18, 1840, he was accosted by a spiritual being whom he understood to be "the Prince of darkness, or the devil." Through prayer and the ministrations of three personages who appeared to help him, he was delivered from peril.

On April 19, 1841, Elder Woodruff boarded the *Rochester* with six other members of the Twelve and 120 converts. After the Atlantic crossing and after spending several months in the East visiting family members and working in local branches, he arrived in Nauvoo on October 6, 1841. Before Wilford's arrival, Joseph Smith had announced the time had come for the Twelve to take their place next to the First Presidency and to remain at home. It required a major adjustment in Wilford's thinking, which was strongly oriented toward missionary work out in the world. But he settled into his new role obediently. He fixed up a home for his family, was appointed to the city council, became an associate editor of the *Times and Seasons,* and engaged in private business.

There was much turmoil in Nauvoo during 1842. Joseph Smith went underground to avoid arrest on the false charge he was an accessory to the shooting of Missouri governor Lilburn W. Boggs. The Apostles were saddened when Orson Pratt was temporarily excommunicated. And Wilford was in bed most of the winter with a severe case of the flu. Things brightened for him in 1843 when he filled a four-month mission to the East to raise funds and to speed the gathering of the Saints to Nauvoo.

1844 was a year of triumph and tragedy—triumph when on May 4 the Woodruffs moved into their new two-story brick home, and tragedy when the Prophet Joseph Smith and his brother Hyrum were murdered. At the time of the Martyrdom on June 27, Elder Woodruff was in Massachusetts promoting Joseph's campaign for the presidency of the United States. He did not learn about the murders until July 9. He was devastated, as were the other Apostles. After venting their grief and realizing that the keys to build up the Church remained with the Twelve, the Apostles who were in the East returned to Nauvoo in early August. There they joined Elders John Taylor and Willard Richards, who were with Joseph and Hyrum at the time of their martyrdom in the Carthage jail. At a general meeting on August 8, the members of the Church unanimously accepted the leadership of the Twelve instead of Sidney Rigdon, who had offered himself as a "guardian" of the Church.

At a meeting of the Twelve on August 12, Elder Woodruff was appointed to preside over the Church in Great Britain "and the adjacent islands and continent." After leasing their new home, storing their belongings, arranging to leave Wilford Jr. with the Benbow family, bidding good-bye to their friends, and receiving blessings from the Brethren, Wilford and Phoebe left Nauvoo on August 28. With them were two-year-old Phoebe Amelia and their thirteen-month-old baby, Susan Cornelia (Sarah Emma had passed away while Elder Woodruff was in England). They traveled first to Scarborough, Maine, where they left Phoebe Amelia with the Carters. After taking care of Church matters in the Northeast, including the excommunication of several apostates in Boston, Elder Woodruff, accompanied by Phoebe and the baby, embarked on the *John R. Skiddy*, a new packet ship, on December 8, 1844. With them were three missionary couples, including Dan Jones and his wife, who had been assigned to serve in Great Britain. It was a rough Atlantic crossing. "The sea was piled up like mountains," wrote Wilford. "When we were in the trough of the sea, waves would arise at our stern as high as the top of the mizzenmast." Later during a particularly bad day, he wrote: "We kneeled before the Lord and prayed unitedly that the Lord would cause the gale to cease and the wind to change, that we might go forward and not backward; and in a little time after the wind instantly ceased and finally changed into the southwest which gave us fair wind."

The travelers arrived safely at Liverpool on January 3, 1845. Soon after, Elder Woodruff rented a house for his family on Museum Place, at the bottom of Virgin Street, and took up his new duties. These consisted of overseeing the work generally throughout the mission, directing emigration, supervising publication and writing of the *Millennial Star*, obtaining the British copyright for the Doctrine and Covenants and having that book printed, and instructing and motivating leaders and members in meetings held throughout the area. To broaden her interests and understanding, Wilford took Phoebe with him when feasible. Together they visited museums, libraries, ancient buildings, and points of historical interest. Phoebe's travels were restricted after July 18, 1845, when a son, Joseph, was born.

As he visited in the branches, Wilford was troubled by an "aspiring spirit" he detected among some. He even found this attitude in the two principal leaders in the mission office, who failed to meet him at the pier when he arrived, who were uncongenial in their relations with him, and who gave him little help as he prepared to leave. Only a few months later, the senior of this pair was excommunicated and the other was disfellowshipped when John Taylor, Parley P. Pratt, and Orson Hyde came to England to investigate reports of official misconduct.

Phoebe and the two children embarked from Liverpool on January 21, 1846, destined for New Orleans, from where they would travel upriver to Nauvoo. Elder Woodruff left a few days later for New York. After picking up Phoebe Amelia in Scarborough and his father and stepmother in Connecticut, and after handling matters in the eastern branches, Elder Woodruff traveled to Nauvoo, arriving there on April 13.

Things were chaotic in Nauvoo. Many of the leaders

and members had been driven out in February and were on their way west. Wilford liquidated his holdings; purchased supplies, wagons, and animals; packed his belongings; and crossed the river on April 30. Later that evening, he and others recrossed the river and dedicated the Nauvoo Temple. Earlier, on April 15, with Phoebe's consent, Wilford was married in the temple to his first plural wife, Mary Jackson. Because of their strict, monogamous upbringing, Wilford and Phoebe struggled to accept the principle of plural marriage. They did so at last due to the instruction of Joseph Smith, whom they sustained as a prophet. Later Elder Woodruff was married to three other plural wives: Emma Smoot Smith, Sarah Brown, and Sarah Delight Stocking. These faithful women bore thirty-three children—nineteen daughters and fourteen sons.

Wilford's forty-eight-day trip across Iowa was marked by the serious illness of Susan Cornelia; an almost-fatal accident to his father, Aphek; the rebellion of his stepmother and her return to Nauvoo to live with his sister, Eunice, who had left the Church; and the constant hassle of keeping his animals rounded up. The family problems continued at Winter Quarters on the Missouri River when little Joseph died and when another baby, whom they named Ezra, died shortly after birth. Phoebe was almost inconsolable with grief that was aggravated by her adjustment to living in plural marriage. To help ease her distress, Wilford built her a new, snug cabin.

Elder Woodruff left for the Rocky Mountains with Brigham Young's Pioneer Company in early April 1847. Compared to the crossing of Iowa, this was a relatively peaceful trek for him. He kept an accurate record of the journey, commenting on the interesting and peaceful contacts with Indians; the awesome appearance of the buffalo herds, which "looked as though the face of the earth was alive and moving like the waves of the sea"; and his first exciting view of the mountains "piled up" to the sky. Near

Fort Bridger, where the company crossed several trout brooks, Wilford broke out fly-fishing equipment he had purchased in England and indulged in his lifelong recreation. "I caught twelve in all," he reported with not a little pride, "and about one-half of them would weigh about three fourths of a pound each, while all the rest of the camp [which used mundane bait of meat or grasshoppers] did not catch during the day three pounds of trout in all." As the Pioneer Company neared the Salt Lake Valley, Brigham Young, ill with mountain fever, transferred to Elder Woodruff's carriage. When the valley came into view, the two Apostles "gazed with wonder and admiration upon the vast, rich, fertile valley." Wilford envisioned "that in not many years . . . the House of God would stand upon the top of the mountains while the valleys would be converted into orchard, vineyard, gardens and fields."

Elder Woodruff remained in the valley from July 24 to August 26, 1847. Except on Sundays, which were devoted to prayers and religious services, he worked each day from dawn to dark, plowing, planting, exploring, cutting timber, making adobes, and beginning a rustic home for his family. He also joined in setting standards for the city, in designating a site for the temple, and in renewing his sacred covenants through rebaptism. Before leaving to return to Winter Quarters, he checked the field and found the corn was a foot high and about to tassel out.

The return trip was marred by conflicts with Indians and the loss of many horses. This slowed the pace of travel as the members of the party had to alternately ride and walk. They arrived at Winter Quarters on October 31, 1847. Wilford learned that three days earlier, Phoebe had given birth to a daughter, whom they named Sarah Carter Woodruff.

In counsel, Elder Woodruff and his brethren of the Twelve sustained and ordained Brigham Young as the second President of the Church on December 5, 1847. He selected Heber C. Kimball and Willard Richards as his counselors. These actions were ratified at a general conference on December 27. A few months later, the First Presidency appointed Elder Woodruff president of the Eastern States Mission, with headquarters in Boston, Massachusetts. He would both supervise proselytizing and administrative work in the mission and direct the emigration of converts from there and abroad.

Again tragedy struck the Woodruff family en route to Boston when baby Sarah died on July 22, 1848. At the time they were visiting Phoebe's sister and her husband, Rhoda and Luther Scammons, near Lost Grove, Illinois. Phoebe would not be comforted. Of seven children she had given birth to, four were dead. Wilford was at a loss to console his wife. The baby was buried in the Scammonses' garden. Wilford put up a limestone slab at the grave site on which he carved the names and dates of birth of all seven of Phoebe's children and the dates of death of those who had passed away.

Arriving in Boston August 12, 1848, Wilford rented a house in Cambridgeport, a Boston suburb, which served as his home and his headquarters for twenty months. From there he traveled throughout the northeastern states and into Canada, ministering to the members, directing missionary and emigration work, and counseling the Saints to move to the new gathering place in the Rocky Mountains. He also conferred with J. M. Bernhisel and Colonel Thomas L. Kane, who were working with eastern politicians to try to obtain statehood for Utah.

It was a stressful and demanding assignment for Elder Woodruff. Not the least of his problems was transportation. In New Brunswick, Canada, for instance, thirty-five miles from his destination and with no transportation, he decided to walk, carrying his bag. "Although I began to be very weary and lame, yet I entered the dark forest before me, and found my last 15 miles a sore, dreary road indeed."

And the circumstances he found at the end of the road were not always pleasant. "I sat all day to settle a difficulty," he wrote about a branch meeting in Massachusetts, "and I heard it until my head, heart, and brain ached. It lasted until night." He found relief from the constant pressure through Phoebe's companionship and by working hard in the little garden he had planted and by fishing occasionally.

Following instructions from the First Presidency in April 1850 to "gather up the Saints" and come west, Elder Woodruff organized a group of two hundred and, traveling on the rivers, arrived at Kanesville, Iowa, in mid-May. There wagons and animals were acquired for the trip to the Salt Lake Valley. Wilford had twelve wagons, twenty-seven yoke of oxen, and thirty cows. Ten of the wagons were loaded with merchandise belonging to his brother-in-law, Ilus Carter. It was a hard trek, marked by several deaths from cholera, a stampede that created havoc, sticky mud caused by heavy rains, and an overturned wagon. The party limped into the valley on October 14, 1850.

After completing a home for his family, branding his animals, and selling the merchandise he had purchased from Ilus, Elder Woodruff settled into a normal routine for the first time since 1844. It was a joy to meet regularly with his brethren and to fill apostolic assignments. The love and respect he had shown toward Joseph Smith was now transferred to his new leader, Brigham Young. "The power of God was upon President Young," Wilford wrote on August 23, 1851, "who is made by the power of God a great, good and glorious man, and a father, indeed, to the church and kingdom of God."

Elder Woodruff also became involved in a major effort at self-improvement. Impressed by Benjamin Franklin's autobiography, he copied lengthy excerpts in his journal, including the author's thirteen virtues with their precepts. He enrolled in Parley P. Pratt's Spanish school and Orson Hyde's grammar school, and he became president of the

Universal Scientific Association. He affiliated with the newly organized Pomological Society, Lorenzo Snow's Polysophical Society, and the Typographical Society. He also organized a school for his children.

Meanwhile, Elder Woodruff became Assistant Church Historian and a member of the territorial legislature, serving as chairman of the standing committees on revenue, libraries, and roads and as a member of the education committee. When in December 1855 the legislature met in Fillmore, Utah, Wilford stayed in the home of a member. His days were filled with legislative business, while letter writing, keeping his journal, reading, and meeting with his brethren occupied the evenings and weekends. At one meeting Elder Woodruff spoke about the responsibilities resting on the priesthood: "I feel that as Prophets, Apostles and Elders we have no time to sleep, slumber and rest. . . . There is a mighty responsibility upon us as a people, and we have no time to lose or throw away if we do our duty to God." Those words reflect Wilford Woodruff's lifestyle and work ethic: he was never idle. Except for occasional recreations or socializing, all his hours were filled with some kind of productive activity, whether mental, spiritual, or physical. And as with his fishing, Wilford's socializing was zestful: "The Governor and Legislative Assembly of the Territory of Utah made the most splendid party ever got up in these mountains as far as a feast and decorations were concerned. The U.S. Judges and military officers were invited. Dancing commenced at three o'clock; dinner at nine; and supper at twelve o'clock." The feasting included "pies, cakes, oysters, etc."

Elder Woodruff and other Church leaders made frequent trips to outlying communities to provide direction and encouragement. It was not always easy to get there. "We have been over the worst road for a few days past that I ever knew wagons to pass over," he wrote of one trip to southern Utah. "We had to draw our wagons up and let them down with ropes [and] it was so sideling we had to hold our wagons up to keep them from turning over." Their arrival at these communities often was greeted by band music, the firing of cannons, and the waving of flags.

In the mid-1850s Elder Woodruff joined with his brethren in conducting a "reformation" among the Saints, some of whom had become negligent in their Church duties. Others were guilty of sexual sins, swearing, smoking, stealing, and other conduct unacceptable for Latter-day Saints. To combat this, the leaders went through all the Mormon communities calling the people to repentance. This effort was spearheaded by Elder Woodruff's good friend, Jedediah M. Grant, who was a member of the First Presidency. Elder Woodruff recorded the crux of President Grant's message in his journal, giving it his endorsement: "When you are right, we will cease to chastise; we will cease to rebuke; we will cease throwing the arrows of the Almighty through you; we will cease telling you to surrender, to repent of all your sins." The speaker also said if the Saints did not repent, the leaders would "continue to throw the arrows of God through you, to hurl the darts of heaven upon you and the power of God in your midst; and we will storm the bulwarks of hell, and we will march against you in the strength of the God of Israel."

Elder Woodruff used the messages of this reformation to evaluate his own status. Wondering whether he measured up, he went to President Brigham Young and offered to step down from the Twelve if the prophet felt someone else could serve more effectively. Brigham declined the offer, assuring Wilford his service was exemplary. Then as Elder Woodruff rose to leave, President Young stopped him: "Come, don't be in a hurry. . . . I want men to stop here who [have] the spirit of God. It rests me."

In the spring of 1857 three federal judges, George P. Stiles, W. W. Drummond, and John F. Kinney, returned to Washington, D.C., bearing false reports that the Mormons were guilty of destroying or hiding court records. Without checking this and other negative reports, President James Buchanan assembled an army to quell an uprising in Utah that didn't exist. This reckless action rightly earned the venture the name "Buchanan's Blunder."

The Mormons learned about the invasion on July 24 at a gathering in the mountains to celebrate the tenth anniversary of their arrival in the Salt Lake Valley. After the persecutions and drivings in Ohio, Missouri, and Illinois, the Saints were resolved to resist the new threat. The Nauvoo Legion was activated; missionaries and leaders were called home; and plans were laid to guard the mountain passes, to harass the army with guerrilla attacks, and, if pushed to it, to scorch the valley with fire and then leave. In the spring of 1858 Elder Woodruff moved twenty wagon loads of belongings, including Church historical records, to Utah Valley. He was prepared to burn and destroy his Salt Lake Valley holdings. When the invading forces saw the same resolve among all the Saints, they were anxious for a truce. When a peace commission met on June 4, it was agreed that Brigham Young would relinquish the governorship to Alfred Cumming, that any claims against the Saints would be dropped, and that the army would be allowed to march through—but not to stop in—Salt Lake City. It was a major victory. "The Lord has heard our prayers," wrote Elder Woodruff, "and the President of the United States has been brought to a point where he has been obliged to ask for peace."

Within a few months another crisis prompted Elder Woodruff to pack the historical records and his personal belongings again in preparation for another move. It occurred when federal judge John Cradlebaugh requisitioned several hundred troops to guard the courthouse in Provo, where he presided at a murder trial. The excitement over the case occurred when the judge attempted to tie Brigham Young to the murders because of false charges that the prophet was responsible for the massacre at Mountain Meadows. Petitions to Washington, D.C., brought censures to the army and the judge. Later, federal judge Charles E. Sinclair, in Salt Lake City, unsuccessfully sought to enlist the help of the army to arrest Brigham Young under a false charge of counterfeiting. On June 29, 1859, Elder Woodruff commented on the end of this charade: "The Deseret News contained Judge Black's letter to the Utah judges, reproving them sharply for their course."

Another Federal official who harassed the Saints was Colonel (later General) Patrick Edward Connor, who arrived in Salt Lake City in December 1862. He came to Utah with the avowed purpose of diluting the influence of the Mormon leaders. To this end, he encouraged his troops to prospect for minerals, hoping to cause another gold rush. He also established a newspaper, the *Union Vedette,* in which he attacked the Church leaders, especially Brigham Young. Following passage of the antibigamy act in 1862, the colonel threatened to use the military to serve a writ on Brigham Young. "There was quite an excitement in the city," Elder Woodruff wrote on March 12, 1863. "Colonel Connor marched out his forces and travelled one mile towards the city. The flag was raised upon the President's house and the people gathered in arms to meet the enemy; but as soon as they came about one mile, they marched back again." Further tension occurred when Church leaders urged members not to mix with the soldiers, and the colonel responded by imposing restrictions on the right of the Mormons to shop at the military post. The enmities continued throughout Colonel Connor's tour of duty but never erupted into physical conflict.

Meanwhile, there was some dissension within the Church. A few dissidents in Weber County were excommunicated for apostasy. Their leader, Joseph Morris, claimed he had been sent to rule over "all of Adam's posterity." A more serious dissension occurred in Salt Lake City when a group called the Godbeites apostatized. Their leaders were prominent businessmen who at first questioned the Church's economic policies, especially its opposition to mineral development. Later their dissent expanded to include doctrinal and other questions. The pages of their publication, the *Utah Magazine*, were used to attack the Church and its leaders. Elder Woodruff, Orson Pratt, and George Q. Cannon were appointed to work with these dissidents. Some of them changed as a result, but others were excommunicated. Wilford mourned over these men, some of whom were former associates in the School of the Prophets.

The 1860s saw a surge in the Church's building program. The foundation of the Salt Lake Temple, covered during the Utah War, was uncovered and then replaced when the original work was found to be inadequate; the Salt Lake Tabernacle was completed; and other Church buildings were completed, including chapels in Bountiful and Farmington. The dedication of a new building was a milestone, accompanied by brass bands, flags, military displays with cannons, and speeches, all capped by a dedicatory prayer. Elder Woodruff was pleased to offer the prayer dedicating the chapel at Farmington: "I dedicated the house from the foundation to the top thereof," he reported, "naming everything I could think of in the building, and the ground upon which it stood."

Following the death of Heber C. Kimball on June 22, 1868, George A. Smith was called as the first counselor to President Brigham Young. Although ten years older than he and senior to him in the apostleship, Elder Woodruff had served as a subordinate to George A. Smith in the Historian's office. After his call as counselor to Brigham Young, President Smith served as Church Historian for two more years until he was replaced by Albert Carrington, who in turn was replaced by Orson Pratt. Not until the death of Orson Pratt in 1881 was Elder Woodruff named Church Historian. For almost thirty years he worked faithfully and uncomplainingly in a subordinate role in the Historian's office, despite his preeminent contributions to Church history. Elder Woodruff always focused on performance, not position.

Twenty years after arriving in the Salt Lake Valley, Elder Woodruff began to enjoy the fruits of his labors. He owned several large, comfortable homes built for his growing family. His family also included foster children, whom he nurtured and protected. He owned farms, gardens, and cattle. He continued to seek self-improvement, was influential in government and civic affairs, and, of course, was prominent in Church affairs as a member of the Twelve. He passed a significant milestone when Wilford Jr. left for a mission in England. "It rejoices my heart that I have lived to see the day when I have a son who is called to go into the vineyard of the Lord," he wrote. After the son's return, Elder Woodruff was pleased to seal Wilford and his bride in the temple. And the arrival of grandchildren opened a new world for him. He was awakened one morning by a two-year-old grandson, Wilford Leslie Snow, while he was visiting in the home of his daughter Phoebe Snow, wife of Lorenzo Snow. The little boy put his hands on his grandfather's head and blessed him: "O Lord, bless grandpa. Give unto him great wisdom, health, strength and peace. Comfort his heart. May he live long upon the earth to do great good." The proud grandfather added, "As Wilford Leslie is young in the patriarchal office, it is right to say he had the assistance of his mother."

Elder Woodruff's wealth was acquired from his own strenuous efforts. Along with his church, family, civic, and political responsibilities, he performed prodigious physical labors—haying, picking strawberries, threshing wheat, gathering peaches, repairing the house, drawing corn and carrots, pulling weeds, tying up grapevines, setting out trees, sowing seeds, and digging ditches to head off grasshoppers. And all these activities were conducted with a zest that belied his advancing years and in a manner that, to some, was inconsistent with his prophetic role. Such as these seem to have forgotten that Adam was commanded to labor by the sweat of his brow all his days; Abraham, Isaac, Jacob, and other biblical patriarchs were herdsmen or farmers; and the Savior was a carpenter, accustomed to working with his hands. Wilford Woodruff was a wondrous worker in that noble tradition.

Several months before Brigham Young died, Elder Woodruff received one of his most notable assignments: he was called to be the first president of the St. George Temple. He and President Young worked closely together for weeks writing down the temple ordinances taught them by the Prophet Joseph Smith. In early January 1877, portions of the temple were dedicated under the direction of President Young. Elder Woodruff dedicated the baptismal font. He remembered the ancient covenants made to Abraham, Isaac, and Jacob and recalled the renewal and extension of those covenants incident to the restoration of the gospel. He also invoked special blessings upon President Young. "Comfort him in his old age," Elder Woodruff implored. "Heal up his body, relieve him of his aches and pains; fill him with the revelations of thy spirit, that he may be able to spread thy word unto the people."

When endowment work began, Elder Woodruff's first act was to serve as proxy for "the Prophet Robert Mason," who had foreseen the restoration of the gospel and had predicted Wilford would become a principal actor in the restored Church. Later Elder Woodruff had vicarious temple work performed for many notable people, including some deceased presidents of the United States.

The dedication of the entire temple occurred in April 1877 as part of the Church's general conference held in St. George. There Brigham Young delivered his last general conference sermon. He died four months later in Salt Lake City. Elder Woodruff was one of the speakers at the funeral and dedicated the prophet's grave. He later chaired the audit committee assigned to straighten out the confusion between Church assets and those of the Young estate, a situation caused by the intermingling of assets necessitated by the unfair provisions of the antipolygamy legislation.

The Saints had said that legislation was unconstitutional in its violation of their freedom of religion. That position was eroded away in January 1879 when the U.S. Supreme Court upheld the constitutionality of the 1862 antibigamy act in *Reynolds v. United States.* Soon after, federal officials sought to arrest high Church leaders who lived in plural marriage. In early February, U.S. Marshall Stokes and three men were seen in St. George, reportedly seeking to arrest Elder Woodruff. He remained in the temple for two days, where a bedroom had been prepared for him. Then under cover of night, he fled west into Nevada with his friend, David H. Cannon. After several days with members of the Church in Bunkerville, he returned to Dixie, spending two weeks shuttling back and forth between Santa Clara and St. George while composing a message to the world. He then decided it was wise to go into hiding again.

This time Wilford headed south into Arizona. Traveling through rugged, desolate country, he reached Moencopi, an Indian trading post, where several Latter-day Saints lived. On an exploring trip out of Moencopi, he met a Mormon missionary serving among the Indians, Jacob Hamblin, who had a copy of the *Deseret News* for April 1, which contained Elder Woodruff's message to the world. In it he had borne testimony, counseled the Saints, and called on all kings, presidents, and rulers to repent.

In May, after suffering a severe illness he called "bilious cholic," Elder Woodruff moved to Sunset on the Little Colorado River near Winslow, Arizona. There, and in the neighboring towns of Brigham City and St. Joseph, the Saints were living the United Order. "I ate my supper of bread and milk at the Sunset table," he wrote. "The center table was fifty feet long; the side table the same. . . . All I talked to seemed to prefer this manner of living."

Lot Smith, president of the Little Colorado Stake, prepared a special room for Elder Woodruff at Sunset. "It is 18 x 16," wrote the Apostle, "well carpeted with a chimney and mantel piece, two good windows, curtains . . . and all very comfortable." Not long after arriving there, he "went into the mountains alone and built an altar of stone and dedicated the land to God for the benefit of the Saints."

Sunset was surrounded by Indian tribes. Elder Woodruff visited the Apache, Zuni, Navajo, Laguna, Islata, and Hopi tribes. He spoke to them and bore testimony to them. He also authorized the purchase of the St. Johns town site upriver from Sunset for 750 head of cattle.

Elder Woodruff's stay in Arizona ended when President John Taylor invited him to attend the April 1880 general conference in Salt Lake City. Shortly before he left, the Saints at Sunset honored him at a party on March 1 to celebrate his seventy-third birthday. More than a hundred guests sat down for the birthday dinner. After the meal there were speeches, recitations, and singing: "A company of little girls sang 'Papa Come Home' while several young ladies sang 'Do They Pray for Me at Home.'" He was showered with gifts.

En route to Salt Lake City, Elder Woodruff spent several days in St. George performing ordinance work and speaking to the Saints. A frigid weather pattern had made it uncomfortably cold in balmy Dixie. After a full day of meetings and half sick with a cold and headache, Elder Woodruff reported, "I went to the house, soaked my feet, and went to bed with a hot stone at my feet."

There were unfounded rumors that the First Presidency would be reorganized at the April general conference. However, the conference was distinguished by the declaration of a jubilee to celebrate the fiftieth anniversary of the organization of the Church. The Church forgave large debts owed to it and gave hundreds of cattle and sheep to the poor. Members were urged to treat their debtors charitably. It was a time of compassion.

The event expected in April occurred in October, when at the 1880 semiannual general conference John Taylor was sustained as the third President of the Church, with George Q. Cannon and Joseph F. Smith as his counselors. Elder Woodruff was sustained as the President of the Twelve.

It also was a time of tension. The aggressive pursuit of polygamists that followed the Reynolds case had subsided temporarily. But all recognized it was only a lull in the storm. To prepare for the onslaught, the general Church leaders emphasized the need for decentralization and the assumption of more responsibility by local leaders. Elder Woodruff and the members of the Twelve were constantly on the move, visiting the stakes, training the leaders, and motivating the members. President Woodruff's comment following a stake conference in Nephi reflected a typical result: "The spirit and power of God rested upon us and the people."

The expected storm struck on March 14, 1882, when the Edmunds Act was passed by Congress. It added tough new provisions to supplement the 1862 antibigamy act. The first case prosecuted under the Edmunds Act was against Rudger Clawson. In October 1884 he was found guilty of unlawful cohabitation, fined $800, and sentenced to four years in the penitentiary. It sent a wave of fear among those who practiced plural marriage. "I find my house watched this morning by a marshal or some spy," President Woodruff wrote three months later. "He walked the street in front of my house until 11 o'clock watching. I did not attend meeting." A few days later Wilford moved into a room in the Seventeenth Ward chapel that had been fixed up for him and Elder George Teasdale. "We are living in perilous times," President Woodruff wrote. "No man who obeys the patriarchal law of marriage is safe. . . . There never has been a more united and determined effort made for our destruction since the organization of the church than now."

During the next two years, Wilford Woodruff was on the run, trying to escape detection and arrest. He traveled incognito and kept out of sight when he was not on the move. He stayed with members who opened their homes and gave him their best: Bishop Edward Bunker in Bunkerville, Nevada; William Squires and Thomas Cottam in St. George; Truman Frink in Salt Lake City; and Henry Woodruff in the Uintah Basin. The kindness and solicitude of these hosts could not compensate for the loss of freedom Wilford suffered. "I feel like a prisoner shut up in the house," he wrote while staying with Brother Squires. To break the monotony, he helped reap his host's wheat field. "Brother Squires reaped one shock of wheat today in his field, the first wheat cut in the county, and I cut another shock in the evening." The seventy-eight-year-old Apostle worked regularly in the field until the harvest was completed, always doing so in the evening to avoid detection. The last day of the harvest was June 3, 1885, when he produced his greatest yield: "I cut twenty four bundles of wheat in the dark," he wrote on that day, "and hurt one of my eyes." In other places he stayed, he was not so fortunate as to have physical work to do. Without it, he devoted all his time to writing letters, keeping his journal, reading, and visiting with the host family. It was a routine that taught patience.

Learning Phoebe was ill, Wilford traveled to Salt Lake City in November 1885. Her condition was worse than he had expected. She died on the ninth and was buried three days later. It was wrenching to lose this beloved companion of almost fifty years, especially because he was unable to attend the funeral. He watched the procession from behind the curtain of his Church office. "The Lord has borne me up in this affliction in a wonderful manner," he wrote of the experience. "I pray to God to still sustain me."

Elder Woodruff dreamed often during his exile. He attached spiritual significance to some dreams; others he dismissed as being driven by physical impulses. In the spring of 1887 he had a series of dreams about President John Taylor. He did not understand them but felt they had spiritual implications. "I dreamed again last night," he wrote on March 15, 1887, "of attending another general conference. President Taylor was present but seemed in poor health. He seemed to think he should pass away. . . . I dream almost every night of these great meetings. I do not now understand what these dreams mean." Three months later the meaning of the dreams came into focus when he learned that President Taylor's condition had worsened. When on July 16 President George Q. Cannon advised that the prophet was not expected to live long, Wilford immediately left for Salt Lake City. President Taylor died before he arrived. Behind the scenes, Wilford offered condolences to the family and counseled with his brethren about the funeral. Again he was unable to attend the services and watched the procession from behind the curtain in his office.

Wilford Woodruff had never aspired to the heavy responsibility that now came to him as the presiding officer of the Church. But he accepted it willingly, confident that God would help qualify him for the task. Pending the installation of a new First Presidency, he was authorized to transact necessary Church business in behalf of the Twelve.

President Woodruff felt impressed to establish a beet sugar industry to provide a money crop for Mormon farmers. Two committees of experienced businessmen recommended against it. Although his business experience was limited, Wilford rejected their recommendations. "Every time I think of abandoning it there is darkness; and every time I think of building it, there is light. We will build the factory if it bursts the church." The sugar industry ultimately succeeded and proved to be a great boon to the Saints. This shows the revelatory quality Wilford Woodruff brought to the prophetic office when he was sustained as the fourth President of the Church on April 7, 1889. He selected George Q. Cannon and Joseph F. Smith as his counselors. He freely sought advice from his counselors and others; but his final judgments were always based upon inner promptings.

Before President John Taylor died, he had approved a provision in a proposed constitution for the state of Utah prohibiting the practice of plural marriage. President Woodruff concurred in this. A few days after his ordination, he traveled to San Francisco, California, to confer with powerful political and business leaders. He obtained their support to urge a change in policies and attitudes in Washington, D.C., toward the Latter-day Saints. In the following months he also traveled around the Church to confer with stake presidents about "the temporal situation in their stakes." Following these actions, President Woodruff issued a temporary ban on the performance of plural marriages. And when he discovered the ban had been violated in one instance, he ordered the dismantling of the Endowment House. All this led to the action President Woodruff took on September 25, 1890, when he issued the Manifesto, which discontinued the teaching and practice of plural marriage in the Church. This did not mean the principle of plural marriage is wrong or that Joseph Smith was not inspired in initiating it. It only meant that God had spoken through Wilford Woodruff as the living prophet, directing that the practice be suspended.

The Manifesto was unanimously accepted by the Church at the general conference on October 6, 1890. Later a few dissidents refused to accept it, inexplicably affirming the principle of continuing revelation through a living prophet while refusing to accept the revelation given through this living prophet.

This paved the way for the completion of the Salt Lake Temple and its dedication in April 1893. It also paved the way for Utah's statehood on January 4, 1896. Two years later, on September 2, 1898, President Woodruff died in California. His long, productive life attests to his faith, diligence, and obedience. And the "conspicuous" role he played in the restored Church attests to the power of God and the inspiration of President Woodruff's childhood friend, old Father Mason.

NOTE

This chapter is based on Francis M. Gibbons's book *Wilford Woodruff: Wondrous Worker, Prophet of God* (Salt Lake City: Deseret Book Company, 1988) and works cited therein.

CHAPTER FIVE

LORENZO SNOW

Oliver Snow III and Rosetta L. Pettibone Snow were descendants of solid British and New England ancestors. They had migrated to Mantua, Portage County, Ohio, in search of farming opportunities. There on April 3, 1814, their fifth child and first son, Lorenzo, was born. The Snows were Baptists. That they were open-minded and amenable to new truths is shown by the conversion of the mother and her daughter, Leonora, to The Church of Jesus Christ of Latter-day Saints in 1831. Another daughter, Eliza, followed them into the new church in 1835. These actions had no seeming effect upon Lorenzo, who was imbued with a desire to follow a military career and who showed little interest in religion at the time.

In September 1835 Lorenzo enrolled in the nearby Oberlin Collegiate Institute, intending to pursue his military career. A chance encounter with David W. Patten en route to Oberlin veered Lorenzo from this career path. Elder Patten, an Apostle in the Mormon Church, bore emphatic testimony about the truth of Mormonism. The power of that testimony and the urging of Eliza, who then lived in Kirtland, Ohio, prompted Lorenzo to move there after a few months in Oberlin. In Kirtland he enrolled in a Hebrew school taught by a Jewish scholar, Joshua Seixas. Influenced by Joseph Smith as well as by the Prophet's father, Lorenzo was converted to the Mormon Church and was baptized in June 1836 by John Boynton of the Twelve.

Disappointed his baptism was not accompanied by the spiritual uplift he expected, Lorenzo retired alone to the woods to implore God for a witness. In answer he received "a perfect knowledge that God lives, that Jesus Christ is the Son of God, and of the restoration of the holy Priesthood and the fulness of the Gospel. It was a complete baptism— a tangible immersion in the heavenly principle or element, the Holy Ghost." He experienced the same spiritual phenomenon during several successive nights. The experience turned his life around and set him on a course that would lead far away from a military career and to the pinnacle of leadership in The Church of Jesus Christ of Latter-day Saints. Later Joseph Smith Sr. gave Lorenzo a patriarchal blessing that promised in part that "there shall not be a mightier man on earth than thou. . . . Thou shalt have power over unclean spirits. . . . If expedient the dead shall rise and come forth at thy bidding . . . and Thou shalt have long life."

Soon after, Lorenzo filled a successful mission, laboring without purse or scrip in several counties in Ohio. It humbled him to ask for food and lodging. With that humility came increased spiritual perception. Once a vivid dream warned of a plot to mob him. When the circumstances in his dream occurred in reality, he knew exactly what to do to avoid harm.

Elder Snow found chaotic conditions in Kirtland when he returned. Some Saints had apostatized because of the failure of the Kirtland Bank. He was impressed by Joseph

Smith's poise during the crisis. It had a profound effect on him and helped him develop a deliberate poise and calmness in the face of trouble, which was one of his most notable traits.

In 1838 the Snow family moved to Adam-ondi-Ahman in Missouri. Although still weak from a severe illness, Lorenzo left a few months later on his second mission. He labored in southern Missouri, southern Illinois, and Kentucky for more than a year with good success. During a cold, wet autumn in 1839, he walked five hundred miles from Kentucky to northern Ohio. He laid over in Shalersville, Ohio, during the winter months, teaching school to replenish his funds. Since the Saints had been driven from Missouri during his absence, Lorenzo went to Illinois in the spring, joining his family at LaHarpe, near Nauvoo. Within weeks of his arrival, he was called on a third mission, this one to England where the Apostles and other missionaries were laboring. After arranging a loan at high interest to pay his way, Lorenzo left for England on May 20, 1840. He would be gone for almost three years.

After a rough forty-two-day Atlantic crossing, Elder Snow arrived in Liverpool, England, in midsummer. He was assigned first to labor in Manchester, then in Birmingham, where the work was flourishing. Lorenzo's prior missionary experiences, his maturity, and his success in England, especially in Birmingham, prompted the Brethren to appoint him to preside in London. It was an honor that carried a great burden with it.

Elder Snow found an oppressive, stifling spirit in London that was not conducive to effective missionary work. He discovered this emanated largely from satanic influences. One night in his London apartment he was awakened by a strange clamor. To Lorenzo "it seemed as though every piece of furniture in the room was put in motion, back and forth against each other in such terrible fury that sleep and rest were utter impossibilities." This was accompanied by an ominous spiritual essence that filled the room. This disturbance was repeated on several successive nights. To combat it, Lorenzo engaged in a special fast that he ended by reading a chapter from the Bible. He then kneeled in prayer and in an authoritative voice rebuked the evil spirits by the power of the holy priesthood and "commanded them to leave the house." They never bothered him again.

After that experience the work accelerated in London. During the months Elder Snow presided, the branch doubled in size. His service also was marked by a high degree of spirituality. The gifts of prophecy and tongues were shown through him. Once while speaking, he even sang in tongues. He also confided in Brigham Young the couplet that had come to him by inspiration, "As man now is, God once was; as God now is, man may be." Later the Prophet Joseph Smith declared that statement to be "true gospel doctrine." While in England, Lorenzo also wrote and published a tract, *The Only Way to Be Saved*.

In early 1843 Elder Snow led a party of 250 Mormon converts from Liverpool to New Orleans and thence upriver to Nauvoo. While crossing the Atlantic on board the *Swanton,* he healed one of the stewards whom the captain thought was dying and beyond help. Upon reaching New Orleans, several officers and members of the crew were baptized, convinced that Elder Snow was a true servant of God.

Soon after arriving in Nauvoo, Lorenzo learned that his sister Eliza had been sealed to Joseph Smith in plural marriage. This was a shock to him, even though he had received spiritual promptings that the ancient practice would be introduced among the Saints. At Eliza's request, Joseph met privately with Lorenzo to explain the principle to him. He accepted it, although he did not begin to practice it until later.

Elder Snow earned his livelihood teaching school. He

arranged his schedule to enable him to supervise Joseph Smith's Ohio campaign for the presidency of the United States. Lorenzo was in Cincinnati campaigning when he learned that Joseph had been murdered in Carthage, Illinois, on June 27, 1844. He grieved over the death of his mentor while consoling Eliza in her great loss.

When pressures applied by enemies of the Church made it plain the Saints would be forced to leave Nauvoo, Lorenzo began to prepare for the exodus. In the midst of these exertions, he acted on Joseph Smith's instructions about plural marriage by being sealed to four women in the Nauvoo Temple on the same day in 1845: Mary Adaline Goddard (his cousin who had three sons by a former marriage), Charlotte Squires, Sarah Ann Prichard, and Harriet Amelia Squires. Suddenly, at age thirty-one, Lorenzo Snow, the bachelor, became the head of a family of eight. And in the spring of 1848 while at Winter Quarters preparing for the trek to the Salt Lake Valley, he married a fifth wife, Eleanor Houtz.

Elder Snow and his family crossed the Mississippi on February 12, 1846. Their trek across Iowa was interrupted by a lengthy stay at Mt. Pisgah, one of the way stations established by the Saints. Appointed by Brigham Young to preside over the Saints there, Lorenzo created an intricate, smooth-running organization with numerous committees, each responsible for one aspect of the work. He also sponsored theatricals presented in his rustic cabin, which was decorated imaginatively. His philosophy was that life should be lived to the full at the moment, and enjoyment should not be postponed to some uncertain, future date.

Elder Snow was the captain of one hundred families that migrated from Winter Quarters to the Salt Lake Valley in the spring of 1848. All in all, it was a pleasant trek for members of the Snow family. They had ample food, the weather was good, the trail was well marked, and the Indians were friendly. "I managed to discharge my obligations as captain of my hundred very satisfactorily, for which I felt truly grateful to the Lord," he wrote afterward.

At first, the Snows lived in the fort built by the first pioneers. Later Lorenzo built a rustic cabin for his family and then a gracious home on South Temple at Third East. Several months after arriving in the valley, he had become a useful member of the new community as a teacher, a family man, and an active member of the Church. He had no aspirations for office and was content to play the inconspicuous role marked out for him. So he had no idea of what was afoot when he was invited to meet with the First Presidency on February 12, 1849. It came as a surprise when he was called as a member of the Twelve, ordained, and set apart. He was surprised again in October when he was called on a mission to Italy.

Elder Snow traveled east with a group of missionaries, and from New York he embarked for England. He spent two months there, renewing acquaintances with some of his converts whom he affectionately called "my children in the gospel." Crossing the English Channel and continental Europe, he traveled to Genoa, Italy, on the Ligurian Sea. This great seaport, the birthplace of Christopher Columbus, was dominated by the Catholic Church and provided no openings for missionary work. Very soon, therefore, Elder Snow and his companions went north to the Piedmont, where the Waldenses lived. These self-reliant people had resisted all efforts to turn them from their Protestant beliefs. After the miraculous healing of a young boy named Joseph Guy, the elders had success. The climate improved further when Elder Snow dedicated the land for the preaching of the gospel. In the autumn of 1850 he and his companions climbed a mountain near LaTour, where Elder Snow offered a dedicatory prayer. They named the site "Mount Brigham" and called the place on which they stood "the Rock of Prophecy."

Leaving his companions in charge, Lorenzo went back

to England to arrange for the translation and publication of the Book of Mormon in Italian. Returning to the Piedmont after nine months, he was pleased to find the work there was flourishing. The gifts of the Spirit were appearing and people with administrative ability were being baptized. Soon after, a convert named John D. Malan was placed in charge of the branch, and Elder Snow and a companion traveled to Malta. There arrangements were made to publish and distribute Church tracts, including two tracts written by Elder Snow, *The Voice of Joseph* and *The Ancient Gospel Restored*. Time constraints caused Lorenzo to abandon plans to travel to India. Instead, he booked passage to England. Embarking for the United States from Liverpool on June 12, 1852, he arrived in Salt Lake City on July 30. The joy of being reunited with his family was muted by the news that his plural wife Charlotte had died in Lorenzo's absence. His frequent moves had prevented him from receiving the dreadful news. He grieved at the passing of this beloved companion.

Elder Snow soon became heavily involved in the affairs of the community. He was elected to the territorial legislature and appointed to the board of regents of the University of Deseret. He also organized the Polysophical Society, a social group that met regularly in his home. It featured readings, recitals, singing, and dramatic sketches and was one of the forerunners of the Church's Mutual Improvement Associations.

In October 1853 the First Presidency called Elder Snow to lead fifty families to settle an area fifty miles north of Salt Lake City. He became president of the stake that grew up around that settlement, which was later named Brigham City. At first the Snows lived under primitive conditions in an old fort. By the autumn of 1854, however, Lorenzo had built a substantial home that included a living room large enough to accommodate frequent visitors who gathered for entertainments like those sponsored by the Polysophical

Society in Salt Lake City. Later the Brigham City Dramatic Association was organized to stage entertainments on a community-wide basis. Elder Snow felt the need to elevate the cultural life of the community by wholesome recreations. He also stressed education and soon established an efficient school system. And his preaching emphasized spirituality, resiliency, and work.

Elder Snow always performed his duties with a flair. In Salt Lake City he directed an event that celebrated the second anniversary of the arrival of the Saints in Utah. It was marked by elaborate pageantry featuring bands, costumes, parades, banners, and decorations. Lorenzo repeated this on a minor scale when President Young paid his first visit to Brigham City. An escort of uniformed young men riding horses and sixteen young women dressed in white seated in wagons met the prophet at the edge of the town. With a martial band leading the way, President Young was escorted through the streets lined with men, women, and children amid "loud cheers, the ringing of bells and waving of banners."

As Elder Snow put his mark on any enterprise he directed, he also left his mark on the geography surrounding Brigham City. To the east is Mantua, a town named after Lorenzo's place of birth; to the north is Portage, a town named after the county where he was born; and to the northwest is Snowville, which honored the area's most distinguished resident.

During the threatened invasion of Utah by Johnston's Army, Elder Snow activated the Box Elder Battalion of the Nauvoo Legion, although he did not lead it. As part of the "scorched earth" policy, he also led his people to Utah County, settling some of them around what was then called Pond Town, later Salem, where many lived in crude dugouts. When the truce was signed, they moved back to Brigham City.

While he lived at Brigham City, Elder Snow occasionally

117

received ad hoc apostolic assignments. One of these came in 1864 when he and Elder Ezra Taft Benson were assigned to go to Hawaii to investigate reports of misconduct by Walter Murray Gibson. Included in the party was young Joseph F. Smith, who, having returned from a mission to Hawaii, would serve as translator. When the schooner *Nettie Merrill* arrived near the mouth of Lahaina Harbor on March 31, 1864, there was a stiff wind and the sea was running high. A mile away, waves could be seen breaking over the coral reefs that guarded the narrow mouth of the harbor. Believing there was no danger, the two Apostles decided to transfer to a small boat with their gear and go on to the beach so they could begin their work. Joseph F. Smith, who was familiar with these waters and the treacherous weather of the islands, said it was too dangerous and warned against going. When he saw they intended to ignore his warning, he said he would go with them only if directed to do so. Not wanting to order him to go, the Apostles went ahead with a crew, leaving Joseph F. behind. Later Elder Snow said he had the impression at the time this young man would one day be the President of the Church. He was impressed by his self-confidence as well as his willingness to go contrary to his own judgment if directed to do so by priesthood authority.

Joseph F. Smith's concern about the danger proved correct—the boat capsized crossing the reef. Elder Snow was drowned but after an hour was miraculously brought back to life by those who recovered his body and worked over him. After a probe, Walter Gibson was excommunicated, and Joseph F. Smith was left in charge of the mission.

After returning from Hawaii, Elder Snow began to organize the system of cooperatives for which he became noted. Moved by the desire to make his people self-sufficient and to stir a spirit of enterprise among them, he initiated a system of "home industries." The nucleus was the Brigham City Mercantile and Manufacturing Association, which he and three associates had founded. He persuaded his associates to use some of their surplus to fund the first home industry, a tannery. The investors and the tannery workers and managers received stock interests in the new enterprise. Boot- and shoe-making units as well as saddle- and harness-making units were spun off from the tannery. Then came a woolen mill, and a group of satellite units were spun off from it. A prolific number of other home industries were organized afterward, intended to fill every need of the community. These included a dairy; a horticultural unit; a machine and maintenance unit with a blacksmith shop; a construction unit with sawmills and brick and adobe, lime kiln, carpentry, masonry, and architecture departments; tin and pottery shops; rope, broom, and brush factories; a greenhouse and nursery; a public works department to supervise the construction of roads, bridges, and irrigation projects; an education department; and even a tramp department that gave handouts to hobos in exchange for menial labor. When President Young founded the United Order in the mid-1870s, stock interests in the Brigham City enterprises were converted into "stewardships," and the activities were carried on in much the same manner as before.

"Because of many losses and disasters," Elder Snow explained on July 20, 1880, "we have discontinued some of our enterprises and curtailed others. Yet for a period of fifteen years, our union has prevented division in mercantile business; to say nothing about many other things which have been done by our union, and I have nothing to regret of all we have accomplished, . . . and in all these matters we did them by common consent." In time all the home industries were dissolved, having fulfilled their purpose.

A major factor in the ultimate dissolution of the home industries was the completion of the transcontinental railroad on May 10, 1869. Less expensive and more plentiful manufactured goods then became readily available in Utah from the East and the West. Because the transcontinental line bypassed both Salt Lake City and Brigham City, many, including some Mormon dissidents, believed that Corinne, a town west of Brigham City on the main line, would become the economic center of Utah. Not wanting to lend credence to that idea, Brigham Young and Lorenzo Snow, and most other high leaders of the Church, deliberately stayed away from the ceremony on May 10 at Promontory Point, west of Corinne, which linked the Union Pacific and Central Pacific lines. A week later, Lorenzo Snow joined with Brigham Young and other general Church leaders near Ogden where ground was broken for the Utah Central Railway, which would connect Ogden with Salt Lake City. That line was completed in January 1870. Later the Utah Northern Railway constructed a line running through Brigham City that connected Franklin, Idaho, with Ogden, Utah. These events, which gave Salt Lake City and Brigham City rail access to eastern and western markets, minimized the status of Corinne, causing it to wither and leaving Brigham City the main economic center in that area.

In October 1872 Elder Snow, along with his sister Eliza, was invited to join President George A. Smith and a small party to tour the Holy Land. Lorenzo and Eliza chronicled the trip by sending regular dispatches to the *Deseret News*. The reports were compiled and published later. Visiting the Holy Land was a signal event of Elder Snow's life.

En route to Palestine, the party visited England and Italy where Elder Snow was able to relive his missionary experiences in those countries. Along the way, libraries, museums, art galleries, cathedrals, castles, and other ancient buildings claimed their attention. In Egypt the vivid impact of the Sphinx and the pyramids was eclipsed in his mind by the kind and charitable character of the Egyptian people.

Their guide and his assistants met the party at Jaffa with the equipment, food, and animals to make their two-week tour of Palestine enjoyable. The equipment included four large, carpeted tents, three for sleeping and dining and one for food preparation. On the way to Jerusalem from Jaffa, the party passed through the Plains of Sharon and the valleys of Ajalon and Elah, the last being the scene of the battle between David and Goliath. Elder Snow was in awe of Jerusalem, although he doubted whether the sites shown them were the actual places where significant events occurred. He also doubted whether the Church of the Nativity in Bethlehem stands on the exact site where the Savior was born. Despite his skepticism, there were aroused in him "impressions never to be forgotten" when he saw in the Grotto of the Nativity the inscription *Hic de Virgine Maria Jesus Christus natus est* ("Here the Virgin Mary gave birth to Jesus Christ"). Although Lorenzo was a special witness of the Savior's reality and divinity and often had felt his presence or influence, when he visited this place and read the simple inscription, he was filled with a sense of awe and commitment that was never to abate during the remainder of his apostolic ministry.

On March 2, 1873, the party gathered in a tent on the Mount of Olives for a sacrament and testimony meeting during which President Smith dedicated the land of Palestine for the gathering of the Jews. He also invoked divine assistance in the rebuilding of Jerusalem and expressed gratitude for the restoration of the gospel.

While this was the crowning event of the visit to Palestine, Elder Snow was equally moved by his visits to Nazareth, Cana, and the Sea of Galilee. "The Savior came down from the hilly country of Galilee," wrote Lorenzo, "and made his home upon these shores, chose his twelve apostles, taught the people in their towns and villages, and on the seaside as they flocked around him in multitudes."

Leaving Galilee, the party traveled northeasterly past the Fountain of Dan, a main source of the Jordan, to Caesarea Philippi. Lorenzo recalled that there Jesus counseled with his disciples following their first missionary effort when Peter boldly testified that Jesus was "the Christ, the Son of the living God" (Matthew 16:16).

After visiting Damascus in Syria and Beirut in Lebanon, the party embarked for Constantinople (Istanbul) and then for Athens, where they spent five days visiting the ruins of that ancient Grecian city. Unknown to him, Elder Snow was sustained as a counselor to President Brigham Young while the party was in Athens. The action was taken during the April 1873 general conference and was affirmed by a setting apart when he returned to Salt Lake City.

After cruising through the Grecian islands, the party disembarked at Trieste. From there the itinerary included stops in Munich (where Lorenzo and Eliza were astonished at the 800,000-volume royal library), Vienna, Berlin, and Hamburg. Elder Snow was both excited and oppressed by the prevalence of military personnel on the continent. "As in all other countries which we have visited," he wrote of the tour in Germany, "soldiers, in military costume, are seen almost everywhere in great numbers." The excitement came from his dormant desire for a military career, the oppression from knowing that the basic purpose of an army is to kill. This was repugnant to one who gave up hunting when he heard a wounded animal cry as if it were human.

Since the traveling party disbanded upon reaching New York, Lorenzo and Eliza decided to take a side trip alone to the Snow family home in Mantua, Ohio. Elder Snow had been there only once during the previous thirty-seven years, and Eliza had never been back. They were given celebrity treatment by relatives and friends. "Indeed, it was one continual ovation, from first to last," wrote Eliza to the *Woman's Exponent.*

At home, Elder Snow learned that his call would not require moving to Salt Lake City. His duties in the First Presidency consisted mostly of traveling throughout the Church to teach the principles of cooperation and the

United Order. He also met periodically with President Young and the other counselors in Salt Lake City and filled special assignments given by the prophet.

One of these was to participate in the dedication of the St. George Temple in April 1877 and in the general conference to be held in connection with it. In St. George, Lorenzo learned that members of the Twelve were to be released as stake presidents and that other stake presidencies would be reorganized as well.

On the way home following the conference, Elder Snow reorganized stake presidencies in Kanab and Panguitch. Then he joined in reorganizing the Salt Lake Stake. Later he reorganized the stakes in Ogden, Morgan, and Cache Valley. Meanwhile, other counselors in the First Presidency reorganized additional stakes. However, President Young decided to reorganize the Box Elder Stake himself. He and a party from Salt Lake City traveled to Brigham City for the occasion. The party received a typical Lorenzo Snow reception with all its trappings. President Young, who was a guest in Elder Snow's home, delighted everyone present by singing a hymn solo, something he had done often in the early years but seldom did later on. It was the last time the President Young sang a solo—he passed away less than two weeks later.

President Young selected Oliver G. Snow, Lorenzo's son, as the new stake president. At the meeting on August 18, 1877, when the change was made, he said, "Brother Lorenzo Snow, who has had charge of you, has set the best example for the literal building up of the Kingdom of God of any of our presiding elders."

The releases as stake president and, when President Young died, as a member of the First Presidency relieved Elder Snow of heavy responsibilities he had borne for many years. He continued, of course, to perform duties as a member of the Twelve, serving on *ad hoc* committees. These duties, however, were hardly sufficient to fill up the days of one accustomed to performing sustained and important labors in a leadership role. For a period of three years, therefore, he shifted the main focus of his efforts from church to family and personal matters. In many ways it was a change he welcomed and enjoyed.

The U.S. Supreme Court decision in the Reynolds case in 1879 introduced much uncertainty into Elder Snow's life and the lives of other Mormon polygamists. This case upheld the constitutionality of the 1862 antibigamy act and undercut the legal position of Elder Snow and his brethren that the 1862 act was void because it violated their freedom of religion. Their uncertainty escalated dramatically when congress passed the Edmunds Act in 1882. This bill added tough punitive and enforcement provisions to the 1862 act. The result was that Lorenzo and his brethren dropped into the underground to avoid arrest and prosecution.

Elder Snow spent many months in northern California, living quietly and incognito. He mingled behind the scenes with members whom he could trust. In July 1885 he received an assignment from President John Taylor to work among the northern Indian tribes. In response, he labored among the Nez Perce, Umatilla, and Blackfoot tribes in Idaho and among the Shoshone and Arapahoe tribes in Wyoming. Receiving word that things had quieted down in Brigham City, he went home to visit in the autumn. When he learned that federal officials were in the area, Elder Snow took refuge in a concealed space below his bedroom. Armed with a warrant for his arrest, the officials inspected the house but found nothing. Upon leaving, they saw the Snows' dog, Nero, sniffing at a vent below the bedroom. Correctly assuming that a familiar smell wafted from the vent, they reentered the house and found Elder Snow. When he was satisfied their credentials were in order, he submitted to arrest.

A reporter at the hearing noted that Elder Snow was

"calm and dignified," that the "tenor of his disposition was unruffled," and that "he exhibited no trace of excitement whatever." He showed the same disposition throughout his eleven-month incarceration in the Utah Penitentiary. There he joined more than forty members of the Church who had been convicted of unlawful cohabitation. Lorenzo became their leader. These men reflected a character unlike that of other prisoners. Some wrote, some painted, some sculpted, and some composed. Others banded together to learn the manual arts or to study languages, mathematics, or history. And all of them devoted much time to studying the scriptures and to fasting and prayer. Included among the "cohabs" were Abraham H. Cannon of the First Council of Seventy; Rudger Clawson, a future Apostle; James Moyle, the patriarch of an influential family; and Andrew Jenson, assistant Church historian. During the April 1886 general conference, Elder Snow felt impressed to lead his brethren in the "Hosannah Shout," normally reserved for sacred ceremonies in the temple.

Elder Snow was released from prison on February 8, 1887, following a successful challenge to his conviction under a writ of habeas corpus. The U.S. Supreme Court decided that the procedure under which he had been tried was fatally flawed. A large crowd greeted him at the gates of the penitentiary. Later he was honored at a celebration in the Social Hall and at a meeting in the Tabernacle. There he rejoiced in the legal victory that had set him free, while cautioning the Saints about trials that lay ahead. "[We] must pass through the narrows and learn by sacrifice," he told the audience.

One of those trials emerged the following month when on March 3, 1887, the Edmunds-Tucker Act became the law of the land. This was the last and the toughest of the laws aimed at the Church and those who practiced plural marriage. It effectively ended the existence of the Church as an organized legal body in the United States, though the members retained the right of assembly.

Following the death of President Taylor on July 25, 1887, the Manti Temple was dedicated in May 1888. Elder Snow, who was immune from further arrest, presided since President Woodruff was still living in the underground. These services were marked by unusual spiritual outpourings; some participants reported that they heard ethereal voices singing heavenly music and sensed the presence of Church leaders who had passed away earlier.

Wilford Woodruff was sustained as the fourth President of the Church at the April 1889 general conference. At the same time, Elder Snow was sustained as the President of the Twelve. A year later, President Woodruff announced the Manifesto, a revelation by which the teaching and practice of plural marriage were discontinued in the Church. At the general gathering where the Church members accepted the Manifesto, Lorenzo Snow made the motion of acceptance. In the years that followed, this action led to a gradual return to normalcy in the affairs of the Church.

On the recommendation of Elder Snow, Rudger Clawson became president of the Box Elder Stake following his release from the penitentiary. Although Elder Snow was the older of the two by forty-three years, there was an unusually close relationship between them. In March 1891 they joined in raising Ella Jensen from the dead. Ella had died at 10:00 A.M. on a Sunday morning. Her father, Jacob Jensen, Elder Snow's brother-in-law, traveled from his farm to Brigham City to tell Lorenzo. Called out of a meeting, he took Rudger Clawson with him. By the time they reached the farmhouse, Ella had been dead two hours. All were surprised when Elder Snow, after meditating, asked for consecrated oil. He had Rudger Clawson anoint Ella, and Lorenzo sealed the anointing. According to Brother Clawson, in the blessing Elder Snow said "in a commanding voice, 'Come back, Ella, come back. Your walk upon the earth is not yet completed, come back.'" An hour after Elder Snow and Rudger Clawson left, Ella's spirit returned to her body. She later married, gave birth to eight children, and lived to age eighty-six.

In April 1892 Elder Snow led the Hosannah Shout at the laying of the capstone of the Salt Lake Temple. And a year later, when the temple was dedicated, he was named the first president of the temple. He selected John Winder and Adolph Madsen as his counselors. President Snow's deep spirituality was a perfect fit for this sacred calling. His countenance and very presence radiated a celestial quality. He was much loved by the temple workers. After a year of service, they honored him at a ceremony in which he was eulogized and given an ebony black, gold-handled walking cane. He reciprocated by hosting them and the First Presidency on a "sacred excursion" to Brigham City and Mantua.

In August and September 1896, Lorenzo took his only known vacation. In company with his wife Minnie and their daughter, Maybelle, he traveled to San Francisco. During a two-week stay, they visited places of interest in the city and surrounding areas. He also met his brother, Samuel, whom he had not seen for many years. It was a joyous reunion. Boarding the coastal vessel *Walla Walla,* the vacationers sailed north to Vancouver Island, B. C., ferried to the mainland, then traveled by train to Lethbridge through the grandeur of the Canadian Rockies. They were driven by coach to Cardston, their ultimate destination. President Snow left Cardston in mid-September, leaving Minnie and Maybelle there with friends. A few months later, Minnie gave birth to another daughter, Lucille, the last of the forty-one natural children born to Lorenzo's nine wives. In addition, he raised Mary Adaline's three children of a previous marriage. President Snow was almost eighty-three years old when Lucille was born.

On September 1, 1898, Elder Snow learned that

President Woodruff was gravely ill in San Francisco. He immediately went to the temple to pray for his recovery. As he walked through a hallway after he left the special room where he had prayed, President Snow was startled to see the Savior of the world, standing before him in the air, who gave him detailed instruction about the reorganization of the First Presidency. President Woodruff died the next day. On September 8, funeral services were held in the Tabernacle, where Elder Snow and others eulogized their friend. At a special meeting of the Twelve five days later, Lorenzo Snow was sustained as the fifth President of the Church. He was ordained and set apart on October 10 after being sustained at general conference.

The Church's shaky financial status was the major problem facing President Snow as he began his prophetic ministry. The Church had never recovered from its legal dissolution and the escheat of its properties before the Manifesto. Since then it had operated on borrowed money. Indeed, shortly after his ordination, President Snow had to borrow a million dollars to finance the administration of the Church.

Struggling to find a solution to this problem, the prophet was impressed to go to St. George. He and his party traveled there in April 1899 to hold a series of meetings. "It was during one of these meetings that my father received the renewal revelation on tithing," wrote Leroi Snow, the prophet's son. "God manifested to him . . . [that] through strict obedience to this law . . . not only would the church be relieved of its great indebtedness . . . but this would also be the means of freeing the Latter-day Saints from their individual obligations."

President Snow explained the significance of the occasion to the audience: "The word of the Lord to you is not anything new. It is simply this: The time has now come for every Latter-day Saint, who calculates to be prepared for the future and to hold his feet strong upon a proper foundation, to do the will of the Lord and to pay his tithing in full." In other meetings in St. George he elaborated on this theme. On the return to Salt Lake City, he held many meetings along the way where the message was repeated. He repeated it again to the youth leaders at their conference in June. They approved a resolution, committing themselves to pay an honest tithe and to teach others to do likewise. In July President Snow convened a solemn assembly attended by stake and ward leaders. They made the same commitment. Afterward, he traveled widely holding many meetings in which he preached the law of tithing and urged members to obey it.

The results were astonishing. Within a year, the amount of tithing paid in the Church had doubled. Moreover, there was a notable improvement in the financial condition of individual members. While the finances of the Church did not change overnight, this inspired initiative marked the beginning of a new era in the Church. It saw the Church become wealthy with ample means to promote its interests and to expound its message on a global basis. It is a testimonial to the prophetic calling of President Snow and to the verity of Malachi's promise (see Malachi 3:10).

Coincident with his move to increase the revenues of the Church, President Snow moved promptly to assert control of the management and the disbursement of Church funds. He dismantled a network of committees that had been set up to diffuse the control over Church finances and returned control to the First Presidency. He also canceled a lease that had given control over the *Deseret News* to an individual. Moreover, he became active in promoting the candidacies of George Q. Cannon for the U.S. Senate and Brigham H. Roberts for the House of Representatives. He wanted the Church to have a voice in those chambers that so long had passed legislation inimical to the interests of Latter-day Saints. He vigorously rejected complaints of critics who protested his support of political candidates, asserting that his role in the Church did not deprive him of his civic rights. Meanwhile, he initiated an expansion of missionary work, calling Heber J. Grant to open the work in Japan, and taught stake presidents to lead out in nurturing and training their people.

This flurry of activity by an eighty-seven-year-old man is reminiscent of another promise of Patriarch Joseph Smith Sr., who through inspiration had declared to Lorenzo that "age shall not come upon thee." President Snow retained vigor of mind and body and a youthful outlook upon life until the very end. The end came for the prophet on October 10, 1901, following a short illness with pneumonia. Funeral services were held three days later in the Tabernacle, which was decorated in a spectacular yet tasteful way that would have won his approval. The base of the massive organ was covered with white, draped bunting in the center of which hung a floral tribute in the form of the Salt Lake Temple. Above it was a full-sized portrait of President Snow, and above the portrait was the word *UTAH* and the Star of David. The elevated stands where the General Authorities and officers of the Church were seated were similarly draped with bunting, as were the balustrades of the choir seats and the front portions of the balcony on both the north and south sides of the building. Also, the four front columns supporting the balcony on either side of the building were wrapped with the white bunting in barber-pole fashion. Numerous floral displays adorned all levels of the stand, the most prominent one bearing the motto "As God Is, Man May Be."

After the services in which President Snow was appropriately eulogized by his brethren, his body was taken to Brigham City, where he was buried in the Snow family plot in the city cemetery. There, with Mantua, Portage, and Snowville nearby, the prophet would have felt comfortable and at home in the place where he had performed some of his most significant work.

NOTE

This chapter is based on Francis M. Gibbons's book *Lorenzo Snow: Spiritual Giant, Prophet of God* (Salt Lake City: Deseret Book Company, 1982) and the sources cited therein.

CHAPTER SIX

JOSEPH F. SMITH

Mary Fielding, a convert to the Mormon Church from Canada, married Hyrum Smith, a widower with five living children, on December 25, 1837, in Kirtland, Ohio. Mary's first natural child, Joseph F. Smith, was born on November 13, 1838, in Far West, Missouri. At the time, his father was imprisoned in Richmond, Missouri, under false charges arising from the persecution of the Mormons by mobs and by Missouri's officialdom. Mary and her baby and the other Smith children were driven to Quincy, Illinois, under Missouri Governor Lilburn W. Boggs's order to exterminate the Mormons. Hyrum joined them there in April 1839. The parents then established a home at Nauvoo, originally Commerce City, Illinois.

For several years Joseph F. lived a privileged life. Hyrum Smith, one of the most influential men in the community, was a counselor to his brother Joseph Smith, who was the President of The Church of Jesus Christ of Latter-day Saints. The boy's security was shattered on June 27,

1844, when his father and uncle were murdered by a mob in Carthage, Illinois. "The bodies of the martyrs lay in their coffins," a mature Joseph F. Smith recalled. "I remember my mother lifting me up to look upon the faces of my father and the Prophet, for the last time." Two years later the Smiths suffered further trauma when they were driven from Nauvoo by enemies of the Church. Mary sold her Nauvoo real estate to purchase teams, wagons, and supplies for the trek west. At the reins of one wagon was a budding young teamster, Joseph F. Smith, age seven years, seven months.

After Hyrum's death, Mary Fielding Smith was both mother and father to the family. Her leadership showed both sensitivity and tough resilience. Joseph F. was impressed by her spiritual sense when he saw how she, through prayer, located a lost team of oxen and how she asked priesthood brethren to anoint and bless their feeble oxen on the trek to Utah. Joseph F. also was impressed by his mother's staunch independence, revealed when she stood up to a wagonmaster who sought to exclude her from his caravan because of concern she would cause delay. The spunky widow told her critic she would hold her own and would beat him into the valley, a prediction she fulfilled. These same qualities of spiritual sensitivity and forthright independence were evident in her son Joseph F. Smith throughout his life.

Widow Smith established a rustic home in the Mill Creek area of the Salt Lake Valley. Despite the prominence of her husband, she lived almost anonymously, quietly keeping the commandments and teaching her children. She died at age fifty-one on September 21, 1852, when Joseph F. was thirteen. "By the massacre of Carthage, June 27, 1844," read her obituary in the *Deseret News,* "she was left the sole guardian of a large family of children and dependants, for whom, by her indefatigable exertions, she provided the means of support, and removal, from Nauvoo to this peaceful valley of the mountains." Her example motivated Joseph F. Smith all his life.

Joseph F. Smith's boyhood ended at age fifteen when he was called to serve a mission in Hawaii. The call came from the stand of the Old Tabernacle during the April general conference in 1854. After being ordained an elder and endowed, he left for the mission field with twenty other elders on May 27.

Because he traveled without purse or scrip, Joseph F. worked in San Bernardino and San Francisco, California, to earn money for his passage to Hawaii. After a rough voyage of nineteen days on the *Vaquero*, he arrived in Honolulu in late September. His mission president, Francis A. Hammond, assigned him to labor in Kula on the island of Maui, which consisted of a group of scattered villages. Here he began to exhibit a remarkable gift of tongues promised him when he was set apart. Very soon, aided by Elder Pake, a native companion, he learned to speak the Hawaiian language with eloquence. He also was endowed with a special gift of healing.

At a conference in July 1855, sixteen-year-old Joseph F. Smith was called to preside over the island of Maui. Later he presided over the Hilo and Kohala conferences on the large island of Hawaii and over the island of Molokai. At Molokai he became very ill and was nursed back to health by a kindly Hawaiian woman, Ma Mahuhii. Years later when he returned to the islands as the President of the Church, Ma Mahuhii, then blind and very old, brought the prophet a few choice bananas, calling him by name, "Iosepa, Iosepa." He took the aged woman in his arms, kissed her, and patted her on the head, saying over and over, "Mama, Mama, my dear old Mama."

As an orphan and because of his youth, Joseph F. occasionally felt lonely and inadequate. While in the islands, he had a vivid dream that soothed those feelings. In it he saw himself at the door of a mansion where he was admitted by the Prophet Joseph Smith, who said to him, "Joseph, you are late." He answered, "Yes, but I am clean, I am clean." Other aspects of the dream, in which he also saw his father, had a profound effect upon him. "When I awoke that morning I was a man although only a boy," he wrote later. "There was not anything in the world that I feared. I could meet any man or woman or child and look them in the face, feeling in my soul that I was a man every whit."

When Joseph F. returned to Salt Lake City on February 24, 1858, Utah was threatened with invasion by the United States Army. He soon joined the Nauvoo Legion and, under the command of Colonel Thomas Callister, was constantly in the saddle, "prospecting and exploring the country between Great Salt Lake City and Fort Bridger." He also served on picket guard duty under Orrin Porter Rockwell and helped to evacuate Salt Lake City.

When the war scare ended, he worked for the territorial legislature. Meanwhile, he courted his cousin, Levira Smith, a daughter of his uncle, Samuel Harrison Smith, one of the Eight Witnesses of the Book of Mormon. They were married on April 5, 1859. The following year, Joseph F. was called on a mission to Great Britain. One of his companions was Samuel Harrison Bailey Smith, Levira's brother. On the way to the East Coast, the Smith cousins stopped in Nauvoo. There they visited their aunt Emma, the Prophet Joseph Smith's wife, and her sons, Joseph Smith III, Frederick, Alexander, and David. While Emma and her children were friendly to the visitors personally, they were cold and critical as to the "Utah Church" and its leader, Brigham Young. The attitude of three sisters of Joseph and Hyrum whom the missionaries later visited in Colchester, Illinois, was far different. These aunts were grateful to their nephews for holding religious services with them in which Church doctrine was discussed.

The arrival of two nephews of the Prophet Joseph Smith, one of whom was the son of Patriarch Hyrum Smith, created much excitement among the British missionaries. Soon the newcomers were admired not alone for their lineage but also for their performance. Joseph F.'s long service in Hawaii enabled him to be productive from the beginning. He was soon called as the president of the Sheffield Conference. Later he served as a "pastor" over several conferences, training and motivating the missionaries and instructing members of the branches. The eloquence he had shown in the Hawaiian language was duplicated in his native tongue. It was a gift that would distinguish him throughout his career. Many who had heard Church leaders speak in the Tabernacle for decades said none excelled Joseph F. Smith as a preacher of righteousness. The impact he made was a combination of fluency, a pleasing voice, his presence in the pulpit, his spirituality, and his emphatic delivery.

George Q. Cannon's appointment as the president of the European Mission in May 1862 began a long association between him and Joseph F. Smith. They were instantly attracted to each other. Elder Cannon, who was then a member of the Twelve, took Elder Smith with him on a tour of Denmark and worked closely with him in Joseph F.'s role as a pastor. Later they would serve successively as counselors to Brigham Young, John Taylor, Wilford Woodruff, and Lorenzo Snow.

Joseph F. returned to Salt Lake City in September of 1863. A few months later he was called on a third mission. President Young asked him to accompany Elders Ezra T. Benson and Lorenzo Snow of the Twelve to Hawaii to investigate reports of misconduct by a missionary, Walter Murray Gibson. Joseph F. served as translator. The party's schooner, the *Nettie Merrill*, anchored a mile from the harbor of Lahaina on March 31, 1864. A stiff wind was up, and the sea was running high, which warned Joseph F. there would be danger in trying to maneuver the schooner's small freight boat through the narrow, reef-guarded channel that led to the harbor. Ignoring his warning, the two Apostles decided to go ashore anyway to begin their work. Joseph F. refused to join them unless ordered to do so by priesthood authority. Not wanting to do that, the Apostles left him on the schooner and headed for shore with the freight boat's crew. The boat capsized when it was crushed against the reef. Elder Snow was drowned. He was revived after a rescue crew worked for an hour to resuscitate him. Elder Snow reported later that when Joseph F. refused to enter the boat, the spiritual impression came that Joseph F. would one day become President of the Church. The younger man's confidence in his own judgment as opposed to that of the Apostles, combined with his willingness to be subordinate to priesthood authority, revealed a character of unusual wisdom and faith.

When Gibson was excommunicated, Joseph F. Smith was placed in charge of the mission and Elders Benson and Snow returned home. Unfortunately, the apostate continued to exert strong influence on Lanai, where the Church had acquired property, the title of which had become vested in Gibson's name. Joseph F. remained in Hawaii a few months longer, helping reestablish order among members who had been confused by Gibson's apostate teachings. Later, on Joseph F.'s recommendation, the Church acquired a large plantation on the island of Oahu on which the Hawaii Temple and Church college were constructed.

Joseph F. arrived home in December 1864. He was employed in the Historian's Office, served as a secretary to the First Presidency and the Twelve, and was the recorder at the Endowment House. At the Historian's Office, he met, and with Levira's consent, courted and was sealed to Julina Lambson in plural marriage. Later Joseph F. Smith was sealed to four other wives: Sarah Richards, Edna Lambson, Alice Kimball, and Mary Schwartz. Except for Levira, who was unable to bear children, these wives bore forty-three children. In addition, there were two adopted children, and three children fathered by Alice's first husband, who were raised in the Smith home. Each child was loved and cherished by the father. "Children, the greatest of all earthly joys," he wrote. A great sadness in his life occurred when Levira, distraught because she was barren, separated from the family.

Joseph F. Smith's life was changed forever on July 1, 1866. On that day, following a meeting with the Brethren, President Young, moved by a spiritual impulse, ordained him an Apostle and set him apart as one of his counselors. Fifteen months later, he became a member of the Twelve. Still in his twenties, Hyrum's son was now on the path that would lead him to be President of the Church. Meanwhile, he gained prominence and sound reputation in civic circles, serving in the territorial senate and house and on the Salt Lake City Council. Charles W. Nibley left a description of Joseph F. Smith at this stage of his career: "I heard him preach in the old meetinghouse at Wellsville, and I remarked at the time what a fine specimen of young manhood he was—strong, powerful, with a beautiful voice, so full of sympathy and affection, so appealing in its tone, that he impressed me, although I was a youth of but eighteen. He was a handsome man."

At the October general conference in 1873, Joseph F. was called to preside over the European Mission. He left Salt Lake City in late February 1874 and arrived at Liverpool on March 21. He would spend fifteen months there, living at 42 Islington. He had authority over all Church affairs in Great Britain and Europe. He was the editor-in-chief of the *Millennial Star.* He also was in charge of converts immigrating to the United States. For instance, he saw 150 off on the steamship *Wyoming* on October 14, 1874. A presidency of W. N. Fife, James Bywater, and V. King was appointed to shepherd the group to its destination. Elder Smith reported this was the sixth immigration company to leave Liverpool in 1874, totaling "1996 souls."

His office duties, frequent travels, and multiple meetings usually kept his mind off home and family. Yet there were times of homesickness. "I had peculiar feelings," he wrote after receiving a letter and pictures from home, "went into my room and wept and prayed and wept again and felt relieved." His prayers were filled with expressions of gratitude for his family. "I live in the pure unsullied love of my darling children," he wrote. "My wives can trust me. . . . O! My Father, preserve me in Thy holy keeping from the power of temptation."

When he returned to Utah in the autumn of 1875, Elder Smith was placed in charge of the Saints in Davis County, north of Salt Lake City. In two years he prepared them for stakehood. The organization took place in June 1877. Meanwhile, at the dedication of the St. George Temple in April that year, he was called again to preside over the European Mission. His wife Sarah and their son, Joseph Richards, accompanied him. They arrived in Liverpool six weeks later. Sarah had barely begun to make a real home out of the barnlike building at 42 Islington when word came of President Young's death. They repacked their things and returned home.

For a year Elder Smith was preoccupied with the Twelve, charting the course of the Church during another interregnum and sorting out the snarled condition of President Young's estate. The problem arose from intermixing Church assets and the prophet's personal assets because of unfair restraints imposed by the 1862 antibigamy act. Joseph F. served on the committee that worked out a settlement between the Church and the Young family. When that problem was resolved, he received one of the most enjoyable assignments of his career.

On September 3, 1878, Joseph F. left Salt Lake City with Elder Orson Pratt for the East on a mission to gather historical data. Elder Pratt was the Church Historian and Elder Smith his chief assistant. Their first stop was Independence,

Missouri, where they interviewed William E. McLellin, an original member of the Twelve who had been excommunicated, and Mrs. William Eaton, the remarried widow of John E. Page. Mrs. Eaton, who was abrupt and frosty, knew little of historical value. Mr. McLellin was critical of the "Brighamite" church but was friendly and helpful. He took the visitors on a tour of the city, pointing out things of historic interest. At Richmond, Missouri, the Apostles were pleased with the attitude of David Whitmer, who answered many questions about the early history of the Church. He described how the angel Moroni exhibited the plates. He also showed them the printer's copy of the Book of Mormon manuscript in Oliver's handwriting but resisted efforts to have it placed in the Church archives. At Far West Joseph F. saw, for the first time since his infancy, the place where he was born. The reception at Kirtland, Ohio, was chilly. Here Joseph F. paid homage at the grave of Jerusha Smith, his father's first wife.

The high point of the tour came at Palmyra, New York. At Hill Cumorah the Apostles "prayed long and fervently for all Israel and for the interests of Zion." Afterward, they blessed each other. The main disappointment of the tour came on the way home at Plano, Illinois, where Joseph Smith III refused to show Joseph F. the Prophet Joseph Smith's revision of the scriptures. Unlike their meeting in the early 1860s at Nauvoo, the Prophet's son was cold and distant toward Joseph F. The main value of the tour was the preservation of valuable historical data; and for Joseph F. personally, the tour gave him a new sense of proximity with the past.

Three months after the eastern tour, the Church was thrown into confusion. This resulted from the Reynolds decision on January 6, 1879, in which the Supreme Court held that the 1862 antibigamy act was constitutional. This eliminated the legal basis on which the Church had ignored the 1862 act. Concern escalated when Congress passed the

Edmunds Act in 1882, which added tough new provisions aimed at the Church and Latter-day Saint polygamists. An early decision interpreting the Edmunds Act held that each day one lived in plural marriage was a separate offense. This terrorized Mormon polygamists and hastened their flight into the underground to avoid arrest and prosecution. Joseph F. was especially vulnerable because he had charge of the Endowment House records. Thus extraordinary efforts were made to apprehend him, not only because he was Second Counselor in the First Presidency but also because he had information that could convict others. To avoid this, it was decided that President Smith would go into exile in Hawaii.

Returning from a trip into Old Mexico with President John Taylor and other Church leaders, Elder Smith separated from the party in California. He then waited in San Francisco for Julina and their baby. The three of them boarded the *Mariposa* on February 2, 1885. Arriving safely at Honolulu, they went immediately to the Church plantation at Laie across the island of Oahu. This would be Joseph F.'s home for more than two years.

Had it not been for the threat of arrest and the absence of most of his family, this would have been an idyllic period for President Smith. He was with a devoted wife and their child and among people whom he loved and who revered him. He had time to read, to reflect, and to write. There was opportunity to fulfill his apostolic duty by teaching and motivating the members and the missionaries at Laie. There was physical work on the plantation to provide a diversion and to help keep him fit. And there was leisure to enable him and Julina to explore the beauties of the islands. "It seemed like a new ethereal world," he wrote of a visit to Haleahala on Maui, "or as though we had started on an aerial flight to some distant sphere, and could behold our own terrestrial globe far below, wrapped in fleecy robes; and reflecting from its watery surface, through the rifts in the clouds, their beautiful and ever-changing light and shade." The beauty and precision of this writing belie the limited formal education of its author.

A few months after arriving in the islands, President Smith made a discovery that aroused his historical instincts. He learned that a man named L. L. Rice, an Ohio retiree who lived on Oahu, had the manuscript written by Solomon Spaulding. Enemies of the Church had said this was the origin of the Book of Mormon. Through lengthy negotiations, Joseph F. was able to borrow and to copy the manuscript. There is no real resemblance between the two documents. Finding the Spaulding manuscript exploded a false theory that enemies of the Church had promoted for decades. It was a satisfying find for a professional historian to make.

President Smith's daughter Donnette came to Laie to help her mother, who gave birth to a son, Elias Wesley, in April 1886. Later Donnette's duties expanded to nursing her father when he became very ill. A deep bronchial infection, accompanied by alternate sweating and chilling, sapped his strength and put him in bed. His refusal to stay down until he was fully recovered caused several relapses and needlessly prolonged the illness. After he had healed, it was decided that Julina would return to Utah with Donnette and the two babies. "When once alone," he wrote after seeing them off on March 15, 1887, "my soul burst forth in tears and I wept their fountains dry and felt all the pangs . . . of parting with my heart's best treasures on earth."

The separation ended sooner than expected. When word came the following July that President John Taylor was critically ill, Joseph F. returned to Utah. He arrived on the eighteenth, a week before President Taylor died. After the prophet's death, the Church entered another interregnum, being led by the Twelve, who were sustained at the

October general conference with Wilford Woodruff as their President.

Passage of the Edmunds-Tucker Act, which became effective March 3, 1887, increased the pressure on Elder Smith and other polygamists. He did not attend the October conference for fear of arrest. Further, he took special precautions to preserve his anonymity when walking on the streets and when traveling from Utah to Washington, D. C., in February 1888.

In Washington, Elder Smith took charge of all Church affairs in the eastern United States. In addition to the usual duties of shepherding the Saints and missionary work, he directed the emigration of converts from Europe and led the team that lobbied for statehood. Most of this work was done behind the scenes. When he ventured forth, he made every effort to avoid being recognized. On a trip to New York, he negotiated a contract with a shipping firm to carry converts, then traveled to Newport News, Virginia, to inspect the ships. A veteran of many ocean crossings, this inlander knew more about ship accommodations than most maritime workers.

When the First Presidency was reorganized at the April 1889 general conference, Joseph F. Smith was sustained as Second Counselor to President Wilford Woodruff. "I would rather have taken a mission to Vandeman's land as an elder," he confided to his diary, "than to be called to the responsibilities of a counselor in the First Presidency if my own choice was to be consulted." He had no illusions about the work, nor aspirations to high office. He accepted the call willingly, determined to serve devotedly.

President Smith continued to work behind the scenes. He used an office in the Gardo House, located across the street from the First Presidency's offices. First Presidency meetings usually were held there so that he could stay out of sight as much as possible.

There had been discussions among the leaders about

discontinuing polygamy. All Latter-day Saints knew this could occur only through revelation. In September 1890 President Wilford Woodruff and his counselors, George Q. Cannon and Joseph F. Smith, spent two weeks alone in San Francisco discussing and praying about this sensitive matter. On September 25 President Woodruff was inspired to take the historic action. Known as the Manifesto, this revelation was approved at the general conference in October. President Woodruff later declared he would have continued teaching plural marriage forever "had not the God of Heaven commanded me to do what I did do; and when the hour came that I was commanded to do that, it was all clear to me."

This action began a process of healing. It ended the underground for men like Joseph F. Smith who now could live normally. Polygamists were granted amnesty for plural marriages solemnized before the Manifesto. Church properties escheated to the government were returned. And judges and prosecutors administered the laws benignly so as not to disrupt relationships created before the Manifesto. While a small group of Saints rejected the revelation, the great majority accepted it, recognizing that the prophetic authority that began plural marriage could end it and that ending it did not imply it was morally or theologically wrong.

The dedication of the Salt Lake Temple in April 1893 symbolized the dawning of a new day for the Latter-day Saints. It gave hope that the Church could go forward unimpeded to fulfill its global mandate to preach the gospel and to prepare a people ready to receive the Savior at His second coming. Yet that hope was overshadowed by two major problems facing the Church. One was political. The other was financial. Joseph F. Smith played a key role in solving both.

After the Manifesto, statehood for Utah was the main political goal for Church members. A barrier to that was the

People's party, which was dominated by the Saints. Wise leaders like President Smith knew chances for statehood would increase if the People's party was dissolved and if its members joined the national political parties. That objective was achieved through the influence of men like Joseph F. Smith, although the action was taken as individuals, not under the umbrella of Church authority. After statehood was attained, President Smith was a key actor in formulating the Political Manifesto, which precluded General Authorities from seeking political office without the approval of the President of the Church.

The fight over polygamy ruined the Church financially. For several years after the Manifesto, the Church operated on borrowed money. This condition existed when Lorenzo Snow became President of the Church in September 1898. At the April 1899 general conference, several of the Brethren talked about tithing. In his remarks on the subject, President Smith said in part: "I believe the Lord designs in this principle to test the obedience of the people." The Saints soon were put to that test in a remarkable way.

In May, Joseph F. accompanied President Lorenzo Snow and other leaders to Dixie in southern Utah. The prophet had no exact purpose in making the trip but felt a strong urge to go. He learned why he was there during a talk in St. George. As he spoke, God revealed to him that the financial distress of the Church and its members would be lifted by keeping the law of tithing. "I knew," he explained later, "it was a command of the Lord that the people should repent and reform from the great neglect that we had all been guilty of more or less."

This launched a tithing crusade. For months afterward, President Snow and his brethren used every opportunity to encourage tithing faithfulness. "We are doing [this]," Joseph F. explained in his talk at the October 1889 conference, "that there may be something in the storehouse of the Lord with which to meet the necessities of the people; for the necessities of the Church are the necessities of the people." The results were striking: tithing doubled during the first year, and within a few years, the Church was debt free and the members enjoyed increased prosperity.

President Smith now enjoyed the freedom to travel openly without fear. At this period he made separate trips to Old Mexico, Canada, and southern Arizona. When possible, he took members of the family with him. Alice and their two young sons accompanied him to Thatcher, Arizona, where they stayed with Alice's twin brother, Andrew Kimball, the stake president. Among the Kimball children was a ruddy-cheeked boy, Spencer, who one day would become President of the Church.

When President Lorenzo Snow died in October 1901, President Joseph F. Smith became the sixth President of the Church. He selected John R. Winder and Anthon H. Lund as his counselors. The prophet reemphasized the role of the priesthood and continued to stress tithing faithfulness. President Smith's impressive stature, his experience, his eloquence, and his exemplary family gave him great influence with the members of the Church.

The prophet faced an ordeal when he was called to testify before the Senate Committee on Privileges and Elections that was considering challenges to the seating of Senator Reed Smoot. President Smith was on the stand three stressful days. When the hearings developed evidence that some Church leaders had performed plural marriages after the Manifesto, the prophet took disciplinary action against the offenders. And at the April 1904 general conference, President Smith announced the Worldwide Manifesto, which affirmed that the restraint on teaching and contracting plural marriages applied globally.

As the centennial of the Prophet Joseph Smith's birth approached, President Smith decided on a memorial that would appropriately honor him. In July 1905 a granite monument thirty-eight and a half feet high was commissioned.

Its height symbolized the Prophet Joseph Smith's age when he was martyred. President Smith led a party to Vermont to dedicate the monument. The ceremony took place on December 23, the Prophet's birthday. The inscriptions on the monument memorialized both martyrs, Joseph and his brother Hyrum. The event and the location—the state where both his father and uncle were born—produced a powerful emotional response in President Smith. In accepting a gift after the unveiling, his voice choked with emotion and his eyes filled with tears. "My heart is like that of a child," he told the audience. "It is easily touched, especially with love; I can much easier weep for joy than for sorrow. I suppose perhaps it is due to some extent to the fact that all my early remembrances were painful and sorrowful."

After the dedication, President Smith and members of his family visited Topsfield, Massachusetts, the place where Robert Smith, their first ancestor in America, had lived; Palmyra, New York, where they visited the home of Joseph Smith Sr.; and Kirtland, Ohio, where they visited the temple and the home of Hyrum Smith, where Joseph F. Smith was conceived. These experiences deepened his love for family and the Church and reinforced his testimony of the gospel, a testimony he never tired of repeating. While the words might vary, the essence of his apostolic message never altered: "I bear my testimony to you," he told a Tabernacle audience, "that the Lord God Omnipotent reigneth, that He lives and that His Son lives, even He who died for the sins of the world, and that He rose from the dead; that He sits upon the right hand of the Father; that all power is given unto Him; that we are directed to call upon God in the name of Jesus Christ . . . and every moment of our lives we should live so that the desires of our hearts will be a prayer unto God for righteousness, for truth and for the salvation of the human family."

As the head of the Church, President Smith felt the need to share this testimony personally with as many as possible.

He traveled often both locally and abroad for that purpose. On July 21, 1906, he left Salt Lake City with a party for a two-month tour of northern Europe. Their steamer, the *Vaterland,* took them to Antwerp, Belgium, where the tour began. A meeting in Rotterdam was attended by a young boy named John Roethoff, who was losing his sight and had had to leave school. He had told his mother that if the prophet would look into his eyes, he would be healed. The mother led her son to President Smith, who lifted the bandages and looked at the boy's eyes, saying something neither the son nor his mother understood. Later the boy's faith was rewarded—his sight was fully restored.

President Smith and his party traveled throughout Holland, Belgium, Germany, Switzerland, and France, holding many meetings with the Saints. They then crossed the Channel, touring in Scotland and England. In London the party was joined by four of President Smith's sons who were serving missions in Europe: Alvin Fielding, Heber Chase, Willard Richards, and George Carlos. It was a joyous reunion.

A few weeks after the group returned home, joy turned to sadness. Stirred up by former U.S. senator Thomas Kearns, who owned the *Salt Lake Tribune* and who blamed President Smith for his defeat, a suit for unlawful cohabitation was brought against the prophet. It stemmed from the fact President Smith had continued to acknowledge and support the wives he had married before the Manifesto. The prophet had never tried to hide this and had admitted it in testimony at the Smoot hearings. Earlier officials had been understanding and had not pressed these suits, not wanting to upset families. But the bitterness and influence of Mr. Kearns reversed this benign policy. President Smith admitted the charges and was fined but was not imprisoned. This incident did not end Mr. Kearns's mean-spirited attacks on the prophet.

In an effort to reduce the negative publicity from this

incident, the First Presidency issued an address to the Church and to the world. It outlined the events leading to the Manifesto and the efforts made later by members and nonmembers to solve a complicated problem with a minimum of upset. Reasonable people understood this. Others refused to try to understand. These rigid people harassed President Smith for several years without mercy.

In a series of general conference talks, President Smith explained the role of the priesthood and the function of each office in the administration of the Church. He distinguished the priesthood and the keys of the priesthood, underscored the need for each one to learn and to perform his priesthood duty, admonished priesthood holders to be humble and teachable, and stressed that priesthood authority is a derivative power. "We are only instruments whom God may choose and use to do his work," he explained. So frequently did President Smith return to the theme of the priesthood that this aspect of his public speaking overshadows all others. Indeed, his whole ministry was characterized by a deliberate effort to strengthen and magnify the priesthood.

President Smith's many duties included service as chairman of the Church Board of Education. He took a lively interest in the secular as well as the doctrinal education of the Saints. While the rural character of most Mormon communities caused him to stress the mechanical and agricultural arts, he was an early advocate of professional schools for the Brigham Young Academy at Provo, Utah, which later became an accredited university. An academic crisis developed in Provo when members of the faculty began teaching classes on evolution. Complaints from students and parents prompted an investigation resulting in the dismissal of three professors. In an article explaining this action, President Smith wrote: "[We] are deciding a question of propriety and are not undertaking to say how much of evolution is true, or how much is false. . . .

The Church itself has no philosophy about the modus operandi employed by the Lord in His creation of the world. . . . God has revealed to us a simple and effectual way of serving Him, and we should regret very much to see the simplicity of these revelations involved in all sorts of philosophical speculations."

In the summer of 1910 President Smith again traveled to Europe and Great Britain. Numerous meetings were held with the Saints and the missionaries. Along the way he met his two missionary sons, Franklin and Calvin Smith, and his grandson Joseph Smith Nelson. The prophet loved his sons enough that he gave them needed counsel. "I am sorry you were not a little more discreet in responding to President Penrose," he wrote to Franklin. "Boys on missions should cultivate amity with all, and more especially with their file leaders and presidents." And, concerned about the length of some of Calvin's letters, he suggested that short letters, well digested, were preferable. Lest the son take offense at this mild reproof, he added a bit of droll humor: "I think you are a very good letter writer, only that your handwriting appears rather small for so large a boy."

Returning home, President Smith spent a month in bed because of a sciatic nerve condition that had bothered him during much of the tour. Being idle was hard duty, so he decided to leave the bed and tough it out. In time the pain abated. He traveled to Washington, D.C., in the summer of 1911 to testify before a congressional committee considering agricultural legislation that affected the Church. While there, Senator Reed Smoot introduced him to President William Howard Taft and other government dignitaries. Everywhere President Smith was received with respect. The changed attitude toward him and the Church was remarkable. It was the dawning of a new day. On the way home, President Smith stopped in Florence, Nebraska, the site of Winter Quarters. He was caught up in a reverie as he recalled the rugged pioneer days, so much in contrast with the luxurious private railroad car in which he was traveling West.

Freed from the restraints of poverty and persecution, and with more efficient means of transportation, President Smith became the most widely traveled of all previous Church prophets. Soon after returning home from Washington, he visited the Northwest, traveling on to British Columbia. On the way home, he detoured to Yellowstone National Park. Then came preaching and training trips to Payson, Utah; Los Angeles, California; Heber, Utah; Morgan, Utah; Cardston, Canada; Lehi, Utah; Chicago, Illinois; back to Los Angeles; to Arizona; and to West Point, Utah. In many places, he dedicated new chapels. In all places he talked mainly about priesthood and the family. His example and personality were as influential as his words. On one trip to Los Angeles, he had dinner with members of the George Romney family, who had been driven from Old Mexico during the revolution. A sixteen-year-old son, Marion, who later became a member of the First Presidency, said he would never forget that the prophet patted him on the head and said, "My boy, never be ashamed you are a Mormon." It was encouragement he sorely needed at the time. It lifted his spirits and gave him hope.

The outbreak of World War I in 1914 presented new challenges to the Church. President Smith anguished over Latter-day Saints in different countries having to fight each other. He saw in the conflict a fulfillment of prophecy. Yet he made it plain that God did not design or will that war should come. "Men precipitate war and destruction upon themselves because of their wickedness," he explained, "and because they will not abide in God's truth, walk in His love, and seek to establish and maintain peace instead of strife and contention." Yet he was optimistic about the future. "This I do believe, with all my heart," he wrote, "that the hand of God is striving with certain of the nations of the earth to preserve and protect human liberty, freedom to worship him according to the dictates of conscience, freedom, and the inalienable right of men to organize national governments . . . and to choose their own leaders."

Several of the prophet's sons served in the army during the war. Only one, Calvin, saw action overseas. Chaplain of the ninety-first division, he was wounded several times. Hyrum M. also was in Europe during the war, serving as mission president. Because of his initials, H.M.S., he was arrested once on suspicion of being a British spy. This oldest son, who was ordained an Apostle in 1901 at age twenty-nine, died of peritonitis in January 1918. Had he lived, Hyrum M. Smith would have succeeded Heber J. Grant as President of the Church. His death was one of the great sadnesses of his father's life. "My soul is rent asunder," the Prophet wrote after Hyrum's death. "My heart is broken and flutters for life! O my sweet son, my joy, my hope! O I love him still. I will love him for evermore."

President Smith traveled to Hawaii frequently. In May 1915, while the war still raged in Europe, he made his seventh trip to the islands. The purpose was to discuss with sugar manufacturing executives the construction of a plant near the Church's plantation. While there, moved by a spiritual impulse, he dedicated the site for a temple. The Brethren later ratified his action. In each of the two succeeding years, he visited Oahu again to check on the plantation and the construction of the temple. "Smothered with leis and gifts of fruits, nuts and candy," he wrote in May 1917, "we boarded the ship (SS Maui) and bid good by to our friends and Honolulu, perhaps for the last time." The prophet provided that emphasis of finality in his journal, something he rarely did. The good-bye was indeed "for the last time." The Hawaii Temple was completed after his death and was dedicated by his successor, President Heber J. Grant. The same is true of the Alberta Temple: the site was dedicated by President Smith, but the temple was dedicated by President Grant after President Smith's death.

Presiding Bishop Charles W. Nibley accompanied President Smith on several of his last visits to Hawaii, as he did on other trips abroad. There was an unusual camaraderie between them. It was Bishop Nibley, a native of Scotland, who introduced President Smith to golf when the prophet was in his late seventies. The game brought out Joseph F.'s competitive instincts. Although he couldn't begin to beat the bishop at his own game, checkers was another matter. Joseph F. was an expert and enjoyed beating the bishop and making due record of his victories. This became their favorite sedentary sport, occupying many pleasant hours during long sea voyages. On the next-to-last voyage to the mainland from Hawaii, Bishop Nibley was making some progress in the game. "Played the Bish today," wrote the President Smith. "He got three out [of] nine games. He is gaining."

Bishop Nibley was an astute businessman. Through his wise financial counsel, President Smith was able to augment the savings he had accumulated over a lifetime with wise investments so that in his later years he had a modest nest egg. Those savings enabled him to build an unpretentious second home at Santa Monica, California. He and members of his family spent many happy hours here, enjoying the beach and the nearby golf courses.

Hyrum's death in January 1918 had a marked effect on the prophet's physical condition. "It is an unusual thing for me to attempt to make any apology for myself," he told the Saints at the April 1918 general conference, "but I am in a condition of health just at this time which may prevent me from taking so active a part at this session of our conference as I have usually taken." A few weeks later, the prophet went to bed, where he stayed for several months. Shortly before the October general conference that year, he had a remarkable vision. In it he saw "the hosts of the dead, both small and great." These, he said, were visited by the Savior, who "preached to them the everlasting gospel." He also saw that the Savior organized the spirits to preach the gospel to those to whom he did not personally preach. The composition of the group that was so instructed included the "great and mighty ones, . . . Father Adam, the Ancient of Days and father of all, and our glorious Mother Eve," as well as Abel, Seth, Noah, Abraham, Isaac, Jacob, and Nephite and Latter-day prophets. He also saw that the faithful elders of this dispensation continue their labors of preaching the gospel when they pass into the spirit world.

This vision was accepted as a revelation of God by the Council of the First Presidency and Quorum of the Twelve on October 31, 1918. It also was accepted as such by the general conference of the Church on April 3, 1976, and is now included as section 138 of the Doctrine and Covenants.

President Joseph F. Smith passed away quietly on November 19, 1918, six days after his eightieth birthday. He was surrounded by members of his large family and his apostolic brethren. Because of the flu epidemic, there was no public funeral, only brief graveside services. His undeviating service in the cause of the Master for over sixty years served as a fitting eulogy. He went to the grave honored by all.

NOTE

This chapter is based on Francis M. Gibbons's book *Joseph F. Smith: Patriarch and Preacher, Prophet of God* (Salt Lake City: Deseret Book Company, 1984) and sources cited therein.

CHAPTER SEVEN

HEBER J. GRANT

When Jedediah M. Grant died on December 1, 1856, his son, Heber J. Grant, was nine days old. At his death, Jedediah, who was only forty, was President Brigham Young's second counselor. At the funeral, which baby Heber attended in the arms of his mother, Rachel Ridgeway Ivins Grant, President Young said, "The very sons of these women that sit here will rise up and be as great as any man that ever lived." Later, Heber C. Kimball, after whom the baby was named, prophesied that Heber would become an Apostle. And at a Relief Society meeting where little Heber was crawling on the floor, Eliza R. Snow, speaking in tongues, with an interpretation by Zina D. Young, predicted young Heber would become one of the high leaders of the Church. Rachel carried these predictions in her heart. As her son grew, she repeatedly told him he had special work to do and to guard his thoughts and words and actions. Heber often brushed these off as being the illusory yearnings of a widow for her only son.

When Heber was seven, Rachel, along with Jedediah's other plural wives, was forced to vacate the Grant family home on Main Street in Salt Lake City where the ZCMI Center now stands. Heber wept at the news, but then, shaking his fist at the house, said, "When I'm a man, I'll buy you back." Later, as the head of a syndicate that controlled the ZCMI property, Heber J. Grant felt he had fulfilled that boyish vow. Herein is revealed a salient quality of the character of the man who became the seventh President of The Church of Jesus Christ of Latter-day Saints. This quality combined the visualization of goals and the persistent pursuit of them over long intervals. It surfaced at different stages of his life and under varying circumstances:

• When classmates laughed at his poor handwriting, Heber pounded the desk and vowed he would learn to write as well as the professor of penmanship. Toiling for months to master the technical skills of his craft, he became a classical penman, earning extra money in his spare time writing greeting cards and invitations.

• Humiliated when playmates mocked his clumsiness and called him a sissy, Heber boldly announced he would play on the baseball team that won the territory championship. Through incessant practice, throwing a baseball against Bishop Edwin Woolley's barn, Heber developed a powerful pitching arm, earning a place on the roster of the championship team. Unaware of what prompted Heber's merciless attack on his barn, the bishop declared Heber to be the laziest boy in the Thirteenth Ward. Upon learning the facts, he became one of Heber's strongest advocates.

• Learning that bookkeepers at the Wells Fargo Bank earned the princely sum of $150 a month, Heber announced an intention to work there, which he did after perfecting his penmanship skills.

• And as President of the Church, Heber J. Grant launched the Church's welfare program, promising the needy would receive care even though it might bankrupt the Church.

Inherent in this quality was a fundamental faith in God and a fundamental faith in his own ability, as a son of God, to achieve unusual things. One of his formulas for achievement was embodied in an aphorism of Ralph Waldo Emerson that Heber modified for his own use: "That which we persist in doing becomes easy, not that the nature of the thing has changed, but that our power to do has increased."

When Heber completed high school at sixteen, he was hired as a bookkeeper by H. R. Mann, an insurance agent. Later, when Mr. Mann formed an insurance and brokerage partnership with Henry Wadsworth, manager of the Wells Fargo Bank, Heber did part-time bookkeeping for the bank, as he did for the Sandy Smelting Company. Both these men took a fatherly interest in Heber. He responded with hard work and absolute honesty. The Mann-Wadsworth agency was dissolved when the partners moved from Salt Lake City. Heber, who was twenty, had learned the business so thoroughly in five years and was so well acquainted in the community that he started his own insurance and brokerage business, acquiring most of the Mann-Wadsworth clientele. Soon after, his business contacts and influence were broadened when he replaced Bernard Schettler as an assistant cashier at Zion's Savings Bank while Brother Schettler filled a mission. President Brigham Young endorsed Heber's $25,000 surety bond, thereby enabling Heber to carry on his own business while working at the bank.

During these formative years, Heber had other goals. He aimed to be mayor of Salt Lake City, a position his father had held, and also aspired to be a U. S. congressman. To this end, he avidly studied local and national politics. Given his intelligence and persistence, it is suspected he would have attained those goals had not a call to Church service interfered. Another goal was to be married before he reached age twenty-one. He reached this goal when he was sealed to Lucy Stringham on November 1, 1877, in the St. George Temple, three weeks before his twenty-first birthday.

The Church service call came in October 1880, when Heber was called as the president of the Tooele Stake. He was not yet twenty-four. While the call came as a shock, it relieved him of an anxiety stemming from a patriarchal blessing he had received as a boy that promised he would be called to the ministry in his youth. He had interpreted this to mean he would be called as a missionary in his teens. When this did not happen, he questioned the inspiration of the patriarch. Only after his call as stake president did he see the significance of the word *ministry* in the blessing.

The Tooele Saints also were shocked when the young man from Salt Lake City was presented as their new stake president. Some did not vote to sustain him, although they did not raise their hands in opposition. At lunch after the morning session, Joseph F. Smith, Second Counselor in the First Presidency, noted Heber had not borne testimony of the truth of the gospel. Heber said he had not done so because he did not know it to be true, only that he believed it. Turning to President John Taylor, President Smith said he felt they should reverse at the afternoon session what they had done in the morning because he did not feel a man should serve as stake president unless he had a testimony. "I did not seek this office," said Heber, "and I will be only too willing to be relieved of it." Addressing President Smith, President Taylor said with a chuckle, "That young man knows the gospel is true just as well as you and I. The only thing that he does not know is that he does know it."

This knowledge became evident to Heber when the Tooele Stake patriarch, John Rowberry, gave him a special blessing. When he had finished, the patriarch said, "I saw something I dared not mention." President Grant said later it was made known to him at that moment he eventually would become the President of the Church. He never divulged this to anyone until it became a fact.

The members of the Tooele Stake soon learned to love and to admire their new president. He was friendly, approachable, and diligent. He fulfilled the pledge made in his first talk never to ask others to do what he was unwilling to do. The members also found his experience and wisdom belied his age. He had been active in the business world for eight years, was married with two children, and was the sole support of his widowed mother. He was not a novice as some originally thought him to be.

Heber's service in Tooele was short-lived. As he entered the Tabernacle in October 1882, he met George Teasdale, who extended his hand, saying, "Brother Grant, you and I are going to—" A coughing spell prevented him from completing the sentence. At that moment it was made known to Heber they would be called to fill the two vacancies in the Twelve. He assumed the action would take place at the conference. When it did not, Heber was unsettled. Eight days later he learned that the impression was correct but that his idea about the timing was wrong. At a meeting with the Brethren, a revelation President Taylor had received was read. Although Heber had been forewarned, he was shocked by the words, "Let my servants George Teasdale and Heber J. Grant be appointed to fill the vacancies in the Twelve." With that and the ordination and setting apart that followed, Heber's life was on a course foretold by prophecy.

Although he was convinced of the divine origin of the call and accepted it without question, Elder Grant was troubled. Why had the call come to him and at such a young age? He also felt inadequate because he had not received the kind of spiritual affirmation he felt was necessary to qualify him as a special witness. He sought answers in fervent prayers. There was no response until several months later when he was with Brigham Young Jr. and others on a mission to the Indians in Arizona. One day as the party traveled on the Navajo Reservation, Elder Grant took a side trail alone. There he experienced an epiphany in which "he seemed to see" a council held on the other side of the veil where there was discussion about filling the two vacancies in the Twelve. He saw his father, Jedediah M. Grant, and the Prophet Joseph Smith in the council, both of whom wanted him to fill one of the vacancies. "It was also given to me," Heber wrote later, "that that was all these men . . . could do for me. From that day it depended upon me and upon me alone as to whether I made a success of my life or a failure." In his dream, Heber saw special signif- icance in the presence of Joseph Smith, to whom his mother was sealed, having been married to Jedediah M. Grant for time only. Therefore, he considered himself to be the Prophet's son in the sealing line. This supernal experience swept away all doubt and clearly illuminated Heber's future path.

During his early apostolic years, that path was strewn with many obstacles. The main obstacle initially was the government's determined campaign to enforce the anti- polygamy laws. The most recent one, the Edmunds Act, had been passed during the year Heber became a member of the Twelve. While he was not a polygamist at that time, he became one two years later, in 1884, when he was sealed to Augusta Winters and Emily Wells. Because the Edmunds Act had been interpreted to mean each day one lived in polygamy was a separate offense, Heber and the other brethren were constantly on guard to conceal evidence of polygamous cohabitation. This entailed establishing resi- dences for the wives in different communities. For a while Augusta lived in Colorado and Emily was in England, where her father, Daniel H. Wells, served as mission presi- dent. Heber and his brethren felt justified in this strategy because they insisted that the antibigamy laws, as well as the court interpretations of them, violated their religious freedom.

Thus Elder Grant performed his Church duties amid heavy pressures. Moreover, because the Church living allowance was minimal, he had to earn money to maintain his growing families. Consequently, he conducted his insurance and brokerage business on the side. He traveled extensively to visit stakes in the Intermountain West and to transact business in the major cities in the East and on the West Coast. In May 1883 Heber traveled to Chicago and New York to cement relations with his insurance contacts; and the following month found him in San Francisco, where he successfully settled an insurance claim for H. B. Clawson arising from an explosion of powder in the Clawson store. Numerous trips on Church assignments during 1884 included one to Sonora, Mexico, where meetings were held with the governor about establishing Mormon communities in Mexico. And in May Elder Grant joined other General Authorities at the dedication of the temple at Logan, Utah.

Conditions worsened in 1887 with the passage of the Edmunds-Tucker Act, under which the Church was disincorporated and its properties were escheated to the government. It was during this period that the syndicate Elder Grant headed acquired the ZCMI property on which the old Grant home had stood.

After years of oppression, and in answer to fervent prayers, President Wilford Woodruff received the revelation to discontinue the teaching and practice of plural marriage in the Church. Received in September 1890, the Manifesto, as it was called, was accepted by the Church the following month. At the time of the Manifesto, Elder Grant's family included eight daughters and a son: Lucy had given birth to five daughters—Rachel, Lucy, Florence, Edith, and Anna—and a son, Heber Stringham; Augusta had a baby girl, Mary; and Emily had two daughters, Dessie and Grace. Three children were added to Heber's family after the Manifesto, all borne by Emily: Daniel Wells, Emily, and Frances. The two sons died as little boys.

Soon after the Manifesto, Lucy became ill. The doctors

were baffled at the cause and could prescribe no remedy. Long periods in the hospital did not help. Distraught, Heber spent many hours at her bedside. "I have shed some bitter tears this afternoon," he wrote in November 1892. "Lucy feels that she cannot get well and as she suffers so much she has little desire to recover." She died two months later. Heber was overwhelmed with grief. He experienced the same agony when Emily passed away in 1908. Augusta survived President Grant, as did all his children except the two sons and his daughter Emily, who died in 1929.

The Book of Mormon prophet Nephi was President Grant's hero. "No other individual has made such a strong impression upon me as did Nephi," he wrote. "He has been one of the guiding stars of my life." That influence was never more evident than during the economic panic of 1891 while Lucy struggled with her illness. The State Bank of Utah that Heber and others had organized badly needed cash to avoid bankruptcy. Before he left for the East, President Wilford Woodruff gave Elder Grant a blessing that promised more money would be offered to him than he needed. "I went out with a feeling of perfect assurance that I would be successful," wrote Heber. We may gauge the extent of his optimism knowing that he intended to sell, without discount, 6 percent ZCMI notes owned by the bank in a volatile market where interest of one-half of 1 percent per day was not uncommon.

On the way east a banker in Omaha, amazed at Heber's audacity, advised him how his bank might work out of its difficulty.

"I told him it was money I was after and not advice," Heber later wrote, "and that I had to go east for $100,000 and that I intended to get it and I would stop on my way home and tell him where I got it." A banker in Chicago gave the same advice and received the same response. When a bank in New York, which earlier had solicited business of the State Bank of Utah, turned him down, Heber wrote a note to its board of directors: "If you do not want to buy notes guaranteed by thirteen reputable men and a bank of a half million dollars capital, take my advice and do not do business so far away from home." This caused a change in attitude and touched off a chain of events that enabled Heber to sell $88,000 worth of ZCMI notes without discount in just two days. Half in jest, he wired the banker in Chicago advising what had happened and asking whether he wanted to buy the last $12,000 note. He received a return wire, "Send the note." Later, through some of his insurance contacts, he had offers of loans that exceeded his requirements. "From the day that President Woodruff blessed me," Heber wrote, "and said I would get all the money I was going for and more if I needed it, I had a perfect assurance in my heart that his promise would be fulfilled, and it was fulfilled to the very letter."

Afterward when President Woodruff was impressed to establish a sugar industry in Utah, Elder Grant became his chief agent in raising the capital needed to finance it. Once the prophet had decided to go ahead, Heber sold stock in the company with the same determination shown in selling the ZCMI notes, even though he originally had doubts about the success of the venture.

At the height of his family and business trials in the early 1890s, Heber also became deeply involved in politics. This seemed to be a carryover from his early aspirations for political office. When the People's party was dissolved in June 1891, Elder Grant joined the Democratic party. He became the party's finance chairman. At the urging of friends, he even considered running for governor and United States senator. He abandoned the idea when he learned that President Woodruff opposed it. Later he helped formulate the Political Manifesto, which precluded General Authorities from seeking political office without approval of the prophet. Two General Authorities, Moses Thatcher of the Twelve and Brigham H. Roberts of the First Council of

Seventy, were unwilling to obey the manifesto and went forward with plans to run for federal office. Elder Grant and Francis M. Lyman of the Twelve were assigned to counsel with Elder Roberts. After spending hours with him, pleading and reasoning, he yielded. Elder Grant was ecstatic. "I made a copy of the letter from brother Roberts," he wrote, "and I did not walk across the road to read it to Brother Franklin D. Richards, but I ran over there." He then read it to everybody in sight. All had tears in their eyes. There was great sadness when Elder Thatcher would not yield.

During the years Elder Grant struggled to save his bank from failure, he incurred heavy personal debt. He still carried this burden in 1900 when, without prior announcement, he was called to preside over the mission in Japan. The unexpected call came at a weekly temple meeting. Heber accepted willingly. Afterward Elder John W. Taylor came to him and said: "Heber, you have made a financial sacrifice today that is the equal, financially speaking, of Abraham offering up Isaac. . . . The Lord has accepted your offering. I know your condition financially, and I prophesy that you shall be blessed of the Lord and make enough money to go to Japan a free man financially." Elder Taylor then gave him the formula for reaching that goal: "I am inspired to tell you [that] you are not to plan to make money, but you are to get down on your knees every morning and tell the Lord you want to make money that day, and then go out and get it, and you will be astonished how easily you will make the money." Elder Grant followed this procedure faithfully for four months, after which he reported: "I paid my tithing on my profits for the four months, and the amount was forty-six hundred dollars. I had earned over two hundred percent more in only four short months than I had previously earned in any four months, and went to Japan a free man, financially."

Elder Grant left for the mission field on July 24, 1901, in company with three companions, Louis B. Kelsch,

Horace S. Ensign, and Alma O. Taylor. They boarded the train at the Salt Lake depot at 11:00 P.M. and once on the sleeper gave vent to their enthusiasm by loudly singing all verses of three favorite Latter-day Saint hymns. This set the tone for Heber's mission in Japan. Sailing from Vancouver on July 30 aboard the *Empress of India*, they arrived in Yokohama a week later. Checking in at the Grand Hotel, they made arrangements for the translation and publication of some Church literature. Before actually starting their work, they gathered in a secluded wood outside the city on Sunday, September 1, 1901, where Elder Grant offered a prayer dedicating Japan for the preaching of the gospel.

The work was hard. Language was a main barrier. Communicating through translators was unsatisfactory, especially because the translators were not members and did not understand Mormon theology. Heber took language lessons. It was slow, tedious, unrewarding work, like hitching a thoroughbred racehorse to a plow. Strong opposition from established Christian sects posed other problems. Determined the Latter-day Saints would not succeed, they attacked the missionaries in the press and raised every possible barrier. Heber answered as best he could, but his efforts were ineffective. After six disappointing months, he decided to return to Salt Lake City to review strategies with the Brethren. As his ship, the *Galic*, eased away from the pier, two Japanese converts, the entire harvest of six months' work, stood with the missionaries waving goodbye. These converts later left the Church.

Heber spent three months in Salt Lake City. He was much in demand as a speaker. He frankly admitted the work was hard and, to that date, unproductive. But he was optimistic about the future. "I have the assurance in my soul," he told the general conference audience in April 1902, "that there is to be a wonderful work accomplished in Japan; that there will be many, yea, even thousands of that people that will receive the Gospel of Jesus Christ." This prediction was not fulfilled during President Grant's life. It began to be fulfilled shortly after his death when, following World War II, Mormon servicemen started teaching the gospel to the Japanese.

Elder Grant returned to Japan in June 1902. Augusta and Mary were with him, along with several more missionaries. He remained there until September 1903. Life was much happier with members of his family present. But baptismal success did not follow. His greatest success as mission president came from training and motivating the missionaries. They never forgot the example of his persistence and drive and his faith in the future despite few immediate results.

"I went out into the woods," Elder Grant wrote of his last days in Japan, "and got down on my knees and told the Lord that whenever He was through with me there, where I was doing nothing, I would be very glad and thankful if he would call me home and send me to Europe to preside over the European Mission." Soon after offering this prayer, he received a cable from the First Presidency, directing him to come home. He arrived shortly before the October general conference in 1903. At the conference it was announced that Elder Heber J. Grant had been called to preside over the European Mission.

Emily and six of the girls accompanied Elder Grant. Because the Church-owned building at 42 Islington was in a rundown neighborhood and was inadequate for the Grant family, a new mission home was purchased at 10 Holly Road in Liverpool. President Grant did his work from there. He not only supervised personally the 114 missionaries laboring in the British Isles, but also edited the *Millennial Star* and directed the work of the mission presidents in Holland, Belgium, Switzerland, France, Germany, Austria, and Scandinavia.

President Grant toured extensively throughout Great Britain and Europe, teaching and motivating the missionaries and instructing the Saints. He usually took members of his family with him, exposing them to the cultural wealth of these ancient countries, visiting museums, libraries, and art galleries. This not only broadened his family's understanding but cultivated in him an appreciation for beautiful art that was later reflected in his purchase of many paintings and the encouragement of young, unknown artists.

Traveling with President Grant was never dull. He was interested in everything and always ready for a novelty. Once while in Stockholm, Sweden, on July 4, he asked his companions what they would like to do to celebrate their country's birthday. When no one had an idea, he suggested they call on King Oscar, the monarch of Sweden and Norway, to extend greetings. He had credentials signed by American officials but had made no prior request for a royal interview. They approached the king's castle, and when the guard walked away from them, Heber went to the front door and asked to see the king. After he had shown his credentials and made his finest sales pitch, the king, unbelievably, came to the door. In the conversation the king told Elder Grant that because of favorable reports he had received about the way his former subjects had been accepted in Utah, the Church would have freedom to proselytize in his realm.

Upon completing his mission, Elder Grant and his family returned to Salt Lake City in December 1907. He had been away from home almost five years and had dipped into his savings to maintain his family. Elder Grant worked hard to shore up his finances while continuing to fulfill his Church responsibilities. His business interests included insurance, real estate, banking, ZCMI, and the Utah-Idaho Sugar Company. When he had built up his resources, he fulfilled a promise made to Emily to build her a new home. It was located at Second Avenue and B Street in Salt Lake City. The happiness of the occasion was clouded by her illness. She had cancer and failed rapidly. "Unless there is a change for the better, she certainly cannot live but a few days," Heber wrote on May 23, 1908. She slipped away two days later. It was "one of the hardest blows" of his life. Quiet family funeral services were held in Emily's home, which she had personally decorated.

Elder Grant had the instincts of a good propagandist. These were revealed in two causes he took up at this time: prohibition and home manufacturing. Using the tools of repetition and dramatization, he turned often to these themes in general conference and other talks. His fight against liquor was broadened later to include speaking out against the use of tobacco, tea, and coffee. He talked about these things incessantly, telling pertinent and sometimes amusing stories to clinch his point. He became famous for quoting a poem titled "The Saloon Bar," which portrayed the evils of alcohol, and for telling a story about a cheap out-of-state suit he had bought that lacked the durability of the good suits made of cloth manufactured in Provo. He was offended once when Elder Francis M. Lyman, President of the Twelve, suggested he discontinue talking so much about liquor, because the people were getting tired of hearing about it. He soft-pedaled it for a while, but not for long. One of the great legacies he left to the Church was the strong emphasis he gave to the Word of Wisdom, the observance of which promoted good health and gave the Church a special mark of distinction.

Elder Grant intermingled his family, church, and business duties with recreations. He did this to preserve his health and to create a sense of well-being. He regularly worked out at the Deseret Gym and later in life took up golf. He also enjoyed sports as a spectator. These outlets helped him keep a proper perspective.

When Elder Francis M. Lyman passed away in November 1916, Elder Grant became the President of the Twelve. A thirty-four-year apprenticeship had qualified him to lead the quorum. Soon after his call, he attended a stake conference in Parowan, Utah. Instead of returning home immediately afterward, he remained for several days, holding special meetings in the wards and branches. The enthusiasm created caused him to urge all members of the Twelve to do the same on their conference assignments. The result was a marked increase in the commitment of Church members everywhere.

As he lay dying, President Joseph F. Smith called Elder Grant to his bedside. Taking his hand and looking steadily into his eyes, the prophet said to him: "The Lord bless you, my boy, the Lord bless you. You have a great responsibility. Always remember this is the Lord's work and not man's. The Lord is greater than any man. He knows whom He wants to lead His church and never makes mistakes."

Heber J. Grant was ordained and set apart as the seventh President of the Church on November 23, 1918. As he and his counselors, Anthon H. Lund and Charles W. Penrose, considered filling the vacancy in the Twelve caused by President Grant's ordination, they focused on Richard W. Young, grandson of Brigham Young and Heber's lifelong friend. A retired general of the army, a lawyer, and a former stake president, he had every qualification to serve in the Twelve. Deciding he was the man, President Grant wrote Richard W. Young's name on a slip of paper before going to the temple meeting where filling the vacancy was to be discussed. In the temple, he removed the paper with the name written on it, fully intending to present Richard W. Young to the council for approval. But for a reason he could never fully explain, he was unable to do so; instead, he presented the name of Melvin J. Ballard, president of the Northwestern States Mission, a man with whom he had had very little personal contact. This experience had a profound influence on President Grant. It taught him to heed the sudden flashes of insight that came to him in making decisions affecting the Church. This quality is reminiscent of his hero, Nephi, who moved forward, step by step, as God inspired him. It was a quality that would be especially important in the development of the welfare program when President Grant led the Church into an uncharted area, one step at a time, to create a vast mechanism to help provide for the needy of the Church.

Because of his many business associates who were not members of the Church, President Grant became a bridge to unite the Latter-day Saints with the non-Mormon community. He was a member of the Salt Lake Rotary Club and of the Bonneville Knife and Fork Club, a dinner club composed of both members and nonmembers. Such was his popularity that he was once introduced as being both the President of the Church and of the Gentiles in Utah.

Despite his eminence as the President of the Church and his influential role in business, President Grant's basic personality never changed. He retained a democratic, down-to-earth attitude toward all. He had a childlike faith in the destiny of the Church and was excited about every advancement it made. The dedication of temples in Hawaii, Canada, and Arizona were occasions of special significance and cause for celebration. He spoke at every session of the dedications of these temples. Because he had personally known all the Presidents of the Church except Joseph Smith, and because his mother had known Joseph and was sealed to him, he used these occasions to reflect on the prophetic character of his predecessors. "I have attended, as a child, family prayers in the Lion House," he said at the dedication of the temple in Alberta, Canada, "and I have actually turned and looked when Brigham Young was praying, for it seemed to me as though the Lord must be standing there. He seemed to be talking as one man speaking to another when praying to the Lord. There are few men that I have ever listened to that seemed to me could get so close to the Lord in prayer as did Brigham Young." President Grant had the ability to make these past events and personalities come alive in the minds of his listeners. Occasionally he enlivened his talks by singing. Although he was tone-deaf, he had practiced so tenaciously that he was able to sing very well and enjoyed singing as much as his audiences enjoyed hearing him.

A year before the market crash of October 1929, President Grant became concerned about the economy, even though on the surface it seemed to be robust. These anxieties were shared by other Church leaders and were reflected in policies adopted by the Church and the corporations it owned or controlled. New building and expansion were strictly controlled; indebtedness was eliminated where possible; and fixed assets or stocks were kept to a minimum. Also, members were taught to set their individual affairs in order, to live frugally, and to avoid debt. President Grant stressed the danger of installment buying, often quoting an amusing, satirical poem, "Simon Called Simple," about a boy who thought he could buy pie without cash. These precautions enabled the Church, and the members who listened, to enter the Great Depression in a condition as sound as possible. No one, even those who tried to prepare for it, was prepared for the depth of the Depression or for the despair it brought.

Nor was President Grant prepared for the personal shock caused by Utah's vote to repeal the Eighteenth Amendment in 1932. And he was humiliated that Utah's vote provided the margin of victory for the pro-liquor forces. He was confident that free access to alcohol would be a scourge to the nation. With loss at the ballot box, President Grant increased his efforts to persuade Latter-day Saints to observe the Word of Wisdom.

The 1932 election that eliminated prohibition also brought President Franklin D. Roosevelt to power and generated the flood of New Deal legislation intended to lift the Depression. President Grant strongly opposed those facets of the New Deal that encouraged dependency on government. He felt inspired to lead the Latter-day Saints in a different direction. The result was the creation of a system of Church welfare designed to abolish idleness and "the evils of a dole" and to create a sense of "independence, industry, thrift and self respect" among the Latter-day Saints. To help achieve his vision, President Grant engaged the assistance of able men, chief among whom were his counselors, J. Reuben Clark and David O. McKay, and a young stake president, Harold B. Lee. Over several years, and despite many obstacles, the welfare system became firmly established as an important feature of the Church, organized to aid its members in time of need. It stands as a monument to the vision and persistence of President Heber J. Grant.

While President Grant worked to provide economic security for the Saints through Church welfare, he also promoted Church education. He was instrumental in establishing the Church seminary and institute program and discontinuing the system of Church academies where both religious and secular subjects were taught. As a sound businessman, he realized it was financially impossible for the Church to continue to provide secular education for its members. Two exceptions to this policy were Brigham Young University and Ricks College, which the Church continued to support. President Grant was one of their chief boosters.

He also supported other good causes with his time and his money. He seldom refused aid to anyone who sought it. And much of his charity was anonymous. He enjoyed paying off the mortgages of friends and widows who were in financial straits. One of the General Authorities who was the recipient of such a gift was overwhelmed by it. "President Grant was the most liberal and generous man with his personal means that I have ever known," wrote his long-time secretary, Joseph Anderson. "In fact, I doubt if any have excelled him in this respect. He was a man who thoroughly enjoyed making money, but not for the purpose of accumulating it. His only desire was to have money that he might do good with it."

Brother Anderson was more than a secretary to President Grant. He also was his friend, his confidant, and his almost constant traveling companion. A trip they took to southern California in January 1940 marked a major turning point in President Grant's ministry. Following several vigorous rounds of golf, intermixed with Church and business meetings, President Grant suffered a stroke that paralyzed his left side and seriously impaired his speech. After convalescing for several months in California, he returned home.

While the paralysis and the impairment to his speech were handicaps, they did not prevent President Grant from fulfilling his prophetic duties. He was able to work a few hours each day. He delegated many tasks he formerly performed himself. In this way he retained ultimate control, charting the course, while easing off on his personal involvement. For a while he entertained the thought he could recover his former strength. He began carrying a rubber ball in his left hand, regularly squeezing it to build up and tone the muscles. Eventually he accepted the fact his disability was permanent. This was a crucial incident; from that point he began to reorder his habits. The hours away from his office were spent reading, dictating, planning, and resting. He enjoyed taking rides around the valley or into the canyons. He always took others with him, members of his family or friends and associates. In good weather this was almost a daily occurrence. He enjoyed watching the changing seasons and seeing the animal and bird life in the mountains. For the first time, he developed a more calm and contemplative attitude toward life.

The prophet continued to speak briefly at general conferences until April 1942, when he spoke in public for the last time. Thereafter, his talks were read by others. During his last years he called three new members of the Twelve who ultimately became Presidents of the Church: Harold B. Lee, Spencer W. Kimball, and Ezra Taft Benson. He also called Mark E. Petersen to the Twelve during this period to fill the vacancy caused by the excommunication of Richard R. Lyman. The fall of Elder Lyman was one of the great sorrows of his life.

Near the end of 1944 the prophet's health began to weaken. He discontinued making his daily diary entries. His condition continued to wane until May 14, 1945, when he quietly passed away. Because of his advanced age and his life of achievement and service, the funeral was almost like a valedictory. As the funeral procession proceeded east on South Temple, the bells of the Catholic cathedral at Third East tolled their acknowledgement while the priests stood on the sidewalk to bid farewell to their friend. The prophet was laid to rest in the cemetery high on the east bench, overlooking the valley he loved.

NOTE

This chapter is based on Francis M. Gibbons's book *Heber J. Grant: Man of Steel, Prophet of God* (Salt Lake City: Deseret Book Company, 1979) and the authorities cited therein.

CHAPTER EIGHT

GEORGE ALBERT SMITH

When George Albert Smith was born on April 4, 1870, his grandfather and namesake, George A. Smith, was a counselor in the First Presidency of The Church of Jesus Christ of Latter-day Saints. President George A. Smith's father, John Smith, who once served as an assistant counselor in the First Presidency, was a brother of Joseph Smith Sr., father of the Prophet Joseph Smith. And George Albert's father, John Henry Smith, who became a member of the Twelve Apostles when George Albert was ten, later became a counselor in the First Presidency. A patriarchal blessing George Albert received at age twelve intimated his eminence in the Church would exceed that of these three forebears, leading him to the prophetic office. "Thou shalt become a mighty prophet in the midst of the sons of Zion," he was told, "for none of thy father's family shall have more power with God than thou shalt have, for none shall excel thee."

The inconspicuous circumstances in which George

Albert was reared belied this promise of future distinction. He was just one of the children of the many polygamous families who lived in the neighborhood near Temple Square in Salt Lake City, where he was born. He was an active, likable, friendly boy who enjoyed sports as well as home-staged theatricals. He also was known to have independent views that he defended vigorously. After his primary schooling, he was educated at the Brigham Young Academy in Provo, Utah, and at the University of Deseret in Salt Lake City. At Brigham Young Academy he came under the influence of Karl Maeser, whose admonition "Don't be a scrub" and whose teaching about personal responsibility, especially the control of one's thoughts, provided lifelong incentives toward personal excellence.

George Albert's serious eye injury at a summer job on the railroad while at the University of Deseret ended his formal academic career. For a while he held menial jobs at ZCMI. In time, his outgoing personality, his persuasiveness, and his genuine interest in people led him into sales. He became a successful salesman for ZCMI, with a route that took him from Salt Lake City to southern Utah. He became a favorite with the other salesmen because of his geniality, his singing ability, and his musical skill on the guitar and harmonica. He also acquired their respect for observing the Word of Wisdom, while not condemning others for disobeying it.

Later, George Albert was called to serve a mission to work with young people in the same area where he had worked as a salesman. He and a companion attracted hundreds of youths to their meetings by their teaching and testifying as well as by their entertaining skits featuring music and colorful costumes.

George Albert married Lucy Woodruff, a granddaughter of President Wilford Woodruff, on May 25, 1892. Several weeks later, the groom left for the Southern States Mission. Lucy joined him there in a few months. Elder Smith served as mission secretary under Elder J. Golden Kimball, although he often was in charge of the mission during President Kimball's absences. In this way the future Church President learned about Church administration and prose-lytizing. He also learned about bigotry and anti-Mormon hatred. He once was threatened with death by angry mob-bers who shot their guns into the corners of a cabin in which he and a companion were staying. And he learned about the love and faith of many other Southerners who befriended him and who joined the Church.

The Smiths had a belated honeymoon when they returned from the South via Niagara Falls. At home George Albert resumed his sales work at ZCMI and became active in politics. Indeed, he and his father, who was chairman of the Utah Constitutional Convention, were prime movers in organizing the Republican party in Utah. Afterward both of them unsuccessfully sought election to the United States Congress. However, the political prominence they gained resulted in George Albert's being appointed receiver of the U.S. Land Office in January 1898, one of the first Mormon appointees to important government office after Utah state-hood in 1896.

Meanwhile, Lucy gave birth to her first child in November 1895, a daughter named Emily. A second daugh-ter, Edith, was born in November four years later; and six years after that, in September 1905, the Smith's last child, George Albert Smith Jr., was born. The father cherished his wife and children. And he was justifiably proud of his numerous ancestors and relatives who had filled high Church offices. Yet he abhorred nepotism and once at a stake meeting was heard to whisper that if one more Smith were presented for office, he intended to walk out. Just then his name was announced as a counselor in the Salt Lake Stake's Young Men Mutual Improvement Association (YMMIA).

George Albert again was surprised by a call and felt

anxiety about too many Smiths occupying Church office when in October 1903 he was called to the Quorum of the Twelve Apostles. He was not advised of the call beforehand and was not even present at the meeting. The nepotism issue weighed heavily with him because there were five Smiths among the twenty-six General Authorities. He feared that his father, who was then in the Twelve, had influenced the call. Assured this was not so, he later received spiritual confirmation that the call had come by divine inspiration through the prophet.

During the first three years of his service in the Twelve, Elder Smith received assignments that usually kept him close to home. This enabled him to work at the land office during the week. After leaving employment there in 1906, his assignments began to entail heavy travel. Wherever he went, whether touring missions or presiding at stake conferences, he delivered upbeat messages of love, faith, and optimism. Karl Maeser's "don't be a scrub" philosophy found its way into many of Elder Smith's admonitions to missionaries and the youth. He also warned young people to guard their thoughts and "to stay on the Lord's side of the line."

Elder Smith began his long career in acquiring and promoting Church historical sites when in the summer of 1907 he negotiated the purchase of the Joseph Smith Sr. farm near Palmyra, New York, for twenty thousand dollars. He paid cash, which had been sewn into Lucy's skirt. His influence later resulted in the purchase of other Church historical sites in the Palmyra area, including the Hill Cumorah, which was purchased from the descendants of Pliny T. Sexton, whom he had befriended.

Elder Smith's health was fragile. His frequent travels and heavy speaking schedule took their toll. In February 1909 he returned from a tiring trip to the East to speak at a prohibition meeting in the Salt Lake Theatre. He retired the night of the twenty-fourth "feeling quite used up." The next day Elder Smith suffered a general collapse and was unable to rise from his bed. Several years of subsequent poor health prevented him from fulfilling his duties in the Twelve. The nervous tension at the root of his disability was worsened by worry he was shirking his duty. Doctors' orders that he should rest only intensified the problem. Finally yielding to the advice, Elder Smith went to Ocean Park, California, in April 1909, where he lived in a beach cottage for four months, resting as much as his conscience would allow. He showed no improvement. In November 1909 he went to St. George, Utah, and spent six months in a tent near a house where his family lived. His brother Nathaniel, who built the wood-floor tent, was a constant companion and an aide to assist Lucy in George Albert's care. During this stay George Albert never changed to street clothing. Still there was no improvement in his health.

In the summer of 1910 Elder Smith spent three months in a small apartment on the Saltair pier, where he enjoyed the buoyant waters of the Great Salt Lake each day. This regimen helped but did not effect a cure. He then spent several weeks in a sanitarium where special treatments were administered. This helped for a while, but after several months of activity, he suffered a relapse. In February 1912 George Albert returned to Ocean Park, where, except for brief trips to Utah and Arizona, he spent sixteen months. In the summer of 1913 he was able to return to his Church duties, although his health was still fragile.

During the long months of George Albert's convalescence, two vivid dreams and a letter from his father were anchors of spiritual strength to him. In the first dream he saw his grandfather George A. Smith, who said, "I would like to know what you have done with my name." In answer, George Albert said, "I have never done anything with your name of which you need be ashamed." With that the powerful grandfather, who had weighed over three hundred pounds in life, took the frail grandson in his arms.

When George Albert awakened, his pillow was wet with tears of gratitude that he could "answer unashamed." In the second dream he saw many of his relatives assembled, including his father, who had recently passed away. The spirit of peace and love that pervaded the scene was ever after a source of comfort to him. Elder Smith's frequent allusions to these dreams suggest the strong impact they had upon him.

The letter from his father arrived while George Albert was in St. George. These words were like a rod of iron to the son: "Keep up good fortitude and good faith; don't waiver in your determination to live. The bitter experience through which you are going is but designed for your purification and uplifting and qualification for an extended life work."

Once he was able to resume his apostolic duties, Elder Smith also became involved in a myriad of business and civic affairs. He became a member of the board of several corporations, including ZCMI and Utah First National Bank. He also became very active in the Sons of the American Revolution (SAR) and in irrigation and reclamation affairs. And for several years, President Joseph F. Smith called on him for special services.

President Joseph F. Smith died in November 1918. George Albert chaired the committee for his funeral arrangements. Two months later, Joseph F.'s successor, Heber J. Grant, called George Albert Smith to preside over the European Mission. Elder Smith was excited by the call. Lucy was less enthusiastic, being concerned about her husband's health, which still was not robust. Nor did she relish leaving her new home at 1302 Yale Avenue. She was consoled by a prediction of President Grant that George Albert's health would improve in the mission field. The prediction was fulfilled, although a temporary relapse a few months after the Smith family arrived in Liverpool was cause for concern.

Edith and George Albert Jr. accompanied their parents

into the mission field. Emily was married to Robert Murray Stewart and remained in Salt Lake City. In Liverpool the family settled comfortably into Durham House, the mission home that also served as headquarters for the *Millennial Star*, which George Albert would edit.

A shortage of missionaries caused by wartime restrictions was Elder Smith's most immediate concern. After several months of persistent diplomacy, that lack was remedied. Meanwhile, Elder Smith traveled extensively throughout the British Isles and Europe. Members of the family usually accompanied him. Albert, who had been set apart as a missionary, was his most frequent companion. The relationship between father and son replicated the close association between George Albert's father and grandfather, who had occupied adjacent homes across the street west of Temple Square. Such close living arrangements seemed to be a Smith family trait, reflected in George Albert's purchase of a vacant lot next to his Yale Avenue home where he hoped Albert ultimately would build after marriage.

Elder Smith's legacy to the European Mission was the sense of buoyancy and optimism his leadership imparted, especially to the young missionaries. His appointment as superintendent of the YMMIA when he returned home in 1921 positioned him to exert a similar influence upon young men throughout the Church. And the close working relationship he developed with the leaders of the Young Women Mutual Improvement Association (YWMIA) enabled him to extend that influence to the young women.

Elder Smith served as YMMIA superintendent for thirteen years. With the help of his counselors, Elders Richard R. Lyman and Melvin J. Ballard of the Twelve, and a board of distinguished educators and youth leaders, he effected a revolution in the activity programs of the Church. Churchwide basketball and other athletic programs, as well as music and dance festivals and the dramatic arts, flourished under his leadership. Most important, perhaps, was the emphasis he gave to Scouting and to the development of the Vanguard and M-Men programs. His leadership in this field drew national attention when he was elected to the National Executive Council of the Boy Scouts of America, the first Utahn so recognized. He was awarded the Silver Beaver and Silver Buffalo awards in recognition of his service to Scouting. The citation that accompanied the Silver Buffalo award acknowledged his "indefatigable" service and his "enthusiasm" for Scouting as largely accounting for "the fact that Utah stands above all other states in the percentage of boys who are Scouts."

Elder Smith's emergence as a national leader in Scouting was accompanied by an increased stature as an executive of the Sons of the American Revolution. He had been active in the Utah affairs of the SAR for several years. In 1922, when he attended its national convention, he was elected a vice-president general representing western states. This began twenty-six years of active service in the society's national leadership. He became a favored speaker among SAR groups around the country, known for his fluent delivery and anecdotal style. He won many friends for the Church among influential people across the land. And he was diligent in retaining contact with these friends, as also with other people of influence. On one trip east, for instance, to attend an SAR meeting, he stopped in Washington, D.C., to renew acquaintances with President Warren Harding, one of eight presidents of the United States with whom he was personally acquainted.

Through Elder Smith's influence, the national SAR convention was held in Salt Lake City in 1924. His handling of the event, which included a public meeting in the Tabernacle and interesting side activities for the delegates, drew wide praise. The flair for organization this event revealed found a further object for exercise the next year when he chaired the celebration of the fiftieth anniversary of the Mutual Improvement Association (MIA). Later, Elder

Smith was appointed general chairman of the Church's centennial celebration. This featured the drama *Message of the Ages*, staged in the Tabernacle during April and May 1930.

These events foreshadowed a meeting in Elder Smith's home in August 1930. Present were several friends, members and nonmembers, who were interested in preserving history through monuments and markers. This led to the creation of the Utah Pioneer Trails and Landmarks Association the following month. Elder Smith was its first president and prime mover. It would occupy much of his time and effort during the remainder of his life. Under his leadership, the association placed 120 markers extending from Nauvoo, Illinois, to San Diego, California. The association's crowning achievement was the "This Is the Place" monument, dedicated in 1947 as part of the pioneer centennial. Brief, carefully researched statements on plaques succinctly tell the stories of historical events that occurred at or near the monuments. This means of communicating knowledge was fitting for one whose impaired eyesight precluded him from extensive study and writing.

The success of the association lay with Elder Smith's skill as a visionary, an organizer, and a publicist. He brought together people of different backgrounds with abilities in research, writing, art, engineering, and law, all of which was necessary to bring a project to fruition. He then infused them with his enthusiasm and vision and created wide interest by publicity he was able to generate through his influence and contacts. The willing support of nonmembers was guaranteed when the first project undertaken by the association was a marker at Provo, Utah, commemorating the Catholic priests Escalante and Dominguez, who were the first Europeans to trek through the area. And that ecumenical spirit was perpetuated in the creation of other monuments, especially the "This Is the Place" monument, which honored not only the Latter-day Saints but also early explorers, trappers, and missionaries who were not members of the Mormon Church.

While Elder Smith's public life during the 1930s was rewarding as he chaired the centennial celebration and geared up for his work with the Trails and Landmarks Association, his private life was marked by trial and trauma:

• His daughter Emily, who had been a member of the Primary General Board for many years, became involved in a controversy with the president of the Primary. It revolved around differences of opinion concerning how the Primary Children's Hospital should be administered. When Emily directly opposed the president, she was dropped from the board. Feeling that his daughter had been mistreated, Elder Smith sought to have her reinstated. This brought him into conflict with Elder David O. McKay, who was the adviser to the Primary and who felt obligated to support the Primary president. This controversy rocked along for many months, causing great emotional stress to Elder Smith. The matter was never resolved to his or Emily's satisfaction. Despite the temporary resentment this incident created, Elder Smith called Brother McKay as his Second Counselor in the First Presidency when he became the President of the Church.

• Elder Smith's son-in-law George Elliott, Edith's husband, almost died from accidental asphyxiation from a faulty heater at his place of employment.

• George Elliott and Elder Smith's brother Winslow Smith were indicted and convicted of mail fraud arising from the interstate sale of certificates issued by the mortuary where they were employed. While their innocence was vindicated later by a presidential pardon, the prolonged affair wore heavily on Elder Smith's fragile health and exhausted his resources in defense costs.

• Over a period of several years, Lucy's health steadily declined. Weakened and distressed, she quietly passed away on November 5, 1937. Elder Smith was deeply distraught by Lucy's death. She had been such a bulwark of strength to him during his years of illness, always sympathetic, kind, and consoling. He felt lost.

Elder Smith mourned for two months, groping ineffectually for a new identity as a widower. President Heber J. Grant, desiring to give him a new focus, called Elder Smith to tour the missions in the South Pacific. He left in late January 1938 with a group that included Matthew Cowley, who had been called as president of the New Zealand Mission. In Hawaii, Elder Smith was joined by Rufus K. Hardy of the First Council of Seventy, who would be his companion during the tour.

After holding a stake conference and other meetings in Hawaii, the two General Authorities traveled to Pago Pago, capital of American Samoa, where they participated in a *huitau*, the native version of a conference. Elder Smith was impressed by the friendliness of the people and was intrigued by their colorful costumes and dances.

After a brief stop in Fiji, they traveled on to Auckland, New Zealand, where Elder Cowley was installed as the mission president. Then came touring in Australia with mission president Thomas D. Rees. Over a period of six weeks, missionary and member meetings were held in Sydney, Brisbane, Melbourne, Adelaide, and Perth. Returning to Auckland, they spent four weeks touring the New Zealand Mission with President Matthew Cowley. Most of the Saints there were Maoris, natives who had keen spiritual perceptions. This was illustrated at the death of Rufus K. Hardy in March 1945. His long association with them caused the Maoris to look upon Elder Hardy as "their" General Authority. As they mourned his passing, feeling bereft of a prized connection with Church headquarters, one spoke up and said: "There's nothing to worry about. When President Cowley gets home, he'll fill the first vacancy in the Council of the Twelve Apostles, and we'll still have a representative among the Authorities of the Church." Seven months after that prediction, Elder Cowley was called to the Twelve to fill the vacancy created when George Albert Smith became the President of the Church.

After leaving New Zealand, George Albert and Elder Hardy completed their tour with visits to Tonga and Western Samoa.

Elder Smith returned home in mid-July. Six months in the South Pacific had helped to ease the sadness of Lucy's death and to crystallize his future plans. He decided never to remarry, which prompted the decision for Emily and her family to move into his home so that, with household help, she could care for his needs and act as a social hostess. This enabled Elder Smith to resume his Church duties without concern about the home and with the assurance of a warm, loving welcome when returning from his wide-ranging travels.

Elder Smith became a devotee of air travel in the 1930s when commercial flights were something of an oddity. He saw it as the transportation wave of the future. While presiding over the mission in Europe, he and Albert had flown from the continent to London. After that first flight, Elder Smith vowed he would never fly again, a resolve that faded when he realized how flying could multiply his effectiveness. He was the first General Authority to use air travel regularly, often flying to the West Coast and returning the same day, doing in one day what would have taken several days by train. He actively promoted air travel, writing and talking about it, giving airlines suggestions about improving passenger interest and safety, and taking a personal interest in legislation affecting it. As a result of this interest, Elder Smith was appointed to the board of directors of Western Airlines. This was not an honorary appointment, but one that brought to the board a seasoned traveler whose perspectives, influence, and dedication to flying were invaluable in setting policy.

Whenever Elder Smith traveled, he always carried a briefcase stocked with an assortment of Church pamphlets and books. He distributed these to fellow travelers whose acquaintance he deliberately cultivated. And when he had a layover in a city away from home, he often would contact and introduce himself to influential people and, when appropriate, leave Church literature with them.

At home Elder Smith discharged his apostolic duty in a distinctive way. He was the classic good neighbor, calling on the sick, encouraging the lonely and misfits, and helping the disadvantaged. For many years he was president of the Society for Aid of the Sightless in Utah. His own sight problems gave him special empathy for those who couldn't see, and that empathy was broadened to include anyone who had problems. He was an easy mark for those who sought help, financial or otherwise. Hundreds of people were the recipients of his anonymous liberality. Once while walking along a Salt Lake City street on a cold winter day, he gave his overcoat to a vagrant. This trait was the reflection of a personal creed he formulated that included the sentiment "I would be a friend to the friendless and find joy in ministering to the needs of the poor."

Elder Smith's charitable efforts were driven by his benevolent nature and the mandates of his apostolic calling. He had a compulsion to help people. He seemed to have a sense of global responsibility to cure the ills of all mankind. In this he was a notable exemplar of the Savior's teachings. He went about doing good, and he went about trying to persuade others to do good and to rely upon the influences of God. When he taught missionaries how to follow the promptings of the Spirit in their work, he admonished them to "give the Lord a chance." He meant that if they, like Nephi, would begin to act, to move forward toward a goal, God would open doors and guide their steps in a miraculous way.

Those whom Elder Smith could not influence in person

he endeavored to influence by mail. His correspondence was voluminous, and never a one-shot affair. He would write again to those who did not respond to his letters. George Albert kept up a correspondence with one man in England for more than fifteen years. His letter writing had multiple objectives: to uplift another, to create a friend for himself or the Church, and to help bring about a conversion. If the conversion did not occur, he did not stop writing.

Special objects of George Albert's writing and, where possible, his personal contacts, were dissident members of the Smith family. He mourned that many of his relatives failed to join the Mormon exodus west and became affiliated with the Reorganized Church or other splinter groups. He kept track of these cousins, and whenever he traveled to an area where they lived, he looked them up. So while he was in Brisbane, Australia, he contacted Ina Inez Smith Wright, a daughter of Alexander Smith, one of the sons of the Prophet Joseph Smith. Mrs. Wright, the mother of ten children, was a member of the Reorganized Church. At first she was reluctant to meet this official of the "Utah Church." However, Elder Smith's friendly, disarming manner soon dissolved her reticence as the pair enjoyed tracing relationships and sharing Smith family lore. George Albert also made special efforts to befriend Frederick Smith, one of the Prophet Joseph Smith's sons. Once he drove with him from Nauvoo, Illinois, to Independence, Missouri, following a ceremony celebrating the centennial of the creation of Nauvoo. During that long trip, George Albert spoke plainly to his cousin, emphasizing their common heritage and their shared convictions about the Restoration and urging that the Smith family come together under the umbrella of a single church. Of course, George Albert had The Church of Jesus Christ of Latter-day Saints in mind. Frederick did not concur. That dissent, however, did not deter George Albert in his efforts to bring the family together.

The year 1943 saw significant changes in Elder Smith's

status. With the death of Rudger Clawson in June, George Albert became the senior member of the Twelve. This was officially recognized on July 12, when he was set apart as President of his quorum. Meanwhile, two new members of the Twelve were called during the summer: Spencer W. Kimball and Ezra Taft Benson. They filled vacancies caused by the deaths of Elder Clawson and Elder Sylvester Q. Cannon, who had passed away in May. The qualities of leadership Elder Smith brought to his new calling were noted by his cousin and associate in the quorum, Richard R. Lyman: "Under the direction of George Albert Smith the members of the Council of the Twelve are sure to be tied together by bonds of genuine affection, and unitedly and individually every member will have the freest possible opportunity, encouragement, and inspiration to do his best." This tribute by George Albert's friend and long-time assistant in the YMMIA made more poignant Elder Lyman's excommunication in November. It was one of the great sorrows of George Albert's life. He later gathered his family together to explain what had happened, to emphasize that high status in the Church does not guarantee immunity from temptation and error, and to warn them to be vigilant and obedient. Several months later, Elder Mark E. Petersen was called to replace Richard R. Lyman in the Twelve.

Elder Smith's new position brought new responsibility. He now coordinated and supervised the work of all members of the Twelve. He also continued to fill his share of stake conference and mission tour assignments. And he did not fail to administer to the needs of the sick and the downcast. Meanwhile, other responsibilities came with his new status. He was elected to the boards of a sugar company and the Heber J. Grant Company while he continued to serve on the boards already mentioned. The added pressures took their physical toll; he suffered intermittent attacks of nervous tension. Long experience had taught him how to combat them with added rest and a more relaxed approach to his duties.

While Elder Smith sought to balance the demands of his new office with his physical limitations, he watched with sadness as President Heber J. Grant continued to weaken. The prophet had suffered a stroke several years before, which had slurred his speech and created partial paralysis. Although he had fought valiantly against these disabilities, he had progressively become more fragile and feeble. On April 30, 1945, when he returned from a stake conference in Vernal, Utah, Elder Smith received a telephone call from the home of President Grant advising the prophet wanted a blessing. Elder Smith took his brother Winslow with him. They found President Grant lying in bed. He seemed not to be in pain, but he was lethargic and restless. After President Grant weakly greeted his visitors, Winslow anointed him with consecrated oil and George Albert sealed the anointing, pronouncing a blessing of comfort, peace, and freedom from pain. It was the last time George Albert saw his old friend alive. Two weeks later, on May 15, as he traveled east by train, Elder Smith received word that President Grant had passed away.

Elder Smith's first act upon arriving in Salt Lake City was to visit President Grant's widow, Aunt Augusta Winters Grant. Later at the funeral he extolled the virtues and achievements of his lifelong friend. Shortly afterward, on May 21, 1945, at a meeting in the temple, he was ordained as the eighth President of The Church of Jesus Christ of Latter-day Saints. He selected J. Reuben Clark and David O. McKay as his counselors, the same counselors who had served President Grant.

The nature and quality of George Albert Smith's leadership as President of the Church was reflected in counsel he gave to his brethren at a meeting in the temple shortly after his ordination. "I counselled the brethren to love the people into living righteously," he wrote following the meeting.

And later he told members of the Church at the October 1945 general conference, at which time he was sustained as President of the Church: "Let us love one another that our Heavenly Father may be able to bless us; and he will bless us if we love one another and do good to all his children." These sentiments characterized all of George Albert Smith's actions during the years he served as the President of the Church.

Two important events occurred between May and October 1945. First, in August the war suddenly ended in the Pacific, having ended earlier in Europe. This was an immense relief to all, especially to President Smith, a man of peace. Second, in September President Smith presided at the dedication of the temple in Idaho Falls, Idaho. "We pray that thou wilt accept this temple as a freewill offering from thy children, that it will be sacred unto thee," he said in his dedicatory prayer. The gleaming white building on the banks of the Snake River symbolized the three things most important to George Albert Smith: his God, his family, and the church over which he presided.

The death and destruction caused by the war had created chaos among the thousands of Latter-day Saints in Europe. President Smith's first prophetic initiative was to try to alleviate their suffering. He appointed Elder John A. Widtsoe of the Twelve to direct the relief effort. He and others accompanied Elder Widtsoe to Washington, D.C., to help clear away any government red tape. President Harry S Truman promised his cooperation. True to form, George Albert gave President Truman a leather-bound copy of *A Voice of Warning* before leaving the Oval Office. In doing so, he informed President Truman that the Latter-day Saints regularly prayed for him.

When health problems later prevented Elder Widtsoe from filling his assignment, Elder Ezra Taft Benson was appointed to replace him. There was a close rapport between President Smith and Elder Benson: they shared an intense commitment to Scouting; they lived in the same neighborhood, attending the same ward; and they bore the names of ancestors who had preceded them in the apostle-ship. It was President Smith who had encouraged Elder Benson to use his full name to distinguish him from his great-grandfather even as President Smith had used his full name to distinguish himself from his grandfather.

For many years President Smith had primary responsi-bility for the Lamanites. After he became President of the Church, he delegated that responsibility to Elder Spencer W. Kimball of the Twelve, appointing him to chair a Lamanite committee that included Elder Matthew Cowley. Soon after this committee was organized, President Smith accompa-nied Elders Kimball and Cowley to the Navajo Indian Reservation to hold meetings with tribal leaders. Present were representatives of other churches who complained that Mormon elders had visited some of their members in the hospital. In his mild response, President Smith said: "My friends, I am perplexed and shocked. I thought people went to the hospital to rest and get well. If I were ill, it would please me very much if any good Christian missionary of any denomination would be kind enough to visit me and bind up my wounds and pour on the sacred oil." President Smith's diplomatic strategy in dealing with tribal leaders, a strategy followed by Elder Kimball, opened many doors that otherwise would have been closed.

In May 1946 President Smith turned his diplomatic skills to a complex problem in Mexico. For several years a group of excommunicated members who called themselves the Third Convention had created dissension among the Mexican Saints. Several General Authorities had failed to solve the problem. President Smith held a series of meetings with these dissidents in Mexico City. After hearing their complaints privately, his first step was to reduce the Church court sanctions against them from excommunication to dis-fellowshipment. Then in a public meeting he stressed that all were brothers and sisters, spiritual children of the same Heavenly Father, who should be charitable toward each other and reconcile their differences in love and forgiveness. As a result of these meetings and other similar meetings in neighboring cites, most of the dissidents returned to the Church. The qualities of love and compassion shown by the prophet in his words and actions were a powerful sermon to Church members, reducing the need for him to continually emphasize repentance, restitution, and confession.

During the summer of 1946 President Smith joined a group that traveled from Nauvoo, Illinois, to Salt Lake City, paralleling, as far as possible, the route followed by the Latter-day Saints during the exodus. This was a prelude to the many events held the following year to commemorate the pioneer centennial. During the April general conference, whose sermons dwelled mostly on the pioneers and the legacy of their hard work and privations, President Smith expressed gratitude for the quality of life inherited from his ancestors. "I do not know of anybody who has ever had a happier life than I have had," said he. "I have not had very much money—maybe that is the reason I have been happy—but I want to tell you that I have had the comforts and necessities of life and the companionship of the best men and women and boys and girls that have lived upon the earth. And I have lived in an atmosphere of peace and happiness and stand here today to thank my Heavenly Father in your presence of that fact."

President Smith knew he would not have enjoyed such a measure of peace and happiness had his early ambition for political office been realized. Therefore, he never regretted not having fulfilled that early ambition. Yet he retained a lively interest in politics throughout life, maintained a close acquaintance with politicians of both parties, and carefully monitored the public issues of the day. As President of the Church, he refrained from expressing political preferences. Yet as a matter of Church protocol, he never failed to grant interviews to politicians of either party requesting them. So during the 1948 presidential election campaign, he received President Harry S Truman and candidate Thomas E. Dewey, attending meetings in the Tabernacle for both while maintaining a discreet neutrality. A few months after the election, President Smith received former president Herbert Hoover, who asked for counsel about a study he was making of the federal government.

President Smith's diplomatic skills shone again in 1949 when a tract highly critical of the Church and sponsored by a group of Catholics was widely circulated in Utah. President Smith quietly defused what could have been a volatile public issue by going to John Fitzpatrick, who was Catholic and publisher of the *Salt Lake Tribune*, to discuss the tract. Mr. Fitzpatrick went to the Catholic bishop, who advised the tract had no official church sanction. The bishop then took steps to discontinue circulation of the tract and to censure those responsible for it.

Although the prophet had recurring health problems at the end of 1949 and the beginning of 1950 and was hospitalized for several weeks, he revived to have one of his most active years as Church President. In March he traveled to San Diego, California, to participate in a ceremony honoring the members of the Mormon Battalion; in May he dedicated a monument honoring Brigham Young at Whittingham, Vermont, President Young's birthplace; in June he dedicated a monument in the rotunda of the Capitol in Washington, D.C., further honoring Brigham Young; and later in the summer he spent two weeks in Hawaii to commemorate the centennial of the commencement of missionary work in the Hawaiian Islands. He then presided at the October general conference, speaking several times with vigor.

On October 20, 1950, he fainted. This fainting spell was President Smith's harbinger of death. He later suffered a stroke. Bedridden, he continued to be mentally alert but was unable to attend to his duties at the office. His counselors were in frequent touch to report and to receive instructions. Throughout this period he was more solicitous about those around him than about his own condition. On the day he died, April 4, 1951, his eighty-first birthday, Albert and others present turned him over in bed so he would be more comfortable. As they did so, he said, "Be careful that you don't hurt yourselves." These were his last words.

President George Albert Smith's funeral services were held Saturday morning, April 7, 1951, in the Tabernacle on Temple Square. A general session of conference that had been planned before he died was canceled for the funeral. The essence of the great man's character and the basis of his universal appeal were captured by President J. Reuben Clark, who said: "His real name was love. I think no man that we have ever had in the church had a greater love for humanity than President George Albert Smith. He gave his love to all, . . . and the sense of the love which came from him . . . is what has brought together this great gathering to pay tribute to his memory." As the funeral cortege passed the Catholic cathedral on Third East in Salt Lake City, the cathedral bells pealed their salute to a great friend. The prophet was buried in the Salt Lake City Cemetery next to Lucy, his companion in life and in eternity.

NOTE

This chapter is based on Francis M. Gibbons's book *George Albert Smith: Kind and Caring Christian, Prophet of God* (Salt Lake City: Deseret Book Company, 1990) and the sources cited therein.

CHAPTER NINE

DAVID O. McKAY

David Oman McKay was the son of immigrant parents. His father, David, was a native of Thurso, Scotland; his mother, Jennette Evans, was born in Merthyr Tydfil, South Wales. The McKay home, where David O. was born on September 8, 1873, was in Huntsville, Utah, in the Upper Ogden Valley. The father welcomed this oldest son and third child as one who in the future could help shoulder the burdens of his labor-intensive ranching and farming operation. David O. fulfilled that hope along with several brothers who later were born into the family.

From their earliest childhood, the McKay children were taught to work. They also were encouraged to embrace the teachings of The Church of Jesus Christ of Latter-day Saints, their parents' adopted religion.

Religious principles were reinforced by the parents' exemplary Christian conduct, family prayers, scripture study, and attendance at Church meetings. Special focus was given to the Church when David left his family to fill a mission in his native Scotland and later when he was called to serve as bishop of the Huntsville Ward.

When David O. completed his primary schooling in Huntsville, he was enrolled in the Church-owned Weber Stake Academy in Ogden, where he lived with his grandmother Evans. At the academy he came under the influence of Superintendent Louis F. Moench, a German immigrant and scholar who imbued him with a love for learning and a desire for higher education.

After David O. taught school in Huntsville for a year, he and his brother Thomas E. and their sisters Jeanette and Annie enrolled in the University of Utah in Salt Lake City. At first they shared a rented house. Their tuition and other expenses were defrayed in part by a $2,500 legacy their mother had received. They worked to cover the deficit.

David O., called "Dade" by his friends, soon emerged as a leader at the university. A member of the football team, he was elected class president; he also excelled at his studies. He formed many enduring friendships: James E. Talmage was president of the university; Richard R. Lyman and Joseph F. Merrill were on the faculty; and his classmates included J. Reuben Clark, Stephen L Richards, and George Q. Morris. All these men later shared the apostleship with David O. McKay.

While attending the university, David O. met his future wife, Emma Ray Riggs. At the time, he boarded at the home of Emma Ray's mother. There was no romantic involvement between David and Emma then, for she was dating another man. Their courtship and marriage came several years later.

David O.'s plan was to teach school upon completing his education so he could help the family financially. He had received an attractive offer to teach in Salt Lake County, but an unexpected letter from "Box B" upset the plan. The letter from President Wilford Woodruff called him to serve a mission in Great Britain. He accepted willingly.

After brief training, he was ordained a seventy and set

apart by Seymour B. Young, endowed in the Salt Lake Temple, and assigned to accompany twenty other elders to England. They arrived in Liverpool on August 25, 1897. The mission president, Rulon S. Wells, immediately assigned Elder McKay to labor in Glasgow, Scotland. Living with several elders in the Glasgow conference house, he shared expenses, including the cost of hiring a housekeeper and cook. He soon was transferred to Stirling to labor with Peter G. Johnson.

The work there was slow and seemingly unproductive, which troubled Elder McKay. His sense of unease heightened following a visit to the Stirling Castle. Several hours spent touring this ancient building with Elder Johnson was enjoyable but made Elder McKay feel guilty. As they walked home, David saw an inscription above the door of an unfinished building: "What e'er Thou Art, Act Well Thy Part." The idea seemed to crystalize a resolve in his mind to work with more diligence and purpose. The idea also became a ruling principle that guided Elder McKay throughout his life.

Elder McKay was called as president of the Scottish Conference in June 1898. As such he supervised all the missionaries, directed all the members in Scotland, and was spokesman for the Church there. He served as conference president until his release in August 1899.

At a conference meeting near the end of Elder McKay's mission, James L. McMurrin, a counselor in the mission presidency, prophesied that if David remained faithful, he would eventually sit in the leading councils of the Church. This prediction and other spiritual phenomena evident in the meeting gave Elder McKay a personal testimony of the truthfulness of the Church, something he had prayed for since his youth. The experience convinced him that all sincere prayers are answered, sometime, someplace. Before leaving Great Britain, he was privileged to visit the birthplaces of his parents in Thurso, Scotland, and Merthyr Tydfil, Wales.

When he returned home, David O. immediately joined the faculty of the Weber Stake Academy. Three years later he was appointed principal upon the retirement of Louis F. Moench. David O.'s tenure was marked by an expansion of the curriculum, the athletic program, and the student body, as well as by the construction of a new building, the funds for which he had to raise. Meanwhile, he courted Emma Ray Riggs, who was teaching school in Ogden. They were married on January 2, 1901, in the Salt Lake Temple. In the coming years, they had seven children, six of whom lived to maturity.

Soon after returning from Great Britain, David O. McKay was appointed to the Weber Stake Sunday School Board, then as an assistant superintendent. Under his leadership the stake developed a creative system of teacher training that attracted wide attention, including the attention of Joseph F. Smith, President of the Church and General Superintendent of the Sunday Schools. In 1905 President Smith invited Superintendent McKay to write an article for the *Juvenile Instructor,* the organ of the Sunday School. The article was entitled "The Lesson Aim: How to Select It, How to Develop It, How to Apply It." At the 1906 April general conference, President Smith called thirty-two-year-old David O. McKay to the Twelve. He was ordained a high priest and an Apostle and set apart as a member of the Twelve on April 9.

Elder McKay continued to serve as principal of the Weber Stake Academy until 1908. Meanwhile, he filled his apostolic duties, meeting regularly with his brethren in Salt Lake City, attending stake conferences, and touring missions. Because of his youthful appeal, Elder McKay was sought by many young people to perform their temple marriages and to speak at their missionary farewells. His speaking style was measured and analytical, and the themes of his talks were reinforced both by scripture and by quotations from the writings of noted secular authors. This reflected his love for classical literature and his admiration for precise writing and expression.

Elder McKay's calm and assured manner in the pulpit masked an inner turmoil he suffered while speaking in public. Not long before he became President of the Church, he made this confession before a Tabernacle audience: "It is always more or less an ordeal for me to face an audience, and particularly a congregation in this historic Tabernacle. I've been in hopes for years that I would outgrow that feeling, but I still think, study, and pray in anticipation; I tremble as I stand before you with the sense of inadequacy to give a timely message as it should be given; and after it's over, worrying in self-reproachment for having failed to do justice to the cause."

Soon after his induction into the Twelve, Elder McKay was called as an assistant to President Joseph F. Smith in the general Sunday School superintendency. In this role, he implemented a Churchwide system of teacher training and correlation used so successfully in the Weber Stake Sunday Schools. Emphasis also was given to gospel scholarship. He gathered around him a group of scholars and teachers who helped formulate and coordinate this innovative change. They included James E. Talmage, John A. Widtsoe, Stephen L Richards, Richard R. Lyman, and Joseph F. Merrill. After the death of President Joseph F. Smith in November 1918, Elder McKay was appointed General Superintendent of the Sunday Schools by President Heber J. Grant. He occupied this position until 1934, when he was called as Second Counselor to President Grant.

Elder McKay received an unusual assignment from President Grant in the autumn of 1920 when he was appointed to make a tour around the world. His instruction was to observe the operation of the Church in remote areas while strengthening and motivating members and leaders;

to study the administration of the Church school system in the Pacific; and, if he felt inspired to do so, to dedicate China for the preaching of the gospel. Hugh J. Cannon was appointed to accompany him.

The travelers went by train from Salt Lake City to Vancouver, British Columbia, from where they embarked for Yokohama, Japan, on December 7, 1920, on the *Empress of Japan*. Accompanied by mission president Joseph M. Stimpson, the travelers visited education and government leaders in Japan, as well as members in Tokyo, Osaka, and Kofu. On to Peking (Beijing) via Korea and Manchuria, Elder McKay dedicated China for the preaching of the gospel on January 9, 1921. The site was a quiet grove within the walls of the Forbidden City. "A hallowed and reverential feeling was upon us," wrote Elder Cannon of the occasion. The companions then retraced their steps to Japan and from thence traveled to Hawaii, where they held meetings on several islands. On Oahu Elder McKay inspected the Church school at Laie and visited the temple. There followed stops in Fiji, Samoa, Tonga, New Zealand, and Australia. The Church college at Hastings, New Zealand, received Elder McKay's special attention. From Australia the companions traveled to the Holy Land via Batavia, Singapore, Rangoon, Delhi, Bombay, Port Said, and Cairo. Elder Cannon reported that Elder McKay was "deeply moved" by visits to the historic shrines in Jerusalem and around the Sea of Galilee. Traveling to Aintab (Gaziantep) from the Holy Land, Elder McKay delivered to the local Saints money raised by a special fast. They regarded the gift as providential because there had been great suffering among them following the war. After stops in Rome and in Lausanne, Switzerland, where Elder McKay greeted his oldest son, Lawrence, who was on a mission, the companions traveled to Liverpool, England. There they embarked for New York and from there traveled by train to Salt Lake City. They had been gone one year.

As the tour progressed, Hugh Cannon became more deeply impressed by Elder McKay's spiritual qualities. Paramount among these was a buoyant faith in the face of extreme uncertainty. An experience in Australia accentuated this trait. Elder Cannon had met difficulty obtaining travel clearance. Showing no concern, Elder McKay told him to remain to work on the problem and to meet him at another city, from where they would depart for Java. Gradually, doors that had been closed began to open. The documentation was issued just in time to leave for the rendezvous. "Herein lies an important lesson," wrote Hugh J. Cannon, "which Brother McKay never failed to emphasize. Even though a stone wall appears to cross your path, go as far as you can, and you will usually find an opening through which you can pass." This character trait surfaced often throughout Elder McKay's long career. It accounts largely for the success of many programs in which he was involved, especially the welfare program, which, in its early years, was developed through the faith, the tenacity, the will, and the self-confidence of men like David O. McKay.

Another test of faith came shortly after Elder McKay's return from the world tour when he was called to preside over the European Mission. The McKays, with children Lou Jean, Emma Rae, Edward, and Robert, left for Liverpool on November 8, 1922. The family settled comfortably into Durham House, 295 Edge Lane. From there Elder McKay directed missionary and member work in Great Britain and supervised the work in missions on the continent. His greatest challenge was to blunt the abusive attacks on the Saints and the Church by the press. His approach was to reason with editors, calling for fair play. He stimulated missionary work by initiating a program called "Every Member a Missionary." When he became President of the Church, this was adopted as a Churchwide program. His greatest contribution in Europe was imbuing the missionaries with the motivation to excel. And the power of his testimony was an incentive for them to seek a personal witness: "I accept Jesus Christ," said he, "as the personification of human perfection—as God made manifest in the flesh—as the Savior and Redeemer of mankind. So it is with the church which Christ has established. Since it is founded by the Perfect One, it follows that when properly interpreted it too approaches perfection." Elder McKay took the Savior as his exemplar and sought to fashion his life after him. He also sought to help the Church conform more fully to the Savior's commands.

Elder McKay's ability to exert influence on the structure and the performance of the Church was magnified when he was sustained as Second Counselor to President Heber J. Grant on October 6, 1934. At the same time his friend J. Reuben Clark was sustained as First Counselor, replacing Anthony W. Ivins, who had passed away. Eighteen months earlier, President Clark had been called as Second Counselor, filling the vacancy created by the death of Charles W. Nibley. Although their responsibilities would change, these friends would serve as companions in the First Presidency for exactly twenty-seven years, until October 6, 1961, when President Clark passed away.

The main problem facing the First Presidency in October 1934 was the poverty of many Latter-day Saints caused by the Depression. During the next two years, under the overall direction of President Grant, the First Presidency formulated what was first known as the Church Security Plan, later called the Church Welfare Plan. Since President Clark was away from Salt Lake City much of the time during those years, President McKay led out in laying the foundations of the plan under delegation of authority from the prophet. He was assisted by Harold B. Lee, who later became the managing director of Church welfare.

The plan was announced officially by President Grant at the October 1936 general conference. The prophet declared its purpose was to create a system "under which the curse of idleness would be done away with, the evils of a dole abolished, and independence, industry, thrift and self respect be once more established amongst our people." During the conference, President McKay said that "the greatest blessings that will accrue from the church security plan are spiritual" and that "permeating, inspiring and sanctifying" all welfare work "is the element of spirituality." He stressed this aspect of the plan repeatedly. Later, when his outside commitments diminished, President Clark became the member of the First Presidency chiefly involved in welfare matters. But President McKay always retained an active interest in them.

During these years, President McKay also became intensely involved in business activities. This included service on the boards of directors of Zion's Securities Corporation, Utah Home Fire Insurance Company, the Heber J. Grant Company, Beneficial Life Insurance Company, and the Utah State National Bank. He also was involved in dealings with the Layton Sugar Company and the Amalgamated Sugar Company. Meanwhile, his family obligations continued to multiply. And at Church headquarters, he had principal responsibility to direct missionary work. He strengthened the work by counseling newly called missionaries in the temple and by teaching proselytizing skills in the mission home.

President McKay spent his first day in the hospital as a patient in April 1938 at age sixty-five. It resulted from a painful kidney infection that struck him as he sat on the stand at general conference. Two weeks' rest in California restored him to health. Twenty months later he was hospitalized for a double hernia operation. Disabled for several months, he recuperated in California and Arizona. He returned to work to direct the recall of missionaries from foreign lands prompted by the outbreak of war in Europe. When possible, he met the ships carrying the recalled missionaries. In early November 1940, for instance, he met a ship in San Francisco carrying fifty-seven missionaries from the Pacific. A few weeks later he met a ship in New York carrying thirty-two missionaries from South Africa. He instructed these missionaries and directed their reassignment to missions in the United States.

The outbreak of war in Europe fueled the enlistment of many Latter-day Saints. As the numbers increased in early 1941, the First Presidency appointed Hugh B. Brown to coordinate the Church activities of LDS servicemen. He worked closely with President McKay. That association foreshadowed prophetic calls President McKay extended to Elder Brown to serve as an Assistant to the Twelve, as a member of the Twelve, and as his counselor in the First Presidency.

President McKay traveled to Hawaii in August 1941 to dedicate a new stake center and tabernacle in Honolulu and to hold other meetings. A young teenager, Yoshio Komatsu, spoke impressively at one of them. Confusion with another Yoshio Komatsu later caused the young man to use the name Adney Y. Komatsu, the name by which he later became known as a General Authority of the Church.

President McKay was stirred by the love he saw between members of different racial and cultural backgrounds in Hawaii. He also was impressed by the poise and dignity of Captain Mervyn Bennion, captain of the battleship *West Virginia* who invited him and his party to dine aboard ship. Less than three months later, Captain Bennion died in the Japanese attack on Pearl Harbor. President J. Reuben Clark, the captain's father-in-law, was devastated. The incident deepened President Clark's pacifist views. He opposed United States involvement in the war in Europe and was reluctant about the United States responding to the Japanese attack at Pearl Harbor. President McKay, on the other hand, took a more pragmatic view, reasoning that retaliation was justified and that citizens were justified in serving in combat. Once the United States entered the war, the members of the First Presidency were unified. Everything possible was done to assist LDS servicemen and to affirm the duty of Latter-day Saints to respond to a call to arms.

The war created special problems in Utah as defense and military installations attracted many nonmembers. The First Presidency urged members to adhere to their standards while maintaining good relations with the newcomers. The war also created anxieties for the McKays when sons Edward and Robert and son-in-law Russell Blood entered the service. Their absence and the scarcity of farm labor imposed heavy duties on President McKay to maintain the family farm in Huntsville. "Worked sixteen hours today," he wrote four days before he turned seventy-one. "Cleared out an irrigation ditch up on the farm; hitched up a colt to a mower and dug out a lot of weeds that were irritating me." This was good therapy, providing a welcome break from his duties at the office. And such workdays were balanced with carefree days when David O. trained and rode his horses. One of these, Sonny Boy, was a favorite who would come running from the field at his master's command.

Events of the spring and summer of 1945 brought many changes: In early May the war ended in Europe. President Grant died on May 15. On May 21, George Albert Smith was ordained as the eighth President of the Church. He selected David O. McKay as his Second Counselor. After the two atomic bombs were dropped in Japan in August, the war in the Pacific ended. Edward was home on leave at the time, and he and his father celebrated in a way peculiar to the McKays: "Ned and I worked on the farm most of the day," wrote the family patriarch.

A month later, President and Sister McKay joined other General Authorities and their wives for the dedication of the temple at Idaho Falls, Idaho. Five years earlier, President McKay had dedicated the site. It was the first temple dedicated in almost twenty years. The impressive white structure standing on the banks of the Snake River symbolized the things most important in the life of David O. McKay: God, family, and the Church.

In this and other temples President McKay performed hundreds of temple marriages and other ordinances. He often met a couple whose wedding ceremony he had performed years before. It was not uncommon to learn that children had been named after him. No story was as unusual as the one told by a couple who stopped him once as he left the Tabernacle. The couple recalled their wedding and then introduced their three children—two boys named David and Oren and a little girl named Kay. They explained apologetically that when Oren was named, they didn't know what the "O" in his name stood for. The humor of the incident was not lost on President McKay, who had a keen wit. He enjoyed, for example, retelling the story of the paper boy who was awed to shake hands with him on the elevator. The boy left the elevator and then, having run upstairs to greet the aged prophet as he exited on the floor above, said, "I just wanted to shake hands with you again before you die."

At the April 1946 general conference, President McKay delivered a comprehensive sermon detailing plans for the upcoming Pioneer Centennial. Eight years before, he had been appointed chairman of the Utah Centennial Committee. President McKay suggested that everyone spruce up their homes and yards for the event. He also offered support to law enforcement officers in efforts to clean up gambling and other vices. One gambling lord was heard to say, "The Mormon Preacher ain't going to tell us what we can do." He learned, however, that the moral persuasion of the "Mormon Preacher" was sufficient to direct what he *couldn't* do, at least during the centennial year, when gambling disappeared in Salt Lake City.

President McKay underwent an emergency operation

for a thrombosis (blood clot) shortly after conference. He convalesced for several weeks. By year's end he felt strong enough to attend the annual Rose Parade and Rose Bowl football game in Pasadena, California. The Pioneer Centennial events in Utah began on January 16, 1947, when Colleen Robinson was crowned Centennial Queen. In the following months, Utah was treated to an unusual series of commemorative events. These included a reception for pioneer immigrants who arrived before the continental railroad was completed in May 1869; a reception for state governors who were convened in Salt Lake City; the NCAA track championship; a national tennis tournament; a centennial performance of Shakespeare's *Macbeth* starring Orson Welles; a concert in the Tabernacle featuring Helen Traubel of the Metropolitan Opera; a state banquet where General George C. Marshall was the speaker; an original play, *Promised Valley,* staged outdoors for several weeks; the unveiling of the "This Is the Place" monument in the mouth of Emigration Canyon; and a gala parade on July 24. In addition, there were special celebrations in outlying communities: Tomato Days in Hooper, the Peach Festival in Brigham City, and parades in Loa, Murray, Manti, Ogden, and elsewhere. As chairman of the Utah Centennial Committee, President McKay attended most of these events.

Taking place after President McKay's surgery, and being interspersed with his customary duties, the grand occasion of the Pioneer Centennial was for him an exhausting yet exhilarating time. "Still rejoicing over the success of the great events that have transpired in the past two days," he wrote following the Centennial Parade. "Now that the peak of the celebration has been reached, our worries will not be so great."

Because he always had been so vigorous, it was difficult for President McKay to adjust his activities to his age. The thrombosis surgery had slowed him only temporarily, and he continued with his physical activity on the farm. He paid the price. In the summer of 1948 he suffered a mild heart attack from overexertion; a few months later he fell while training a horse, severely bruising an arm and shoulder; and in April 1950 he suffered torn muscles and ligaments when a huge tree stump he was trying to remove with a team of horses fell on him. He was seventy-seven at the time. He promised to restrain himself but found the promise hard to keep.

A year after this last accident, on April 4, 1951, eighty-one-year-old President George Albert Smith passed away quietly on his birthday. When President McKay administered to the prophet shortly before his death, the experience moved President McKay to tears, an uncommon occurrence for him. The funeral was held on April 7, and at a solemn assembly two days later, President David O. McKay was sustained as the ninth President of the Church.

All were surprised when Stephen L Richards was presented as First Counselor to President McKay and J. Reuben Clark as Second Counselor. President McKay explained the choice was dictated by spiritual promptings, by President Richards's seniority in the apostleship, and by President McKay's long association with President Richards as boyhood friends and in the Sunday School superintendency, and not because of any rift with President Clark. President Clark accepted the decision in good grace, saying the important thing is not where one serves, but how.

In May 1952 President McKay began the first of several lengthy tours he would make into the international areas of the Church. This would be a fifty-one-day tour to Great Britain and Europe that would take him into nine countries and ten missions. Although he was nearly seventy-nine years old and had undergone abdominal surgery and had suffered an inner ear problem during the previous year, President McKay was physically strong and had the appearance of a much younger man. Sister McKay accompanied him.

Symbolically, he went first to Scotland, the land of the McKays and the place where he had served as a young missionary. There he dedicated chapels at Glasgow and Edinburgh, the first built by the Church in Scotland. On the continent he was entertained by Queen Juliana of Holland, had an interview with the President of Finland, and elsewhere met with many other leaders and officials. Meanwhile, he held Church meetings at every stop. At Rotterdam he recalled an experience in 1922 while serving as mission president when he enjoyed the gift of tongues. Back in England he attended a garden party given by Queen Elizabeth II at Buckingham Palace. Returning to Scotland, he announced the acquisition of a temple site in Switzerland where the first European temple of the Church would be constructed. At the time negotiations were under way to acquire a temple site in England. However, they had not progressed to the point to permit a public announcement. These were the first objective steps taken by President McKay to signal a deliberate effort to establish the international character of the Church and to encourage members to remain in their home countries. No longer would it be considered as merely an American church.

Before returning home, the prophet again visited Merthyr Tydfil. He found the small house and saw the tiny bedroom where his mother was born. "I thought, as Sister McKay and I stood in that small bedroom, how different life would be now if two humble elders had not knocked at that door a hundred years ago." His awareness of the benefits that accrue from Church membership was a constant spur to promote missionary work worldwide.

President McKay returned to Salt Lake City amid a contentious presidential campaign. To avoid any hint of partiality, he met with the candidates of both parties, Republican Dwight D. Eisenhower and Democrat Adlai

Stevenson. He also received other political luminaries, including President Harry S Truman, whom the prophet accompanied on a visit to Brigham Young University, and Senator Robert A. Taft. Following General Eisenhower's victory, he allowed Elder Ezra Taft Benson to accept the appointment as Secretary of Agriculture in the new cabinet. "The appointee's high character," said the prophet of his former missionary companion in England, "his experience in dealing with agricultural organizations and problems make him eminently prepared to render efficient service to our country." President McKay shared Elder Benson's concern about "the threatening clouds of Communism and Anti-Christ" and believed he would be able to exert strong influence against them in the cabinet.

While his staff made plans for another trip abroad, President McKay participated in ceremonies honoring the Mormon pioneers at Omaha, Nebraska; attended President Eisenhower's inauguration; and received a briefing at the National Conference on U.S. Foreign Policy. This briefing confirmed his concerns about the threat of Communism.

President and Sister McKay left in early August 1953 for their second trip to Great Britain. With them were son Llewelyn and the Church architect who made preliminary plans for the London Temple. The McKays went on to Scotland, where they visited Thurso, the birthplace of the prophet's father. They found the "Auld Hous," where his father was born, and located a native who remembered stories about the "Black Minister," his grandfather, so named because of his black hair and his Mormon priesthood. The travelers also visited Inverness and gathered valuable family history information there.

Back home, President McKay presided at a solemn assembly in the Logan Temple and at a cornerstone-laying ceremony at the Los Angeles Temple. He also appointed a committee to lay plans for a film presentation of the temple endowment. The committee included Gordon B. Hinckley, now President of the Church, who then occupied a staff position at Church headquarters.

On January 2, 1954, their fifty-third wedding anniversary, President and Sister McKay left on their third trip abroad in twenty months.

They flew first to Johannesburg, South Africa, via London. After holding meetings in Johannesburg, Pretoria, and Cape Town and meeting with government officials, they flew to Rio de Janeiro, Brazil, via Dakar. Their son Robert met them in Brazil and served as his father's secretary during the tour of South and Central America. This included meetings in Brazil, Uruguay, Argentina, Chile, Peru, Panama, and Guatemala. In Montevideo, Uruguay, the prophet laid the cornerstone of a new chapel. In Buenos Aires, he was warmly received by President Juan Perón, who made arrangements for the Church to use an ornate theater for its conference. At Santiago, Chile, the President was met by expatriates Brother and Sister Billy Fotheringham, the only known members of the Church in Chile at the time. Leaving Lima, Peru, the McKays traveled to Central America. Following his report at the April general conference in 1954, the *Church News* noted: "Seldom, if ever before, has the church been given a keener awareness of its universality, and of the great missionary work that is being done and that remains to be done."

President McKay enhanced that vision of the universality of the Church by a trip he and Sister McKay took into the Pacific in 1955. Again they left on their wedding anniversary, January 2, 1955. Their itinerary took them to Hawaii, Fiji, Tonga, Samoa, New Zealand, and Australia. In Tonga he was pleased with the newly completed Liahona College, where Latter-day Saint youth could be trained. In Samoa he dedicated a new chapel at Sauniatu. There he found a monument that had been erected by the Saints following his tour in 1921. In Hamilton, New Zealand, he inspected the new Church college then under construction.

While there he had impressions about the need for a temple. After returning home, he discussed this with his brethren and approval was given for a temple to be constructed in New Zealand. This, along with temples in Switzerland and England, would be the means of helping to anchor members to their own countries.

With only a short interval during which he presided at the April general conference and underwent surgery for the removal of a benign tumor, the eighty-two-year-old prophet continued his world travels. In mid-August 1955 he and Sister McKay left for Europe again. They were joined later by the Tabernacle Choir. Ground was broken for the London Temple, a new chapel and mission home were dedicated in Paris, and from September 11–13 the Swiss Temple was dedicated. Back in the United States, President McKay dedicated the Los Angeles Temple in March 1956; and in April 1958 he took another tiring trip into the Pacific where, on the twentieth, he dedicated the New Zealand Temple.

By this time, the London Temple was nearing completion. Before going there, President McKay underwent complicated eye surgery for the removal of a cataract. This healed in time to enable him to travel to London for the dedication on September 7–9. Because of illness, Sister McKay was unable to accompany him. He felt bereft without her. Another cataract surgery intervened before the prophet traveled to Hawaii for the dedication of the Church college in mid-December 1958.

Only two more overseas trips remained for the aging prophet: In February 1961 he traveled to London again for the dedication of the Hyde Park Chapel and the creation of the London Stake; and in August 1963 he traveled to Wales, where he dedicated the chapel at Merthyr Tydfil. The rendition of "I Know That My Redeemer Lives" by internationally famous contralto Annette Richardson Dinwoodey so touched the prophet that he was unable to speak. She sang a second number while he regained his composure. In his talk preceding the dedicatory prayer, President McKay, touched by memories of his mother, included anecdotal comments, something he rarely did. "I am reminded of a visit I made home when I was in college," he told the audience. "Mother was sitting on my left where she always sat at dinner and I said, 'Mother, I have found that I am the only [one] of your children whom you have switched.' She said, 'Yes, David O., I made such a failure of you I didn't want to use the same method on the other children.'"

By this time, the prophet was almost ninety. His health had been impaired by an accident three months before the trip to Wales. As the saddle blanket was placed on Sonny Boy, the horse became frightened and bolted. "I was knocked down and pulled along the ground for about a block," wrote President McKay. Still he was able to carry on. In September 1963 he received President John F. Kennedy during his visit to Salt Lake City. He was shocked and saddened when the young president was killed two months later. The prophet had maintained a good relationship with President Kennedy, as he had with President Eisenhower. Indeed, following a White House dinner President McKay had attended, Elder Benson quoted President Eisenhower as saying President McKay was "the greatest spiritual leader in the world." The relationship with Lyndon B. Johnson was even closer. President Johnson called President McKay often, stopped to see him in Salt Lake City, and once invited him to Washington for personal counsel. "Let your conscience be your guide," he told President Johnson. "Be true to yourself and your philosophy."

The last years of President McKay's life were marked by an understandable decline in his energy and personal output. For convenience, he and Ray moved from their gracious home on East South Temple to an apartment in the Hotel Utah. They also built a small cottage in Huntsville near the old family home as a hideaway. He continued, however, to give strong leadership to the Church. Work he previously had done personally he now performed by delegation through associates. Following the death of Stephen L Richards, J. Reuben Clark became his First Counselor and Henry D. Moyle was called as Second Counselor. Then followed a series of other counselors, who were called to fill vacancies in the First Presidency caused by death or called to help him fill special needs: Hugh B. Brown, N. Eldon Tanner, Joseph Fielding Smith, Thorpe B. Isaacson, and Alvin R. Dyer. He also called on members of his administrative staff, or on others as the need required, to accomplish his aims.

President McKay passed away quietly on January 18, 1970, in his ninety-seventh year. Emma Ray and five of his six living children were at his bedside. He had fought the good fight and had kept the faith. He had served as an Apostle of the Lord Jesus Christ for sixty-three years, nine months and nine days, longer than anyone else. He went to the grave crowned with honor, leaving behind an illustrious family and an unstained reputation.

NOTE

This chapter is based on Francis M. Gibbons's book *David O. McKay: Apostle to the World, Prophet of God* (Salt Lake City: Deseret Book Company, 1986) and the sources cited therein.

CHAPTER TEN

JOSEPH FIELDING SMITH

Joseph Fielding Smith, the tenth President of The Church of Jesus Christ of Latter-day Saints, was a United States "centennial baby," born July 19, 1876, in Salt Lake City, Utah. He used his full name to distinguish himself from his father, Joseph F. Smith (whose middle name was also Fielding), the sixth President of the Church. The mother, Julina Lambson Smith, the first plural wife of Joseph F. Smith, had been promised that her first son would bear his father's full name. While other plural wives bore sons earlier, including one son named Joseph Richards Smith, none was allowed to use the full name. The name would always be a mark of distinction, recognizing not only Joseph Fielding's father but also his great uncle, the Prophet Joseph Smith; his great-grandfather, Joseph Smith Sr.; and his grandmother, Mary Fielding Smith.

Joseph Fielding's childhood was scarred by family upset when his father was forced to leave home often to avoid arrest because of plural marriage. His father's frequent absences accentuated the parenting role of his mother. Julina once had worked in the Church Historian's Office, where she became immersed in Mormon history. There she first met her husband, who was a fellow employee. Of Mormon pioneer ancestry, she also was deeply religious and a keen student of the scriptures. Given the dominant influence of Julina during his youth, it seems apparent that Joseph Fielding Smith's lifelong love for the scriptures and Mormon history is largely a legacy from his mother. However, as her son matured, as he learned the significance of his ancestors' role in the Church, and as he acquired personal convictions about its validity, his father's influence became more pronounced.

The father's frequent absences in the early years were compensated in part by the presence of Joseph Fielding's numerous siblings and his many aunts, uncles, and other relatives. The Smith family was close-knit and never differentiated between the children of the several wives. No child was regarded as a "half brother" or "half sister." Indeed, members of the family would take offense if such designations were used. All were brothers and sisters without regard to the mothers who gave them birth. Among young Joseph's other relatives was Aunt Mercy Fielding Thompson, the sister of Mary Fielding Smith, who was personally acquainted with Joseph and Hyrum Smith and other early leaders of the Church. Joseph Fielding and Aunt Mercy were very close. From her he learned firsthand about the personalities, the problems, and the perspectives of the first-generation Latter-day Saints.

The Smith family lived frugally. The father, Joseph F., had been raised by a widowed mother who had little means. Ever since his mid-teens, when he was called on a mission to Hawaii, he had been engaged in Church service, which precluded the accumulation of wealth. Because living allowances to General Authorities were minimal, members of his family had to provide for themselves during his absences. Everyone worked. Julina was a skilled midwife who provided needed income. Young Joseph became her chauffeur, driving to and from the homes of her patients in a carriage pulled by their faithful horse Meg. Joseph enjoyed the work except when he had to drive at night or in bad weather. As a boy, it seemed to him that most babies were born at night.

The need to help provide for the family limited Joseph's formal education to primary school and two years at LDS College. When he became strong enough, he acquired a menial job at ZCMI that entailed hoisting heavy bulk goods. The repeated strain on his growing body caused one shoulder to be lower than the other. Later in his teens, he was able to compensate somewhat for his lack of formal education by serving as his father's secretary, writing letters, doing research, and serving as a sounding board for Joseph F.'s ideas. He considered this to be the best education of all because it laid the groundwork for his later apostolic career.

Following the Manifesto and the amnesty granted to Mormon polygamists, life for the Smith family became more normal. The dedication of the Salt Lake Temple added a perceptible spiritual quality to the city. At age twenty Joseph was ordained an elder and was allowed to receive his temple endowment. He also received a patriarchal blessing, which among other things promised he would "preside among the people" and would "live to a good old age."

The large Smith home was adjacent to the University of Utah. As a means of providing revenue, the family agreed to rent a room to Louie Shurtliff, a university student who was the daughter of Lewis W. Shurtliff, a stake president in Ogden, Utah. At first Joseph and Louie paid little attention to each other. She was immersed in her studies and he in his work. In time that changed. A casual friendship progressed to romantic love. They were married in the Salt Lake Temple on April 26, 1898. The following March, Joseph received a call to serve a mission in Great Britain. Louie returned to Ogden to live with her parents while he was gone. Joseph left Salt Lake on May 13, 1899, with a group of missionaries that included his brother Joseph Richards Smith.

Traveling to Philadelphia via Niagara Falls and New York City, the missionaries embarked on a creaky old ship, the *Pennland*.

After thirteen turbulent days on the Atlantic, they arrived in Liverpool, England. Joseph Fielding regained his land legs at mission headquarters, 42 Islington. The mission president, Platte D. Lyman, then assigned him to labor in Nottingham.

Elder Smith first encountered the overt hostility and derision that were then directed toward Mormon missionaries when he arrived in Nottingham. Outside the conference house was a group of street urchins who taunted him, singing in parody to the music of a Church hymn, "Chase me girls to Salt Lake City where the Mormons have no pity." He found this attitude to be pervasive among people of all ages. He also was shocked at the widespread immorality. Wife swapping was commonplace, as were drunkeness and immoral acts committed openly in the public parks. "I have seen more wickedness here in two weeks than I have seen at home in all my life," he wrote.

Elder Smith lived in the Nottingham conference house with several missionaries. They cooked their own meals, sharing expenses and household duties. Their proselytizing consisted mostly of tracting and street meetings. The results were disappointing. Joseph did not baptize a single convert during his entire mission.

After a few months, Elder Smith was transferred to nearby Derby, where he served as senior companion to a missionary nine years his senior. The work there—as unfruitful as it had been at Nottingham—ended with a shock for Elder Smith when he was transferred back to Nottingham to serve as conference clerk under his junior companion, who was appointed conference president. To many this likely would have been a severe blow to self-esteem. It had no such effect on Elder Smith, although it was a disappointment. He served faithfully as conference clerk during the remainder of his mission.

As clerk he handled correspondence, prepared reports, supervised travel arrangements, and directed the work during the absence of the conference president. Elder Smith also performed usual missionary work as time allowed. Most of his free time was spent studying the scriptures, which, combined with the training he had received at home, gave him a special status with the other missionaries, who turned to him for answers to gospel questions. Even the conference president deferred to Elder Smith in matters of doctrine or scriptural interpretation. Joseph also had the gift of healing, a gift promised in his patriarchal blessing. Many who were sick came to him for relief.

At the urging of his father and with the permission of the mission president, Joseph Fielding, his brother Richards (who labored in Leeds), and other British missionaries were granted two weeks' leave to attend the World's Fair in Paris. In the French capital and in London where they stopped en route, they visited places of historic interest. At his father's request, Elder Smith also visited Topsfield in Essex County to obtain genealogical data about Smith ancestors.

At home after his mission, Elder Smith was employed as a clerk in the Church Historian's Office. This began an association that continued during the rest of his life, including service as an assistant historian, Church historian, and President of the Church. He first served under Anthon H. Lund, the Church historian at the time, and with assistant historians Orson F. Whitney, Brigham H. Roberts, and Andrew Jenson. All these assistants were prolific writers, which served as a strong inducement for Joseph Fielding to improve his literary skills. He also gained wide experience as a researcher, helping to compile data to answer charges against the Church raised during the Smoot hearings in Washington, D.C. He also made trips into the field to gather historical data, including a trip to New England to check records about early Smith ancestors, and to Missouri to gather information about persecution against the Mormons in the early days.

Meanwhile, Joseph and Louie built a new home on North Second West in Salt Lake City. Their first child, Josephine, was born on September 18, 1902. They were active in the Sixteenth Ward and the Salt Lake Stake, where Joseph served as a home missionary and as a president of his seventy's quorum. Later he was ordained a high priest and was called to the high council. At the same time he was a member of the general board of the YMMIA while continuing to perform secretarial tasks for his father.

In the secluded environment of the Historian's Office, Joseph began to develop both his research and writing skills. His first published work was a pamphlet, *Asael Smith of Topsfield,* which traced the history of the Smith family in New England. Then followed two other pamphlets, *Blood Atonement and the Origin of Plural Marriage* and *Origin of the Reorganized Church and the Question of Succession.* Later, twenty-two books containing President Smith's writings were published—the most prolific literary output to date of any of the modern Apostles. In all of his writings, he aimed for clarity by using simple words and declaratory sentences. He wanted to inform his readers, not impress them with his learning.

As his reputation as an author grew, Joseph Fielding was more in demand as a speaker. His relationship to President Joseph F. Smith enhanced that demand. Yet he never sought to trade on his father's name or reputation. He was modest at the pulpit, being as economical with spoken words as he was in writing them.

Just as he was coming into prominence, tragedy struck

Joseph Fielding. Louie passed away unexpectedly on March 30, 1908, from complications of pregnancy. She left two young daughters, Josephine and Julina. Joseph was stunned. For a while he tried to manage with a housekeeper to tend the children during the day. It didn't work. He was persuaded to move into the Beehive House with his parents. This was unsatisfactory too. When President Smith suggested he ought to remarry, Joseph prayerfully sought a wife. He was attracted to a pretty young woman, Georgina Ethel Reynolds, who worked in the Historian's Office. She was the daughter of George Reynolds, a member of the First Council of Seventy. Ethel reciprocated Joseph's feelings, and they were married on November 2, 1908.

As Joseph's domestic problems eased, his professional duties increased. He was appointed a board member and treasurer of the Genealogical Society of Utah. Then when the society decided to publish a magazine, he became its business manager and first editor. Soon after, on April 6, 1910, he was sustained as a member of the Twelve. He had no advance notice of the call. He told Ethel of the news with the comment, "I guess we'll have to sell the cow." Elder Smith's family and friends and other members of the Church were pleased with his call. He was overwhelmed by it. "Oh my Father, help me, guide me in Thy truth," he implored in his diary, "and fit and qualify me for I am weak."

Not everyone was pleased. A disparaging editorial in the *Salt Lake Tribune* entitled "The Church of the Smiths" viciously criticized the appointment and the Smith family. The basis of the editorial was that with Joseph's appointment, there were seven Smiths among the twenty-six General Authorities of the Church. "Joseph F. is losing no time unnecessarily in his well defined purpose and process of Smithi-sizing the Mormon Church," it began. After words of ridicule and mockery, it turned to accusations of fraud. Joseph refrained from responding until the October general conference, when he observed it was the heritage of the bigoted to sit in judgment on Church leaders "when it concerns them not at all."

The duties of a General Authority in those days were rigorous. They entailed frequent travel, often under difficult conditions. Automobiles were scarce, and most roads were unsurfaced. Travel away from the railroad lines was by horse and carriage, and in some remote areas by horseback only. Accommodations usually were provided by local members. Sometimes they were meager. The diet varied from place to place. Yet the warm reception the Brethren received was uniform. They were honored everywhere, even revered. Elder Smith loved the people and appreciated every kindness they showed him.

Joseph's preaching intermingled solid doctrine with practical instruction. In one remote stake he talked about the need to pipe drinking water into the homes. In others he urged more efficient farming practices and the development of cooperatives. He was strict in admonishing the Saints to live pure lives and "to endure to the end." His treatment of doctrinal subjects was always supported by scriptural citations. Away from the pulpit he was friendly and approachable and reflected a good sense of humor. He was known to engage in athletic competition with young men during conference visits, revealing a personal liking for sports. For many years he was an active member of the Deseret Gymnasium and encouraged his sons' participation in sports.

Elder Smith's duties at Church headquarters included work in the Historical Department and the Genealogical Society. He also served on several ad hoc committees and continued to assist his father as a secretary. His call to the Twelve enabled him to be of greater personal assistance to his father, for he could represent him officially when directed and could substitute for him in filling speaking assignments.

Elder Smith often traveled with his father. Their last lengthy trip together was in late 1914. Their itinerary took them through the Midwest and into the southern states. They traveled in a private railway car. At Independence, Missouri, the prophet dedicated a new chapel. One of the missionaries who helped prepare the chapel for dedication was President Smith's nephew, Spencer W. Kimball, a future President of the Church. While they were in Independence, President Smith, Joseph Fielding, and others paid a courtesy call on Joseph Smith III, the president of the Reorganized Church, who was in poor health at the time and died soon afterward.

There was excellent press coverage wherever the party stopped. Joseph Fielding helped handle the public relations along the way and joined his father and others in the company in speaking to gatherings of Saints. "The trip through the South has resulted in much good," he wrote in summary, "and the results will be felt by the Elders for a long time to come. We have been entertained by the leading spirits in these communities; Mayors, Magistrates, Potentates, and many prominent men of national renown have paid their respects to President Smith. The newspapers throughout have spoken favorably, showing the great change in sentiment that has come over the people in recent years. Our trip has been most successful and encouraging to the Elders and Saints."

As a member of the Twelve and the son and namesake of the prophet, Joseph Fielding occupied a distinctive status among the General Authorities. This was enhanced by his service as an unofficial secretary and confidant of his father. He had open access to President Smith's office and was privy to his thoughts and plans. This unusual role ended on November 19, 1918, when President Smith died. One of Elder Smith's last services to his father was to record his vision of the dead, which now appears as section 138 of the Doctrine and Covenants. Joseph Fielding's status also had been altered earlier by the deaths of his brother Hyrum M. Smith, a member of the Twelve; John Henry Smith, a counselor to his father; and John Smith, the Church Patriarch. These changes largely ended the criticisms that had been directed toward Joseph when he was called to the Twelve in 1910. He was now regarded, both inside and outside the Church, as a man of ability and integrity and a distinguished leader in his own right. He would no longer work in the shadow of his illustrious father and other relatives but would stand on his own reputation.

As a signal of this change in status, he now began to identify himself as Joseph Fielding Smith instead of Joseph F. Smith Jr. His influence extended into activities outside the Church organizations by service on several boards of directors, including the Beneficial Life Insurance Company and the Zion's Savings Bank. In 1921 he was appointed Church historian by President Heber J. Grant, who had succeeded President Joseph F. Smith as the President of the Church. And the following year his book *Essentials in Church History* was published. This useful work has gone through more than twenty editions and has been translated into several languages, including Spanish, German, and French.

In 1925 Joseph and Ethel built a new family home on Douglas Street on Salt Lake City's east bench. Provision was made for a tennis court and horseshoe pits to accommodate the athletic interests of the children. Two years after moving into their new home, the Smiths' last child, Milton Edmund, was born, bringing the number of children to eleven, which included Josephine and Julina, Louie's daughters. The other children were Emily, Naomi, Lois, Joseph, Amelia, Lewis, Reynolds, and Douglas. When friends were intermixed with the children, the Douglas Street home was alive with activity. Notwithstanding, Ethel's calm personality and literary bent brought a sense of peace to the home.

One of Elder Smith's headquarters assignments at this

time was service on a reading committee. Its purpose was to review manuscripts written by General Authorities to assure there were no factual or doctrinal errors. A manuscript written by Elder B. H. Roberts speculated that there were pre-Adamite inhabitants of the earth. Elder Roberts refused to follow the request of the committee that these speculations be deleted and withdrew the manuscript from publication. (It was eventually published many years after Elder Roberts's death.) There followed a public dialogue between Elder Smith and Elder Roberts in which their conflicting views about pre-Adamites and the age of the earth were discussed. At the request of President Heber J. Grant, they discontinued the public discussion while retaining their private views. Years later, after the deaths of Elder Roberts and President Grant, Joseph Fielding Smith published a book entitled *Man, His Origin and Destiny,* which outlined his views on these subjects.

As the children matured and the older girls were able to assume responsibility around the home, Ethel was able to travel more often with her husband, accompanying him to stake conferences and on mission tours. Because she was a member of the Relief Society General Board, she usually did so in an official capacity, giving training to the women and speaking in the public meetings.

A memorable trip for them was a tour of the Central States Mission, which entailed visits to the Church historic sites in Missouri. To recall the sad events that occurred at Liberty Jail—where his grandfather Hyrum Smith and great-uncle Joseph Smith Jr. had been unjustly imprisoned—and to see the barren tract where the once thriving city of Far West was located aroused in Elder Smith a deep resentment toward the state of Missouri that never abated. Later visits to Carthage, Illinois, where Joseph and Hyrum were martyred, and to Nauvoo, from where his father and grandmother had been driven during the exodus, created similar enduring resentments toward the state of Illinois.

Joseph Fielding and Ethel also took occasional vacation trips with their family. There was great love among them. The practice in President Joseph F. Smith's family of kissing each other upon meeting or parting was perpetuated in Joseph Fielding's family. This was an outward expression of a deep and abiding affection also shown in the kindly way they treated each other, in the family recreations they regularly shared, and in the parental support shown toward the children in their academic or athletic activities. Such closeness made even more poignant a debilitating illness that afflicted Ethel in the mid-1930s. It would not yield to medication or treatment, and numerous priesthood blessings provided only temporary relief. She passed away quietly on August 26, 1937. It was a sad and wrenching time for Joseph and his children, several of whom still lived at home. Because of his frequent travels and the urgent need for someone to supervise the single children, Elder Smith felt it unwise to delay remarriage unduly. After prayerful consideration, his thoughts turned toward Jessie Evans, the Salt Lake County recorder and a well-known contralto who sang regularly with the Salt Lake Tabernacle Choir.

It was awkward for sixty-two-year-old Joseph Fielding Smith to court this popular woman who was twenty-five years younger than he. Because she supported her widowed mother, Jessie Evans had never married. When, through spiritual means, Joseph Fielding decided Jessie was the one, he invented an excuse to contact her. As the Church historian, he offered to help fill gaps in the recorder's records about crucial dates in Salt Lake County's history. This opening led to a series of contacts with Jessie that Elder Smith unromantically referred to as "interviews." These culminated in social outings (he never called them dates), in informal visits with Joseph's children and Jessie's relatives, and, ultimately, in marriage, which was performed by President Heber J. Grant on April 12, 1938.

Jessie was an extrovert, full of fun and good humor. Her

musical talent and political career had given her a public reputation quite apart from her husband. Despite differences in age and temperament, she and Joseph were unusually compatible. He enjoyed her singing and constant effervescence, and she appreciated his wisdom and kindness. In time she persuaded him to join her in singing duets, she playing the piano as they sat on the bench together. Because he had to be coaxed to join her in singing, he came to call these "do its."

Since Jessie was her sole support, Mother Evans moved into the Smith home. It was a good arrangement because she was available to care for the young boys when Elder Smith and Jessie traveled together. Their first long trip was to Hawaii shortly after their marriage. Joseph had received several Church assignments in the islands and took Jessie with him. Aboard ship, she was the life of the party, singing at social gatherings and generally adding zest to all shipboard activities. At meetings in Hawaii, and later at other meetings where he presided, Elder Smith always insisted she sing as part of the program. By his own admission, he was her most ardent fan.

A year later, Joseph was assigned to tour missions in Great Britain and Europe. Jessie went with him. They left Salt Lake City on April 21, 1939, intending to be gone for four months. Because war broke out in Europe while they were there, the Smiths were gone for seven months.

The days spent in England were a time of nostalgic reflection for Elder Smith. He had not been there since his mission forty years before. The long track that led from his clerkship in Nottingham to his present position of eminence in the Church was a source of amazement to him. And to be in the land of his Smith forefathers aroused feelings of filial reverence.

On the continent, the Smiths visited all of the western European countries except Spain. They also toured missions in Scandinavia. The days spent in Italy were like a delayed honeymoon. There were no Church organizations there and few members aside from some expatriates. The Smiths were free, therefore, to enjoy the ancient cities with their treasures of art and architecture. Jessie's interest in music and art led Joseph to places he would never have visited on his own.

As the tour progressed, there were ominous reports of impending war. They were awakened in Florence, Italy, on July 4 by the sound of the jackboots of Mussolini's Brown-shirts as they marched beneath their hotel window. Tensions grew as they toured in Germany. After Germany and the Soviet Union signed a non-aggression pact on August 23, the First Presidency directed that all missionaries be removed from Germany. And when on September 3 England and France announced a state of war existed with Germany, instructions were given to remove all missionaries from Europe. Elder Smith went to Copenhagen, Denmark, where he spent two months directing the removal. He and Jessie returned home in November. In early March of 1940, Joseph met the ship in New York that carried his son Lewis, who had been serving as a missionary in Switzerland.

Because he had witnessed the outbreak of the war firsthand, Elder Smith closely followed its developments. After the fall of France and the crushing defeat of England at Dunkirk, and after the United States offered "Lend-Lease" aid to the British, he foresaw that the United States would be drawn into the conflict. He was concerned because several of his sons were eligible for military service. After the Japanese attack on Pearl Harbor in December 1941, it was apparent that some of his sons would be affected.

Lewis, who was drafted on March 4, 1942, was the first. "This brought sadness to us all," wrote his father on that day. "It is a shame that the clean and the righteous are forced into a conflict of world proportions, because of the wickedness of men." After repeating his conviction that the war not only resulted from disobedience to God's laws but also fulfilled ancient prophecies, he added, "May the Lord guide and protect the sons of the Latter-day Saints and all others who will live righteously." Later, Douglas also was inducted into the army and Reynolds into the navy.

Elder Smith's preoccupation with the war led him to study the ancient prophecies about the causes of war and the consequences of disobeying God's laws. This formed the basis of several talks he delivered at general and stake conferences. Because of the interest these created, he was asked to give a series of lectures in the Lion House, which he titled "The Signs of the Times." Later these lectures were moved to Barrett Hall to accommodate the large crowds who wished to hear them. The lectures were subsequently published in book form. Elder Smith also delivered a series of radio lectures that he titled "The Restoration of All Things," which embodied some of the themes developed in the earlier series. These also were published in book form.

The radio lectures were delivered on Sunday evenings during the last half of 1944. Because of the time needed to prepare them, Elder Smith was temporarily excused from attending stake conferences or conducting mission tours. Throughout this time and earlier, he had a feeling that his sons would survive the war. This and the hopes he had for their future made the events of December 29, 1944, so difficult to accept. "My son Lewis W. was killed today in the service of his country," he wrote under that date. "He was returning from an appointment which took him to India. He spent Christmas day in Bethlehem and from all we know was on his way back to his base somewhere in Western Africa when the plane crashed. We received word from the government January 2 at 5 P.M."

The distraught father took comfort from the reports that his son had shown the character of a devoted Latter-day Saint to the very end. He was buried in Nigeria, West Africa. Later the body was exhumed and reburied in the Smith family plot in the Salt Lake City Cemetery. "Now we feel much better," wrote Elder Smith after the reburial, "knowing that it is here and we are happy because we know he was clean and was worthy in every respect and entitled to every blessing that can be obtained." The war ended only a few months after Lewis was killed. Germany surrendered on May 7, 1945, and the Japanese gave up the following August after atomic bombs were dropped on Hiroshima and Nagasaki.

These changes on the international scene were accompanied by significant changes in the Church. On May 14, 1945, President Heber J. Grant died. He was succeeded by Joseph Fielding's cousin, George Albert Smith. The next month, Joseph Fielding was appointed president of the Salt Lake Temple. He served there four years. The freedom from constant travel this assignment allowed provided a welcome break in Elder Smith's apostolic service. He loved temple work and the quiet reverence that prevailed in the sacred building. As a boy he had avidly watched as the temple walls were completed with huge stone blocks he had seen quarried from solid granite near the mouth of Little Cottonwood Canyon, twenty miles southeast of Temple Square.

The vicarious work performed in the temple coincided with his work in the Genealogical Society, whose research he supervised. It was under his direction that the extensive work of microfilming public records around the world was begun. The merger of these two major responsibilities in one man was unprecedented.

Following the death of Elder George F. Richards on August 8, 1950, Elder Smith became Acting President of the Twelve. Then after the death of President George Albert Smith on April 4, 1951, he became President of the Twelve. As such he supervised and coordinated the work of the Twelve and the First Council of Seventy.

Beginning in the early 1950s, President Smith exerted strong influence on the development of Brigham Young

University in his role as chairman of the Executive Committee of the BYU Board of Trustees. Working with the president of the university, and under the overall supervision of the board, he was instrumental in promoting significant growth in the student body and the physical facilities and in upgrading the BYU faculty. He envisioned that the university would become "a great power for good" throughout the world.

When Elder Smith became the President of the Twelve, the responsibility for missionary work was divided among several groups. In 1954, to avoid overlapping duties and to streamline the work, all authority for missionary work was placed under the Missionary Committee. This committee consisted of members of the Twelve with Joseph Fielding Smith as chairman. A few months later he began a lengthy trip to the Orient, which would have an important impact on missionary work.

At the instigation of Jessie, who traveled with him, a festive party was held for Elder Smith aboard ship en route to Japan to celebrate his seventy-ninth birthday. Amid applause, waiters brought a birthday cake and placed it on Elder Smith's table. Atop the cake was a single candle, which he ceremoniously lit and then blew out as all the diners joined in singing the traditional "Happy Birthday."

Elder Smith divided the Japanese Mission while he was in Japan, dedicated Korea for the preaching of the gospel while he was in Seoul, and then dedicated Okinawa, the Philippines, and Guam en route home.

Despite his age, Elder Smith was active and vigorous. During this period he took up jet flying as a hobby, having become acquainted with several pilots who often took him on flights. He found flying to be exhilarating. This novel recreation continued for almost ten years, until he was nearing ninety. In recognition of his interest in flying, he received the honorary rank of brigadier general in the Utah

232

National Guard, and at age eighty-eight he was given the Minuteman Award.

Also during this period, Elder Smith and Jessie sold the Douglas Street home and moved into the Eagle Gate Apartments, which were less than a block from his office. The Smiths also were near the Salt Lake Temple and Tabernacle, the theaters, and downtown shopping. Because Jessie's mother had passed away and all the children were married, this lifestyle suited the Smiths' personal needs and accommodated their heavy travel schedule.

Between 1958 and 1963, the Smiths made four lengthy international trips, in addition to numerous trips to stakes and missions within the United States. In September 1958 they traveled to England and western Europe. After participating in the dedication of the London Temple, they traveled to Switzerland, where Elder Smith counseled with the presidency of the Swiss Temple and held missionary meetings. Among the missionaries was a grandson, Douglas Myers, who was then laboring in Vienna. Returning to London, Elder Smith dedicated the London mission home before he and Jessie returned to the United States on the *Queen Elizabeth.*

Two months later, they flew to the South Pacific, where they spent three months touring missions and holding special meetings in New Zealand and Australia. They returned by ship from New Zealand to Hawaii and flew from there to the mainland.

In October 1960 the Smiths left Salt Lake City for an extended trip to South America. With them was Elder A. Theodore Tuttle of the First Council of Seventy. Flying to New York, they went by ship to Rio de Janeiro, Brazil. After holding meetings in Rio and São Paulo with mission president W. Grant Bangerter, they traveled to Curitiba for a series of meetings with President Asael T. Sorenson of the Brazil South Mission. In turn, they toured in Uruguay, Argentina, Chile, Peru, Ecuador, and Guatemala. At the meetings held with missionaries, President Smith gave instructions about personal worthiness and spirituality while Elder Tuttle taught the missionaries finding and teaching skills. Arriving home in January 1961, Elder Tuttle "praised President Smith as a 'great traveler' who had energy to spare when other members of the party were tired." The Apostle was then almost eighty-five years old.

President Smith and Jessie returned to Australia in November 1963 to hold a series of meetings. A chief inducement to return there was his daughter Amelia, who was in Australia with her husband, Elder Bruce R. McConkie of the First Council of Seventy. Elder McConkie was the president of the mission in Melbourne, Australia.

The following year, Elder Smith was called as a counselor to President David O. McKay, along with Elder Thorpe B. Isaacson, Assistant to the Twelve. At the time, President McKay's health was declining, and he needed extra help to carry the heavy workload of the First Presidency. President Smith's role was to provide insight in setting policy and to fill special assignments given him by the prophet. He continued to direct the affairs of the Council of the Twelve. In the summer of 1966, Joseph Fielding accompanied President McKay to Missouri to inspect sites of early Church history. Two years later, at the prophet's direction, President Smith dedicated monuments near the Far West Temple site and broke ground for a visitors' center in Independence, Missouri. Later that year, he represented the First Presidency at the annual Hill Cumorah Pageant. Meanwhile, President Smith was absorbed in efforts to maintain the missionary force at a workable level, while struggling with government restrictions on missionary calls occasioned by the Vietnam War. And the First Presidency, as well as all the Brethren, were involved in a major effort to prevent the passage of a Utah state liquor-by-the-drink law being pushed by liquor interests. Ordinarily, Church leaders avoided involvement in political issues, but they made an exception in this case because of its moral overtones.

President David O. McKay passed away quietly on January 18, 1970. Five days later, Joseph Fielding Smith was ordained as the tenth President of the Church. He selected Harold B. Lee and N. Eldon Tanner as his counselors. The new First Presidency was sustained at a Solemn Assembly on April 6, 1970, in connection with the annual general conference.

To oversee the daily, ongoing affairs of the Church, ninety-four-year-old President Joseph Fielding Smith made broad delegations of authority to his younger, more vigorous counselors. However, he retained ultimate authority on all matters and devoted much of his time to temple functions. He installed new presidents in the Los Angeles, Arizona, St. George, and Idaho Falls Temples, while presiding at ground-breaking ceremonies for the new Provo and Ogden Temples. He also accepted a selected few of the numerous invitations he received to speak, conserving his strength for the more important aspects of his work. He also agreed to meet with special visitors who sought interviews, including General William C. Westmoreland and President Richard M. Nixon and others of like stature. President Nixon was in Salt Lake City in late July and spent an hour talking to the First Presidency and members of the Twelve about national and international affairs. With President Nixon were George Romney and David Kennedy, Latter-day Saint members of his cabinet.

During the first months of his administration, President Smith and his counselors made important changes in organization and procedure: three new Church magazines without advertisements, the *Ensign,* the *New Era,* and the *Friend,* were approved; Neal A. Maxwell was appointed Commissioner of Church Education, and Dallin H. Oaks and Henry B. Eyring were appointed presidents of Brigham Young University and Ricks College, respectively; the

Special Affairs Committee was created to monitor government activities that impacted the Church; and the Church departments of Internal Affairs and Public Communications were created. Also, steps were taken to keep the Twelve more fully informed about all aspects of the work by inviting key staff personnel to make reports in the weekly temple meetings.

In early 1971 plans were made to hold an area conference in Manchester, England. It was to be the first of several area gatherings, designed to expose members of the Church outside the United States to the General Authorities and to underscore the international character of the Church. These plans were threatened when President Smith's wife, Jessie, died unexpectedly on August 3, 1971. Following the funeral, the prophet, distraught over his wife's death, said he could not go to Manchester. After reflection, however, and realizing the keen disappointment of the British Saints were he not to attend, he changed his mind. President Smith arrived in Manchester on August 26, 1971, accompanied by his son Douglas; his personal secretary, D. Arthur Haycock; and his personal physician, Dr. Donald E. Smith. Other General Authorities arrived separately. The night before the conference began, a special meeting of the Council of the First Presidency and Quorum of the Twelve was held in the Piccadilly Hotel in Manchester, the first such meeting held outside the United States. It was a time of spiritual renewal and refreshment.

The conference meetings were held in the Bell-Vue Centre, a municipal park in Manchester. In his keynote address, President Smith emphasized that the Church is a worldwide organization, that it had grown to the extent that area general conferences were necessary, and that there was no better place to begin them than in England. He repeated that theme in his concluding address: "We have attained the status and strength that are enabling us to fulfill the commission given by the Lord through the Prophet

Joseph Smith, that we should carry the glad tidings of the restoration to every nation and to all people. And not only shall we preach the gospel in every nation before the second coming of the Son of Man, but we shall make converts and establish congregations of Saints among them." This theme was reinforced by the concluding song of the conference, composed by local members: "This Is Our Place."

When President Smith returned from England, he moved into the home of his daughter Amelia McConkie and her husband, Elder Bruce R. McConkie. Familiar pieces of furniture and other treasured things were used to furnish his private room, and he was made comfortable and given loving attention. He continued to attend his meetings, but not with the same zest as before. He was injured twice from falling, and he fainted twice. It was apparent the end was near. President Smith passed away quietly on July 2, 1972, seventeen days before his ninety-sixth birthday. As his patriarchal blessing promised, he had lived a long life, presiding among the people. He was eulogized reverently and was laid to rest beside the three noble women who had shared his life of selfless service. He had endured to the end.

NOTE

This chapter is based on Francis M. Gibbons's book *Joseph Fielding Smith: Gospel Scholar, Prophet of God* (Salt Lake City: Deseret Book Company, 1992) and sources cited therein.

HAROLD B. LEE

Harold Bingham Lee, the eleventh President of The Church of Jesus Christ of Latter-day Saints, was the second of six children of Samuel Marion Lee Jr. and Louisa Bingham Lee. He was born on March 28, 1899, in Clifton, Idaho, a small farming community in the northern part of the Cache Valley, settled by Mormon pioneers in the 1860s. Harold's Irish and Scottish ancestors, who migrated to the United States seeking economic opportunity, also found a new religion that led them to settle in the mountain valleys of Utah and Idaho. There they worked persistently, helping to build new communities while obeying the strict principles of their religion and rearing large families.

Despite the rural character of his early surroundings, Harold was raised in an atmosphere of culture and refinement. His mother had an artistic flair, and she used carefully chosen colors and fabrics and flowers to decorate the home. His father, who taught school and farmed, was studious and reflective; and as bishop of the Clifton Ward, he introduced qualities of spirituality and a sense of service into their home. The Lee children were given musical training, and Harold learned to play the piano while very young. Later he acquired skill with several wind instruments. The family worked early and late to wrest a living from their small, labor-intensive farm.

After completing eight years of study at Clifton's grammar school, Harold enrolled at the Oneida Stake Academy in Preston, Idaho, several miles southeast of his home. During four years there he gained reputation as a scholar, sportsman, musician, debater, staffer on the school paper, and athletic manager. He formed many enduring friendships at the academy, including one with another young farm boy, Ezra Taft Benson, who was born in nearby Whitney, Idaho, five months after Harold's birth. The predictions of classmates about their future hardly envisioned this pair would become future Presidents of the Church.

After graduating from Oneida, Harold lost no time in pursuing higher education. He immediately took a crash course to qualify him for admission to the Albion State Normal School. He successfully passed the entrance examination and was admitted for the summer semester in 1916.

Albion, Idaho, located two hundred miles west of Clifton, was a new world for Harold B. Lee. Except for brief trips with his parents to Salt Lake City, Utah, and Boise, Idaho, he had never been outside the Cache Valley. And he never before had been associated with students and teachers who were not members of the Church. Moreover, the curriculum, which was devoid of religion classes, included subjects unknown to him, such as educational psychology and political science.

Living off campus with a Latter-day Saint family, Harold devoted himself diligently to his studies. He was successful. At the end of the semester he received a secondary teaching certificate, which qualified him to teach in Idaho grammar schools. He immediately entered into a contract to teach in the Silver Star School near Weston, Idaho, a few miles south of Clifton. His salary was seventy-five dollars a month, which included fifteen dollars for room and board. He gave most of the salary to his father, as he did later when he taught in the Oxford school and earned ninety dollars a month. On weekends he traveled home on his horse. The Silver Star School included grades one through eight. Harold considered the discipline of instructing twenty-five students in eight different grades while maintaining order to be the most significant achievement of his teaching career.

Harold returned to Albion the following summer for additional training. He then contracted to be principal of the larger school at Oxford, north of Clifton, where he also would teach. Assisted by two other teachers, he taught at Oxford for three years while serving as elders quorum president, directing a young women's chorus, and playing trombone in a dance band.

In September 1920 Harold was called to serve in the Western States Mission, with headquarters in Denver, Colorado. His native poise, his schooling, and four years as a teacher and school principal caused Elder Lee to stand out from the beginning. After nine months he was appointed president of the Denver Conference, the largest in the mission. Under his determined and caring leadership, the work thrived with large increases in convert baptisms, many of which were due to his personal efforts.

Many who served under Elder Lee sensed a special spiritual quality about him. It was a quality that was evident from childhood. As a small boy, he was warned by a voice not to go near a collapsed barn. He obeyed that voice. Although it is not known whether harm would have resulted from exploring the barn, the incident suggests an early spiritual receptiveness. In the years that followed, he heard and obeyed that voice often. Once at a meeting in Denver, Sister Harriet Jensen saw an aura of light surrounding Elder Lee's head as he spoke. This phenomenon was repeated years later and was witnessed by others. Afterward, Sister Jensen told Elder Lee, "You are going to someday be the President of the Church."

Elder Lee was admired by his mission president, John M. Knight. President Knight took Harold with him on trips outside the Denver Conference and once assigned him to conduct special meetings alone in another conference. When Elder Lee left the mission field in December 1922, President Knight accompanied him to Utah on the train. In Salt Lake City, they visited Church headquarters, meeting with several General Authorities. In one office President Knight told a secretary that Elder Lee would be called as the president of the Western States Mission. Although this did not come to pass, the statement revealed that John Knight was convinced Harold B. Lee was destined to fill important positions of leadership in the Church.

President Knight had not been released as a counselor in the Ensign Stake presidency when he was called as a mission president. This enabled him to arrange for Harold to speak at the Ensign stake conference on December 22, 1922. President Heber J. Grant and other General Authorities lived in this stake. This unsought recognition was a fitting capstone to Elder Lee's mission.

Before going to Clifton, Harold visited several former missionary acquaintances living in Salt Lake City. Among them was Fern Tanner, who had served under him for a while in Denver. There was a special rapport between them. Later this developed into love and marriage. Among those he also visited was Freda Joan Jensen, the girlfriend of a missionary companion. By an intriguing coincidence, Joan Jensen remained single until she became the second wife of President Harold B. Lee following the death of Fern Tanner Lee.

An injury Elder Lee suffered in Clifton after his return from the mission field aggravated a hernia, requiring surgery. He went to Salt Lake City for the operation. At the invitation of Fern's family, he convalesced in the Tanner home. His acquaintance with Fern continued to grow when Harold moved to Salt Lake City permanently to work and to attend the University of Utah. By autumn 1923 he had qualified for a Utah teaching certificate and was hired as the principal and a teacher at the Whittier School. He later filled the same positions at the Woodrow Wilson School. This enabled him to marry Fern. The ceremony was performed by Elder George F. Richards in the Salt Lake Temple on November 14, 1923.

The newlyweds rented a home from Fern's parents in the Poplar Grove Ward of the Pioneer Stake. Five years later, after Harold became regional manager for the Foundation Press, they purchased a home in the stake. Meanwhile, he was active in ward and stake organizations, including service on the high council. He was surprised in October 1928 when, without prior notice, he was sustained as a counselor in the stake presidency. Two years later at age thirty-one, he was called as the stake president, the youngest in the Church at the time.

During that time, Harold's mission president, John M. Knight, was a Salt Lake City commissioner. After a General Authority criticized Commissioner Knight in a Pioneer Stake meeting, President Lee publicly defended him. When they discussed the incident later, John Knight asked President Lee if he would be interested in filling the vacancy in the city commission caused by the death of another commissioner. After reflecting on it, Harold accepted. With the strong backing of John Knight and the endorsement of other influential people, he was appointed and installed in office on December 1, 1932. After running a skillful campaign, he was elected to a full term the following November.

His dual role as stake president and city commissioner vaulted Harold B. Lee into the public spotlight. This was magnified when he and his associates in the stake began to develop a program to help members impoverished by the Depression. A survey showed that more than half of them needed outside help to survive. The solution was to match resources with needs. A major resource was a large pool of idle manpower, which was drawn upon to help harvest farm crops in exchange for a share of the yield to distribute to the needy. Any surplus was canned or bottled and stored. Volunteer workers at a warehouse obtained by the stake also made clothing, bedding, and furniture. Withdrawals from the storehouse, as it came to be known, were made on the order of bishops. Rather than merely receive a dole, recipients were expected to work or to render service in exchange for commodities. Later a large garden was developed on a vacant lot within the stake and provided supplemental food. Also, idle manpower was employed to construct a gymnasium used for athletic, cultural, and social events. As the Depression deepened, authorization was given to retain tithing funds to help the needy, and some additional funds were provided by the First Presidency. The example of a group of people working together creatively to try to solve their economic problems drew widespread attention, both locally and nationally. At the center of this interest was Harold B. Lee, who was the directing catalyst to promote the group effort.

The members of the First Presidency were among those impressed by the welfare efforts in the Pioneer Stake. For several years some steps had been taken at Church headquarters to combat the deadening effects of the Depression among Latter-day Saints, but no ongoing program had been developed. As the Brethren sought to formulate a general plan, they invited President Lee to brief them on the welfare initiatives undertaken in the Pioneer Stake. He met with President Heber J. Grant and Second Counselor David O. McKay on April 30, 1935. President J. Reuben Clark was out of town but was aware of the meeting and its purpose.

After several hours of discussion, President Lee was asked to draw up a general plan for Church welfare, based upon the model in the Pioneer Stake and the directions given by the First Presidency.

Overwhelmed by the magnitude of such an assignment, President Lee sought divine guidance in humble prayer offered in a secluded grove up City Creek Canyon. It was revealed to him that no new organization was necessary, only the need "to put the priesthood to work." He submitted a preliminary report on June 1, 1935, then revised it in March 1936 at the request of the First Presidency. Through revelation, the First Presidency adopted this revised report as amended by them. A month later, on April 15, Harold B. Lee was called as managing director of the Church Security Department, later named the Church Welfare Department. He resigned from the city commission and was released as president of the Pioneer Stake in order to devote full time to his new calling.

Brother Lee's responsibility was to implement the approved plan, creating welfare organizations in stakes throughout the United States and instructing them in welfare principles and procedures. He did this under the overall direction of the First Presidency, through a general committee chaired by a member of the Twelve. The members of the Presiding Bishopric, who had traditional duties to care for the needy of the Church, were members of the committee. In addition to the objective to help those in need, major goals of the program were to emphasize the overriding role of work in people's lives and to promote attitudes of industry, independence, thrift, and self-reliance.

Qualities of faith, tenacity, staying power, love for the disadvantaged, and indifference to criticism were necessary to establish a broad-based program of this kind. Harold B. Lee had these qualities in abundance. Criticism came from high and low places—criticism, for example, that he was too young and inexperienced or that the program was too unwieldy and complex. However, knowing he had the unqualified support of the First Presidency, Harold ignored the criticisms and stayed the course until the welfare program became an established part of the Church structure, fulfilling its purpose and promise.

When the April 1941 general conference convened, there was a vacancy in the Twelve occasioned by the death of Reed Smoot the previous February. "Before I arose from my bed," wrote Elder Lee on April 5, "I received a definite impression that I would be named a member of the Quorum of the Twelve." He was called that night by President Grant, sustained the following day, and ordained and set apart on April 10. Because Elder Lee was only forty-two, while the average age of the other members of the Twelve was seventy-one, there was a general perception from the beginning of his apostleship that he would one day be President of the Church.

Elder Lee's role as a member of the Twelve was strengthened because of the good character and support of Fern and their two teenage daughters, Maurine and Helen. From the beginning of their acquaintance, Fern had the impression that Harold was destined for high position in the Church. She devoted herself to helping him in every possible way, creating a home of culture and refinement where he could escape from the stresses he faced daily. He reciprocated by showing constant kindness and love and by helping with house chores and maintaining the yards in an attractive manner. The girls were popular with their classmates, musically skilled, and wholly compatible with the high standards of their parents. It was a close-knit and exemplary family.

This family solidarity was essential to withstand the strains imposed by Elder Lee's busy travel schedule. He was away from home most weekends, attending stake conferences or touring missions. As he served in his demanding calling, he reflected the qualities of spirituality and

persistence he had shown in other callings. Inner whisperings and promptings were dominant factors in counseling
or making organizational changes. He was always con-
scious of his subordinate role and sought to do only what
God dictated through the Spirit.

After the United States entered World War II following
the Japanese bombing of Pearl Harbor, Elder Lee was
appointed chairman of the Servicemen's Committee.
Assisted by Elder John Taylor and the military coordinator,
Hugh B. Brown, he supervised the tracking, instruction, and
motivation of LDS servicemen. He traveled extensively to
military bases, was active in encouraging those at home to
write frequently to servicemen, and was instrumental in
preparing pocket-size scriptures that could be easily carried
in their uniforms.

Meanwhile, Elder Lee continued to give direction to welfare work. In the autumn of 1941 he and Elder Marion G.
Romney traveled to Safford, Arizona, to inspect the damage
inflicted by a devastating flood in the Gila Valley and to
review the welfare procedures followed in its aftermath.
They counseled with the stake president, Spencer W.
Kimball, who had directed the relief work. It was the first
real test of the Church welfare program in a disaster situation. A year later, Elder Lee accompanied President
J. Reuben Clark to the Gila Valley for the same purpose. In a
meeting held in Safford, President Clark said it was likely
that Elder Lee would one day become President of the
Church. On the stand was Spencer W. Kimball, who the following year became a member of the Twelve and who
would succeed Harold B. Lee as President of the Church.
Elder Lee struggled to keep such predictions in perspective
and to retain his humility. A forthright brother helped to
foster that quality when he bluntly told Elder Lee he had
spoken too long. "I thought so too," wrote the chastened
Apostle.

Spencer W. Kimball and Ezra Taft Benson were called to

the Twelve in the summer of 1943. A year later Mark E. Petersen was called to fill the vacancy caused by the excommunication of Richard R. Lyman. Afterward, Matthew Cowley, Henry D. Moyle, Delbert L. Stapley, and others were called to the Twelve. These brethren, along with Elder Lee, were referred to as "the younger men" by President J. Reuben Clark, who also called Elder Lee "the dean of the younger men." Probably on the assignment of President Clark, Elder Lee was asked to indoctrinate the new members of the Twelve; and in the cases of Elders Kimball and Moyle, he was assigned to reorganize the stakes over which they were presiding when they were called to the Twelve. This reflected a special, unofficial status that Elder Lee occupied with respect to these men, and with others who were later called to the Twelve, which was apart from the official structure of the quorum.

In late 1944 the Lees and their daughters spent five weeks traveling in Mexico. Driving their own car, they were met at El Paso, Texas, by mission president Arwell L. Pierce and his wife, who then accompanied the Lees. Numerous meetings were held along the way with members who were awed by the presence of an Apostle. It was the last time Elder Lee and Fern were able to take a long trip with their daughters. Helen married L. Brent Goates in June 1946, and Maurine married Ernest J. Wilkins a year later. It was an emotional and rewarding experience for Elder Lee to be able to perform these sacred temple ordinances for his daughters.

In early 1945 Elder Lee gave several radio talks that were later compiled in a book titled *Youth and the Church*. He explained that Maurine and Helen were the "laboratory" from which he gained special insights into the needs and aspirations of the youth. He was popular among young people, and many sought him to perform their temple sealings. During one week in 1948, for instance, he performed twenty-three temple marriages.

Following the death of Heber J. Grant in May 1945, George Albert Smith was ordained and set apart as President of the Church. While the war in Europe ended during that month, the war in the Pacific continued. In July Elder Lee was assigned to go to Hawaii for a stake conference and to check on facilities for Latter-day Saint servicemen. Because Elder Lee was going into a war zone, his father gave him a special blessing before he left. It was a touching experience for both of them. Elder Lee traveled to Hawaii on a crowded freighter but was fortunate to book return passage on a clipper flight.

The war in the Pacific ended the month following Elder Lee's trip to Hawaii. He and the committee then became heavily involved in helping Latter-day Saint servicemen integrate smoothly into civilian life. During 1946 Elder Lee and the Welfare Department geared up to provide massive assistance to the European Saints. And in early 1947 he was stressed when his companion, Elder Charles A. Callis of the Twelve, died in Jacksonville, Florida, shortly after they had created a stake there, the first stake in the South. Elder Lee presided and spoke at funeral services for Elder Callis held in Jacksonville, then accompanied the body to Salt Lake City.

During the war, the number of missionaries had dwindled to include only sister missionaries and a few elders who were deferred from military service because of physical disabilities. At war's end, the Brethren moved promptly to rebuild the missionary force. As the numbers increased, Elder Lee received many assignments to tour missions. Among others, he toured the Western States, Texas-Louisiana, New England, Central States, Northwestern States, and California Missions. Each tour took from three to four weeks, during which meetings and interviews were held with all the missionaries, local leaders were instructed, and general meetings were held. Mission tours were interspersed with the usual stake conference meetings. When possible, stake conferences were scheduled to coincide with mission tours in order to curtail expense and to save wear on the General Authorities.

It was strenuous but rewarding and elevating work. Elder Lee could begin a mission tour feeling drained of energy; yet once the tour was under way, the weariness left as he began to mingle with the missionaries and to feel of their energy and dedication. The tour of the Western States Mission was especially rewarding. It aroused many memories of his own mission, especially as he met with the missionaries in the Denver mission home. It had been only twenty-five years since he had been a young elder laboring there. His reflections on all that had happened since then were tinged with a sense of nostalgia.

At New Haven, Connecticut, the home of Yale University, some missionaries suggested they should alter their presentation because of the high level of education there. Elder Lee disagreed, emphasizing that true conversion comes through spiritual, not intellectual, means. He also laid stress on the different levels of testimony noted in the forty-sixth section of the Doctrine and Covenants, urging those who lacked a personal, spiritual testimony to rely for the time being on the testimony of those who know (see D&C 46:11-14).

Oscar W. McConkie Sr., the father of Elder Bruce R. McConkie of the Quorum of the Twelve Apostles, was president of the California Mission. Despite his distinguished legal career as an attorney and judge, and his notable gospel scholarship, Elder Lee found President McConkie to be humble, submissive, and companionable. As they traveled long hours together, they engaged in lengthy gospel conversations. Once Brother McConkie told of a vivid dream he had had in which Satan appeared to him. After reflecting on the incident and giving his interpretation, Elder Lee shared an experience about how he had rebuked the evil spirit in a woman, and the spirit spoke through her saying,

"You are the head of the Church." President McConkie's interpretation of the incident as recorded by Elder Lee was "that the evil spirit in her had spoken, not of that which I now was, but of that which Satan knew I was ordained to become."

Of the many stake reorganizations Elder Lee effected, none was more memorable than when he installed Aldredge Evans as president of the Ensign Stake. President Evans died a few weeks later. When some questioned the inspiration of calling one who would serve such a short time, Elder Lee explained that calls like this confirm foreordained calls given in premortal existence and that the quality of service, not the length of it, is the crucial thing. Our limited understanding may not grasp the importance of what one might accomplish in a short time, and such achievement may be something others could not do.

President George Albert Smith died on his eighty-first birthday, April 4, 1951. Elder Lee and others were shocked when his successor, President David O. McKay, appointed Stephen L Richards and J. Reuben Clark as First and Second Counselors, respectively. It was a blow to President Clark, who had served as First Counselor to both Presidents Heber J. Grant and George Albert Smith. But President Clark taught the Church a great lesson when he emphasized that the quality, not the place, of service is paramount. During several years afterward, it was a concern to President Clark and Elder Lee that the growth of Church welfare was reined in and some basic changes were made in philosophy, such as when Church employees were placed under U.S. Social Security. This, however, did not affect the permanency of Church welfare, which was later expanded into the concept of provident living, embodying every aspect of life.

The scope of Elder Lee's vision of the Church's mission was enlarged when he was appointed to the executive committee of the Church Board of Education and to the Temple Committee. His experience as a professional teacher brought special insights to his new role in Church education, and his work on the Temple Committee led him into an in-depth study of the temple ordinances. For many years he gave instructions to new missionaries in the temple on the sanctity and significance of the endowment.

After Elder Lee had served eleven years in the Twelve, his body began to rebel at the whirlwind pace he had maintained. In 1952 he suffered from serious abdominal distress and sinus trouble. The Brethren endeavored to give him some relief by sending him to Hawaii for two weeks. The several days' travel aboard the *Lurline,* in company with Fern and away from the telephone and meetings, was therapeutic. And a surgery performed later on his sinuses brought welcome relief.

Returning from Hawaii, Elder Lee delivered the baccalaureate address at the Utah State University in Logan. The provocative title of his address, which he prepared while in Hawaii, was "I Dare You to Believe." At graduation exercises the following day, he received an honorary doctor of humanities degree.

Soon after, Fern suffered a fractured hip in a fall at their home on Connor Street. Elder Lee was solicitous about her as she mended at home following her hospitalization. As she was beginning to move around, Elder Lee received an assignment to make a lengthy tour in the Orient. He was told to time his departure when Fern was well enough to accompany him. They left Salt Lake City on August 3, 1954. After a short stopover in Hawaii, where they stayed in the mission home with friends D. Arthur Haycock and his wife, Maurine, the Lees traveled to Yokohama, Japan, on the USS *Cleveland.* There they began a five-week tour, which included meetings with missionaries, members, and military personnel. Their itinerary included stops in many cities and military bases in Japan, Korea, China, Taiwan, the Philippines, Okinawa, Guam, and Wake Island. Elder Lee met many military leaders who were uniformly complimentary about the conduct of the LDS men under their command. One of these was General Maxwell D. Taylor, who later became the U.S. Army Chief of Staff. In Tokyo Elder Lee addressed a group comprising fifteen different religious denominations. The planned format was for him to speak and to respond to questions during an hour and a half period. They kept him for three hours and seemingly were reluctant to end it then.

As Elder Lee resumed his headquarters duties upon returning from the Orient, temple matters increasingly occupied more of his time. He had been given major responsibility to plan for the dedication of the Los Angeles Temple. President McKay had broken ground for this sacred building in September 1951. As it neared completion in early 1956, Elder Lee devoted much of his time to helping coordinate the complex details connected with the dedication. One night he had a vivid dream in which he saw President McKay giving instructions about the love of God. When President McKay offered the prayer dedicating the temple on March 11, 1956, Elder Lee was startled that the ending of the prayer repeated what he had seen in the dream. The impact on Elder Lee was profound and lasting. He felt it was a special message for him.

A few months after the Los Angeles Temple dedication, Elder Lee was appointed to the board of directors of the Union Pacific Railroad Company. And shortly after that, he was appointed to the board of directors of the Equitable Life Insurance Company. His role in these two major corporations brought Elder Lee into regular contact with some of the premier business leaders of America. He considered the appointments to be a recognition of the Church and not of himself. Therefore, he looked upon this service merely as an extension of his apostolic responsibility. So the day before he was installed on the board of Union Pacific, he engaged in a special fast and prayer to the end that his service would be appropriate to his ecclesiastical calling and would benefit the Church. He served on these boards for many years, traveling regularly to New York for board meetings. He tried to arrange his Church assignments to coincide with the board meetings to economize on time and money.

In July 1957, while he was in New York for a board meeting, Elder Lee accompanied Elder Spencer W. Kimball to the office of a prominent physician and surgeon for an examination of Elder Kimball's throat. The doctor recommended surgery to remove a cancerous growth. Elder Lee emphasized the importance of Elder Kimball's voice and admonished the doctor to use utmost care to preserve it. Elder Kimball, grateful for Elder Lee's presence, felt it was the first time the doctor had truly understood his position in the Church and the need to do all possible to save his voice. Several months after the surgery, Elder Kimball accompanied Elder Lee on several conference assignments as Elder Kimball began to use his voice and to become accustomed to the amplifying equipment that was necessary to make it carry. From then on, a special bond of love existed between these two future Presidents of the Church.

Accompanied by Fern, Elder Lee toured the South Africa Mission in the fall of 1958. Meetings were held, among other places, in Pretoria, Durban, and Cape Town, South Africa, and in Salisbury, Rhodesia. An electric feeling at a meeting in Durban caused the members to remain in their seats at its end. Only after Elder Lee had spoken a second time would they consent to leave. He found much uneasiness in South Africa because of the restrictive principles of apartheid. He deflected questions about the Church policy prohibiting blacks from holding the priesthood by explaining that any change would be based upon revelation from God. En route home, the Lees visited in Cairo, the Holy Land, Athens, and Rome. The historic sites in Jerusalem aroused great interest, especially the Garden Tomb, which Elder Lee felt was authentic. He did not have that feeling at other places.

Despite a serious bleeding ulcer in the interim, which required massive transfusions, Elder Lee, accompanied by Fern, left the following August for a three-month tour of South America. He created the Brazil South Mission, headquartered in Curitiba, after which he spent nine busy days touring the mission with the mission president, Asael Sorenson, who, with his wife, had accompanied the Lees to Brazil. At Porto Alegre in southern Brazil, the gift of tongues was manifested when a young convert suddenly was able to understand Elder Lee perfectly, although she did not speak English. After holding numerous meetings in Uruguay, Paraguay, Argentina, and Chile, Elder Lee created the Andes Mission at a special meeting held in Lima, Peru. During his remarks, Elder Lee was quoted as saying the time would soon come when the descendants of Lehi would be inspired to accept the Book of Mormon and enter the Church in great numbers and that "the Pacific coast of the Americas will become the most fertile proselyting field of the Church." The later rich harvest of converts in Chile, Peru, Ecuador, Colombia, Central America, and Mexico validated this prediction. At Guatemala City, Guatemala, he had "a strong feeling that this place is without question the Lamanite capital of North America and that a temple for the Latin American people should be built here." That impression saw fruition on December 14, 1984, when a beautiful temple was dedicated in Guatemala City.

Not long after returning from the tour of South America, Elder Lee was appointed chairman of the General Priesthood Committee and chairman of the All Church Coordinating Council. In these positions he began the vital work of coordinating the curricula of the Church and organizing all aspects of the work around the priesthood. This entailed creation of the Priesthood Missionary Committee, the Priesthood Welfare Committee, the Priesthood Genealogical Committee, and the Priesthood Home Teaching Committee. All this was done under the overall authority and direction of the First Presidency. His role in this represents one of the most significant contributions of Elder Harold B. Lee during his apostolic ministry.

The most stressful experience of Elder Lee's life occurred when Fern passed away on September 24, 1962. He grieved for months afterward, and life seemed to hold no meaning for him. Elder Lee began to recover from the shock when a friend on the board of Equitable Life, John A. Sibley, told him the loss of his wife was the most difficult ordeal he would ever face. Elder Lee began to heal from that moment. Later he was inspired to renew the acquaintance of Freda Joan Jensen, which culminated in their marriage on June 17, 1963. Joan Lee, who had acquired reputation as a professional educator, was a poised, gracious woman who filled a great void in Elder Lee's life. She provided love, companionship, support, and sound counsel during the remainder of his days. Both she and Elder Lee felt their marriage was destined to be. A priesthood blessing Joan had received years earlier hinted she would marry a distinguished man later in life.

Joan Lee soon learned about the busy life of an Apostle when, not long after their marriage, she accompanied her husband on lengthy trips to Hawaii and Europe. She also learned soon about family trauma when Maurine Lee Wilkins passed away unexpectedly at age forty. Joan had been accepted into the family unequivocally and shared the deep pain of Maurine's loss with Elder Lee, who grieved over the death of his "Sunshine," the pet name he had given Maurine. And Joan also shared the concerns that Fern had had about Harold's health when, in April 1967, he underwent major surgery to remove part of his stomach damaged by an ulcer. This surgery and a later operation to remove a kidney stone mostly eliminated the headaches, weariness, and abdominal upset Elder Lee had suffered from over the years.

Largely through the influence and recommendations of

Elder Lee, the Regional Representatives of the Twelve were appointed in 1967 to provide continuing instruction in the field regarding missionary work, genealogical work, home teaching, and welfare. And the Training Committee, chaired by Elder Thomas S. Monson, was appointed to provide training modes for the Regional Representatives and for the General Authorities at stake conferences.

Following the death of President David O. McKay on January 18, 1970, Joseph Fielding Smith was ordained as the tenth president of the Church. He selected Elder Lee and N. Eldon Tanner as his counselors. A pressing problem that faced the new leaders immediately was the varied and vicious attacks being made on the Church because of its policy that precluded blacks from holding the priesthood. It was decided to take steps to anticipate and to try to forestall such attacks in the future. President Smith authorized Elder Lee to take the lead in this effort. He convened a meeting in New York in February 1970 that included high leaders of the Church and Latter-day Saint leaders in business and the professions. The focus was on taking the initiative in media coverage regarding issues impacting the Church. There also was discussion about streamlining the procedures for preparing and distributing instructional materials throughout a rapidly growing worldwide church.

Out of numerous meetings and discussions that followed, two new departments of the Church were created, the Internal Communications and External Communications Departments. Over the years the names were changed, but the functions remained the same: to take the initiative in media events affecting the Church and to simplify the preparation and distribution of instructional materials. The new First Presidency also took steps to relieve members of the Twelve of administrative responsibilities at Church headquarters; restructured the Church magazines to eliminate advertising; reorganized the Sunday School superintendency, replacing Superintendent David Lawrence

McKay with Russell M. Nelson; combined the responsibility for constructing and maintaining Church buildings under the Physical Facilities Department; began a program for health service missionaries; and installed several new temple presidencies and arranged for the construction of new temples in Provo and Ogden, Utah.

In August 1971 President Lee joined President Joseph Fielding Smith, seven members of the Twelve, and other leaders in attending the first area general conference of the Church, held in Manchester, England. Thousands of Church members assembled from all over the British Isles. Talks given by President Smith and President Lee and others emphasized the international character of the Church and urged members to remain in their home countries.

President Smith passed away quietly on July 2, 1972. A few days later, on July 7, Harold B. Lee was ordained and set apart as the eleventh President of the Church. Before the meeting in the temple where this occurred, President Lee spent long hours alone in the sacred rooms, seeking inspiration and guidance. At the press conference held afterward, he said he had no outlined plan to lead the Church but would rely on the inspiration of the Lord to guide him.

The following month he traveled to Mexico City to preside at an area conference that had been planned before President Smith's death. There he was sustained by a congregation as President of the Church for the first time. He ascribed the remarkable growth of the Church in Mexico to the Spirit of the Lord that "brooded over the land."

Before the October general conference, at which time the general membership of the Church sustained him President of the Church during a Solemn Assembly, he traveled to Europe and the Middle East with Sister Lee and Elder Gordon B. Hinckley and his wife, Marjorie. In Greece and the Holy Land he suffered severe back pains. And in Jerusalem, following an administration by Elder Hinckley and mission president Edwin Q. Cannon, he coughed up clots of blood, which ended his distress. President Lee felt his life had been miraculously preserved. Even so, he had the sense that his remaining days would be few.

Following the Mexico Area Conference, the prophet spent long hours alone in the temple seeking inspiration about filling the vacancy in the Twelve caused by his selection of Marion G. Romney as his Second Counselor. It was revealed to him that Bruce R. McConkie should be called. When he presented Elder McConkie's name to his counselors, N. Eldon Tanner and President Romney, they confided that they had received the same inspiration. Elder McConkie was the only Apostle called by President Lee.

After the Mexico Area Conference, President Lee received a threat of assassination from a group of apostates. This caused a tightening of Church security. Local and federal officers also became involved in trying to capture the criminals. This cast a shadow of apprehension over President Lee and his family that remained during the balance of his life.

Meanwhile, he moved forward confidently in his prophetic role. At his direction the Aaronic Priesthood MIA and the Melchizedek Priesthood MIA were created. The APMIA, which was placed under the Presiding Bishopric, focused on youth activities through the existing Young Men and Young Women organizations. The MPMIA, which was headed by three Assistants to the Twelve—James E. Faust, Marion D. Hanks, and L. Tom Perry—focused on activities for single adults. Because of his lonely experiences as a single following Fern's death, President Lee took special interest in the work of the MPMIA.

The prophet was flooded with invitations to speak. Those he accepted reflected his leanings. Beginning a month after the Solemn Assembly, he addressed large groups of young people in Mesa, Arizona; Pocatello, Idaho; Billings, Montana; Long Beach, California; and Salt Lake City and Provo, Utah. The youth had an almost worshipful attitude toward him, reflected in the way they thronged him. Anxious that this not be overdone, President Lee sought to minimize it. There was no way to eliminate it except to discontinue speaking to them. Unwilling to do this, he later restricted the number of such talks.

But the prophet's magnetic appeal was not limited to the youth; it affected people of all ages. Marion G. Romney "was captivated by his magnetic presence" the first time he met Brother Lee. "I have never been associated with a man who drew more heavily upon the powers of heaven than Harold B. Lee. We who sat with him daily were frequently amazed at the breadth of his vision and the depth of his understanding."

During the last months of his life, President Lee set in motion the initiatives for smaller temples, training by satellite, more careful budgetary control, and the renovation of the Church Administration Building. He also dedicated the new Church Office Building and hosted a reception there at which community leaders were welcomed.

In August 1973 President Lee headed a delegation from Church headquarters to attend the area conference in Munich, Germany. Afterward, he and Joan and Elder and Sister Gordon B. Hinckley visited missions in Vienna and England, where many meetings were held with Church leaders and missionaries.

Throughout this period, there was much tension growing from the earlier threats of assassination. The threats came closer to home when a toxic material was found in President Lee's water pitcher. A diligent search failed to reveal the guilty party, thereby increasing the anxieties.

As the Christmas season approached, President Lee helped Joan shop and decorate their home. They also attended a series of Christmas parties—with the Deseret Industries and Beehive Clothing Mills workers, Church employees, and the officers and staff of Beneficial Life. At the Beneficial Life banquet, the prophet spoke briefly and offered a prayer. Douglas Smith, company president, said: "Most of us were extremely hesitant to open our eyes, because we knew he was talking with the Lord. His deep, compassionate love for all of the children of the Lord—Arab, Jew, and Gentile—was appealingly expressed." He never spoke in public again.

The day after Christmas, President Lee entered the hospital for a checkup that was thought to be routine. That night he suffered a cardiac arrest and passed away suddenly and unexpectedly. The shock of his death was heightened by the fact that most people were unaware of the serious physical problems he had coped with over the years.

The narrative of his life does not begin to tell the story of the impact that President Harold B. Lee had on his times and on his contemporaries, nor upon the organization to which he had devoted his life, The Church of Jesus Christ of Latter-day Saints. As he had said when he came to the prophetic office, the true measure of his achievements will be found only in the hearts and the minds of those touched by his ministry.

NOTE

This chapter is based on Francis M. Gibbons's book *Harold B. Lee: Man of Vision, Prophet of God* (Salt Lake City: Deseret Book Company, 1993) and the sources cited therein.

CHAPTER TWELVE

SPENCER W. KIMBALL

Spencer Woolley Kimball, the twelfth President of The Church of Jesus Christ of Latter-day Saints, was almost named Roberts Kimball. At the time of his birth on March 28, 1895, the baby's father, Andrew Kimball, was a member of the Utah Constitutional Convention. Andrew was so impressed by a talk B. H. Roberts gave to the convention that he wanted to name the baby after him. The mother, Olive Woolley Kimball, resisted the idea. She had nothing against Elder Roberts but emphatically rejected the theme of his talk, which opposed women's suffrage. Since Andrew only wanted to recognize the speaker's eloquence, not his political views, he yielded to Olive's feelings.

The new baby had impressive family credentials. His father, a son of President Heber C. Kimball, was president of the Indian Territory Mission. His maternal grandfather, Edwin D. Woolley, a longtime bishop, was once a business agent for President Brigham Young. His uncle J. Golden Kimball was a member of the First Council of Seventy. And his father's twin sister, Alice, was one of the plural wives of President Joseph F. Smith, then Second Counselor in the First Presidency.

The Kimballs' promising future in Salt Lake City, surrounded by influential relatives and friends, was interrupted in January 1898 when Andrew was called as president of the St. Joseph Stake in the Gila Valley of southeastern Arizona. Andrew moved his family there four months later. Among the five Kimball children was three-year-old Spencer, active, exuberant, and cherubic.

From earliest youth, Spencer sought to emulate his parents, whom he idolized. No man stood higher in his estimation than Andrew Kimball. He said his mother was "faultless, . . . the epitome of perfection. Who could even mention one virtue she had not possessed?" They taught him faith in God, the efficacy of prayer, and the rewards of paying tithing, serving others, and observing the Word of Wisdom. They also taught him to work. Indeed, work became an obsession with Spencer W. Kimball. Except during occasional moments of relaxation or while on vacation, he seemed compelled always to be doing something. This characteristic was evident in all his activities. It was especially conspicuous when he became President of the Church. He sought to imbue all Church members with his penchant for work by encouraging them to lengthen their stride, quicken their pace, and extend their reach. Later these were combined into one punchy admonition: "Do It."

Spencer's industrious habits were first developed around the family home and farm. He graduated from house chores to outside jobs of planting, weeding, haying, and milking. His industry carried over into schoolwork and athletics, and he excelled in both. Popularity among his peers was enhanced by his ability to sing and to play the piano and was illustrated by his regular election as a class officer.

As the boy's character emerged, the father foresaw a distinguished future for him. "That boy Spencer is an exceptional boy," he told a neighbor. "He always tries to mind me, whatever I ask him to do. I have dedicated him to be one of the mouthpieces of the Lord. The Lord willing, you will see him some day as a great leader." Others had similar spiritual impressions about Spencer W. Kimball's future.

After Spencer was baptized, he sought to keep the commandments exactly. He also responded eagerly to challenges. When a visitor from Salt Lake City urged the youth to read the Bible, he started that night and persisted reading in it each day until he had finished. And when he heard the prediction of a critic that the Church would begin to decline in the third generation, he adamantly declared it would not be so, he being of that generation. Such focus and tenacity were reflected repeatedly during his life.

Spencer Kimball was exposed to sorrow early in his youth. During the period of a few months before he reached his teenage years, three of his sisters and his mother died. Olive's death hit him especially hard. He mourned and wept for many days and would not be consoled. The eulogies spoken at her funeral helped to ease the pain, but it was never erased completely. Even in his maturity, Spencer felt occasional pangs of loss at her passing.

The need for a mother in the home and Olive's urging before she died caused Andrew not to delay remarriage. With the approval of the children, he courted and married Josephine Cluff, a schoolteacher and mother who had been married previously.

Aunt Josie, whom Spencer loved and admired, played an important role in his development. Her background in teaching helped him succeed at the stake academy he attended after completing grammar school. At the academy, he excelled academically and socially, as well as in sports. Yet he was not above boyish pranks. He and a partner once concocted a batch of rotten egg gas, which interrupted classes and earned Spencer a B in chemistry, the only blot on his otherwise perfect A record. He also led a protest against a school decree forbidding April Fools' Day jokes.

Spencer and his friends skipped school and spent the day at a nearby resort.

Perhaps concerned about his son's role in the protest, Andrew Kimball announced at the academy graduation that Spencer would not attend the university the next year but would go on a mission. Spencer was surprised but not displeased. He spent the summer working at a dairy near Globe, Arizona, to earn money. His original call was to the Swiss-German Mission, but his call was changed to the Central States Mission because of unrest in Europe.

Spencer left Thatcher on September 30, 1914. During several days in Salt Lake City, he received his temple endowment, was ordained a seventy by his uncle J. Golden Kimball, and was set apart by Elder Seymour B. Young. He left Salt Lake City on October 21 destined for the mission headquarters in Independence, Missouri.

Mission president Samuel O. Bennion assigned Elder Kimball to temporary duty in Independence. He spent a month helping to spruce up the grounds and the interior of a new chapel that was dedicated by his uncle Joseph F. Smith, then President of the Church. Sporadically during this period he tracted and held cottage meetings. His first permanent assignment was to the Missouri East Conference, with headquarters in St. Louis. He first did country work in the Ozarks, then labored in St. Louis and Hannibal. Shortly before Christmas 1915, he was transferred back to St. Louis, where he was appointed acting conference president. It was a great challenge for a "temporary" leader not yet twenty-one to direct thirty-five missionaries, many of whom were older and more experienced than he. Spencer performed so well under pressure that his appointment was made permanent a few weeks later.

He led by example, never asking the missionaries to do anything he had not done or was not prepared to do. The work prospered under his leadership: baptisms increased, the local leaders and missionaries were carefully trained, and he supervised the acquisition and renovation of a chapel in St. Louis.

En route home after his release, Elder Kimball stopped in Independence, where President Bennion commended him for his work; in Salt Lake City, where he reported to the First Presidency; and in Los Angeles and Tucson, where he visited siblings Clare and Gordon and their families. He arrived in Thatcher on December 31, 1916.

Spencer immediately enrolled at the University of Arizona in Tucson. Overcoming an initial sense of intimidation at such a large school, he competed hard and excelled. His aim to be a teacher was diverted when the United States entered World War I in April 1917. He completed the semester, registered for the draft, and then worked temporarily in Los Angeles and on a ranch near Thatcher, helping to drill a well. A newspaper he read at the ranch reported on plans for the coming school year at St. Joseph Stake Academy. The list of teachers included the name Camilla Eyring. Spencer received a spiritual impression that this teacher was to be his wife, though he hardly knew her.

Spencer had decided to attend Brigham Young University in Provo, Utah, while waiting to be drafted. After finishing the job at the ranch, he spent a few weeks in Thatcher. When he caught the jitney bus to Pima one day to visit a friend, Camilla Eyring was on the same bus going home. This began a hurried round of socializing. When Spencer left for Provo, Camilla gave him a box of home-made candy; and later at his request, she sent him her picture. They corresponded frequently. The draft board called up Spencer's number while he was in Utah. When he returned, expecting to leave any day, he courted Camilla, who accepted his proposal of marriage. Because it was not possible for them to travel to the faraway Salt Lake Temple at the time, they were married by the local bishop on November 16, 1917. Spencer wore his army uniform at the wedding. The nuptials were performed in the Eyring home, where they spent their honeymoon.

Changes in army quotas delayed Spencer's call to active duty. When it appeared the delay would be indefinite, he was hired at the Citizens Bank. The newlyweds lived first with Spencer's parents, then with his sister Alice and her husband, George Nelson, and then rented a three-room house in Thatcher. Since Camilla had conceived shortly after the marriage, they wanted a temple sealing before their child was born. They traveled to Salt Lake City in early June for this purpose. The child, Spencer LeVan, was born August 26, 1918. Spencer was then reclassified in the draft, which made his call to active duty unlikely. Any question was resolved with the Armistice in November. When the Citizens Bank was reorganized and its name changed to the Arizona Trust and Savings Bank, the Kimballs moved closer to the bank in Safford and bought a home. After a daughter, Olive Beth, was born on July 31, 1922, their lives seemed picture perfect.

This is not to say that they faced no challenges, however. Aunt Josie died in October, and Spencer leased the Safford home and moved his family back to Thatcher to live with his sorrowing father. Ten months later, when Andrew married Mary Connelly, they returned to Safford. Mary was a member of the YWMIA general board and editor of the *Young Woman's Journal.*

Financial upset occurred the following year when a recession caused the failure of the bank where Spencer worked. Spencer was fortunate to obtain employment at the Bank of Safford, but at a reduced salary.

He suffered deep anguish in 1924 when his father died. President Heber J. Grant spoke at funeral services in Salt Lake City, then traveled to Thatcher for final services where he spoke again. When the St. Joseph Stake presidency was reorganized at a special meeting held afterward, Spencer was sustained as second counselor.

Dissatisfied with his economic progress at the bank,

Spencer formed a partnership with Joseph Greenhalgh in 1927. The firm dealt in insurance, bonds, and real estate. It prospered until the Great Depression, which was signaled by the market crash of October 1929. Conditions worsened for the firm when a bank in which it had deposits failed and when an insurance company that carried some of its policies went under. The Kimball-Greenhalgh Agency managed to survive by careful planning and strict economy. Spencer's meager income from the firm during this period was supplemented by accounting fees he received from several canal companies and a cotton growers' association.

The economy in the Gila Valley improved some when legislation favorable to agriculture was passed by Congress after Franklin D. Roosevelt took office in March 1933. But later that year the Kimballs were rocked by personal tragedy when their three-year-old son, Edward, was stricken with polio. He was hospitalized in Los Angeles for ten weeks. Camilla lived in an apartment near the hospital. Spencer was there intermittently but returned often to Safford to attend to his Church and business duties and to be near the other three children, LeVan, Olive Beth, and young Andrew, who had been born in 1927.

The heavy expense of Eddie's care almost ruined his father financially. The burden was lifted in part by help from the March of Dimes. Ever after the Kimballs were avid supporters of the March of Dimes and liberal contributors to its fund-raising drives.

Three years after Eddie was stricken, and as he was beginning to walk haltingly, he suffered a broken leg in a school-yard accident. Some wondered why an exemplary family like the Kimballs was burdened with such adversity. But the Kimballs did not regard it as a sign of retribution or unfairness. While deeply stressed by the circumstances, they looked upon it philosophically as being merely the natural consequences of living in a dangerous and uncertain world. This same philosophy provided stoic comfort during the many physical ailments Spencer W. Kimball suffered later.

Spencer's leadership talents were showcased when he was appointed chairman of the St. Joseph Stake's golden jubilee celebration in February 1933. The event, which took place over four days, included parades, competitions, dances, dramas, musical performances, and religious services. The highlight was the participation of President Heber J. Grant, who had traveled there from Salt Lake City. Such was the effect of Spencer's expert direction of the jubilee that a member of the stake, Eli Abegg, was heard to say, "I want to tell you in the name of Jesus Christ that Spencer Kimball will one day become an Apostle of the Church."

Spencer's increased stature in the Church was accompanied by a growing prominence in community affairs. In 1936 he was elected by acclamation as the Arizona district governor of Rotary International. He was the first Latter-day Saint to occupy this position. His tenure was marked by a significant growth in membership and a reemphasis on service to others. As a reward, the local Rotary Clubs financed Spencer's attendance at the international Rotary convention in Nice, France, in 1937. Camilla accompanied him at their own expense. The Kimballs also expanded the trip to include a tour of ten European countries over a period of ten weeks. Because Spencer had been released from the stake presidency after twelve years of service, he was able to go on the trip without hindrance to the stake president. Spencer's duties as stake clerk were easily handled by a subordinate.

The Kimballs traveled to Nice via Montreal, LeHavre, and Paris. In Montreal they visited LeVan, who was serving as a missionary. At Nice they joined enthusiastically in all the events of the convention without compromising their standards. When fellow Rotarians who were not members of the Church learned about the Kimballs' commitment to the Word of Wisdom, they were understanding when the couple declined wines and liquors. They did so without any sense of self-righteousness or without impugning the habits of those of their friends who drank.

After leaving Nice, the travelers toured in Italy, Yugoslavia, Hungary, Austria, Switzerland, Germany, France, the Netherlands, Belgium, and England. They took pictures, wrote in their diaries, and gathered literature wherever they went. And after arriving in New York on the return trip, they traveled across the United States, seeing many parts of the country they had never visited before. The experience changed their perceptions of the world forever.

At home again the Kimballs were invited to speak about their trip to several groups in and out of the Church. Because Spencer had been released from the stake presidency and had completed his term as district governor of Rotary International, the Kimballs felt sure they would never again occupy high-profile positions and that they could settle comfortably into their "little niche." To this end they planned and built their dream home with a Spanish and Indian motif and intended to enjoy the good life among their family and friends.

Their plans were somewhat altered a few months later, when the St. Joseph Stake was divided and Spencer was called as president of the new Mount Graham Stake. This role required that he regularly attend the general conferences of the Church in Salt Lake City. Present at the April 1941 annual general conference, Spencer saw Harold B. Lee sustained as a member of the Twelve. He knew Elder Lee well from their work together on welfare matters. This acquaintance became closer following a devastating flood on the Gila River in late September that year. The efficient way President Kimball applied welfare principles in helping victims of the flood and in mitigating the damage it caused attracted widespread attention, especially among welfare leaders in Salt Lake City. It was the first instance in which the welfare plan had been tested in a disaster situation. Harold B. Lee and Marion G. Romney visited Safford shortly after the flood to inspect the damage and to review the procedures President Kimball and his associates had followed. Elder Lee visited again in company with President J. Reuben Clark, and President David O. McKay visited later. Afterward when Spencer attended general conferences in Salt Lake City, he was recognized as he never had been before. On two occasions, for instance, he was invited to stay in the home of President J. Reuben Clark, who was his cousin through the Woolley line.

It was against this background that Spencer W. Kimball was called to the Twelve. At President Grant's request, President Clark extended the call by telephone on July 8, 1943. Brother Kimball was honored but overwhelmed. And he was troubled too. He wondered whether he had been called by revelation or whether it resulted from the publicity given to the flood or from his relationship to President Clark. He was authorized to travel to Salt Lake City to discuss it. On the way he and Camilla stopped in Boulder, Colorado, to visit LeVan, who was studying at the University of Colorado. Early one morning Spencer climbed alone up a mountain west of the city. As the result of anxious, struggling prayers offered there, he received spiritual confirmation that his call had come by revelation. President David O. McKay affirmed this when he met later with Spencer in Salt Lake City.

During a period of several weeks, Elder Kimball closed out his affairs in Safford, selling the business, resigning from various boards and committees, and helping Camilla pack for the move to Salt Lake City. The family left by automobile for their new home on August 26, 1943. It was a sad but exciting time. While everyone was caught up in the adventure of the move, it was wrenching, especially for Camilla and the boys, Andrew and Eddie, to be uprooted and planted in a new place where they were relatively unknown, except for Elder Kimball's prominence as a General

Authority. Over a period of weeks, the initial difficulties of relocating were solved as the family moved into a lovely home leased from Graham Doxey, who had been called as a mission president; as Camilla found relief from a nagging physical problem through treatment at the hospital; and as the boys formed friendships in their new schools.

Elder Kimball returned to Safford in September for the reorganization of the Mount Graham Stake presidency, with Elder Harold B. Lee presiding. At the October 1943 general conference, Elder Kimball was presented and sustained as a member of the Twelve; and he was ordained and set apart by President Heber J. Grant on October 7.

The new Apostle was shocked a month after his ordination when Elder Richard R. Lyman of the Quorum of the Twelve was excommunicated. Elder Kimball learned that high position does not insulate one from temptation or from the consequences of transgression. Elder Harold B. Lee helped compose his feelings during a stake conference assignment they had together shortly afterward. Accompanying other Apostles like Elder Lee on assignment was an important part of Spencer's early training in the Twelve. As he began to conduct stake conferences or mission tours alone or with other Church leaders junior to him, Elder Kimball reflected his own leadership style. This was characterized by a careful analysis of local conditions and personnel and specific suggestions or challenges aimed at improving performance. He was earnest in his public addresses and avoided any hint of levity. In the early years he sometimes dramatized a talk by singing a song whose lyrics were pertinent to his subject. In the homes of the Saints he was jovial and friendly, sometimes playing the piano and singing for their entertainment. In rural areas, he insisted on helping with the chores, such as milking and feeding the animals. The members looked forward to his visits.

Shortly after becoming President of the Church following the death of Heber J. Grant on May 14, 1945, President

George Albert Smith assigned Elder Kimball to the Lamanite Committee. On September 13, 1946, he appointed Spencer chairman of the committee and instructed him to "watch all the Indians . . . in all the world." This fulfilled a promise in Elder Kimball's patriarchal blessing about how his ministry would include important work among the Lamanites. A few weeks later while attending a stake conference in Pleasant Grove, Utah, Elder Kimball had a frightening experience with an evil spirit, which he banished from his bedroom by invoking the power of the priesthood. He equated this with Heber C. Kimball's experience with evil spirits in Preston, England, at the threshold of the work there. Thus began Spencer W. Kimball's lifelong work among the Lamanites and minorities throughout the world, whom he sought to lift and bless by changing attitudes toward them through publicity.

It was during a tour of the Navajo-Zuni Mission in May 1948 that Elder Kimball suffered his first heart attack. It was triggered when he and Golden Buchanan attempted to push their car out of the sand where it had become lodged. That night at the home of Glen Stapley in Phoenix, Arizona, he experienced massive chest pains after a bath. He ignored them and went on for eleven days traveling through rough country in several Indian reservations. Word leaked out what had happened, and the Brethren instructed him to end the tour. Ignoring the doctor's advice to rest, Elder Kimball later suffered another painful episode during a stake conference. This convinced him of the need to rest. He convalesced for several months, first at home, then on an Indian reservation in New Mexico, and finally at Long Beach, California. In late September he was permitted to resume work.

Elder Kimball worked steadily for fifteen months while suffering intermittent attacks of pain. He kept these to himself for fear he would be grounded again. However, in December 1949 they became so severe that he consulted a doctor. The Brethren excused him from all assignments and urged him to rest. He spent several weeks in the Gila Valley, followed by several weeks in California. By the spring of 1950 his condition was much improved, and he was ready to return to work.

Unfortunately, the improvement in his heart condition coincided with the worsening of a hoarseness he had had for several months. It was suspected that he had cancer of the throat, and a biopsy operation was set for April 11, 1950. Although the specimen did not reveal cancer, Elder Kimball was despondent, especially because the operation had temporarily robbed him of speech. Shortly afterward, he received a blessing conferred by President J. Reuben Clark and Elders Harold B. Lee and Henry D. Moyle. He always considered the results to be a miracle. For six years he was able to use his voice normally without discomfort.

When David O. McKay became President of the Church in 1951, he asked Elder Kimball to continue his work with the Lamanites. Spencer also began to travel extensively in the international areas of the Church. He toured in Mexico in company with Elder Harold B. Lee and in Central America with Elder Bruce R. McConkie. During the latter tour in October and November 1952, he dedicated Central America for the preaching of the gospel.

Elder Kimball's most extensive overseas assignment was in 1955 when he spent five months touring missions in Europe and Great Britain. He and Camilla left Salt Lake City in April after general conference. In Europe two things stood out as Elder Kimball instructed the young missionaries— their unusual capability in a new language and the inordinate amount of time being spent in non-missionary work like sprucing up chapels. He admonished them to concentrate on actual proselytizing and to work longer and harder. It was troubling when he learned that word of his message had preceded him into a mission and caused some to tune him out before he had begun. He wondered at first whether he was too strict. But the positive feedback he received from others convinced him the message was needed, so he continued to deliver it without restraint or apology.

Elder Kimball was shocked by the devastation wrought upon Germany during World War II, but he was pleased with the advances the Church had made in that land since then. He also was pleased and honored to dedicate a small chapel in Preston, England, where his grandfather Heber C. Kimball had begun the work abroad in 1837. His tour ended in Switzerland in September 1955, where he and Camilla were privileged to attend the dedication of the temple in Zollikofen, a suburb of Bern.

While Elder Kimball was traveling to Safford for a stake conference in December 1956, his car slid off an ice-covered mountain road near Jacob Lake, north of the Grand Canyon, seriously injuring Camilla. She was taken to Kanab, Utah, where she remained in a clinic until Spencer returned on his way home. And two months later, Elder Kimball's throat problems flared up again. In February 1957 he traveled to New York, where Dr. Hayes Martin performed a biopsy. The patient was ordered not to use his voice for a month. Spencer was concerned because he had not consulted with President McKay before having the biopsy. He had thought the biopsy could be accomplished while he was on an assignment in the East and that he could continue his work without interruption and without troubling the prophet. His failure to consult President McKay created an awkwardness between them for a while. This ended when Spencer submitted a complete report explaining his actions.

When Elder Kimball had to return to New York months later to undergo extensive surgery on his throat, President McKay asked Elder Harold B. Lee to accompany him when he visited the doctor. Elder Lee explained Elder Kimball's role as an Apostle and the vital need to retain the ability to speak. Spencer felt this was the first time the doctor had fully understood his role and the critical nature of the surgery. He was ever grateful to Elder Lee for his presence on that occasion.

Over a period of months following the surgery, Elder Kimball gradually began to use his voice again. He first called it a "still small voice"; later he called it a gruff voice. It actually was a mellow, appealing voice that reminded audiences of the physical trauma he had suffered and caused them to listen to his words more intently. His first talk after the surgery was given at a stake conference in Safford, Arizona, where he told his old friends he had gone east and had fallen among thieves and cutthroats. Later he accompanied Elder Lee to Texas and Louisiana for a series of meetings where he tested his voice under all the conditions he would face when he returned to full duty.

By late 1958 Elder Kimball was ready to accept overseas assignments again. In December he was asked to tour South America. He and Camilla left Salt Lake on January 16, 1959. During a ten-week period they visited and held meetings in Brazil, Uruguay, Paraguay, Argentina, Chile, Peru, and Bolivia. When he returned to Salt Lake City, he was an unabashed booster for South America. He said that Horace Greeley's famous statement—"Go west young man, go west"—should be changed to "Go south young man, go south." He recommended the creation of three new missions in South America and expressed the opinion that in the not-so-distant future, stakes should be created in Brazil, Uruguay, and Argentina. These recommendations were implemented later.

While Elder Kimball was determined in moving the work along, he was usually mild mannered in talking to members and leaders. However, if he detected a spirit of rebellion or obstinacy, he was outspoken in condemning it. Such a situation arose while he toured a mission shortly after returning from South America. "We carried our call to repentance over nearly twenty minutes into the priesthood meeting time," he wrote, "and left it on a note of warning. I told them it was the first step to apostasy and bore down weightily." There were steel and fire in this man that usually were concealed under a cloak of benign goodwill.

In October 1960 the Kimballs left for the South Pacific. Elder Kimball created two new stakes in Australia and two in New Zealand. He also held a stake conference in Sydney, Australia, reorganized the Auckland New Zealand Stake, and toured the New Zealand and New Zealand South Missions. Originally he also was assigned to tour two missions in Australia but was excused from that when word reached Salt Lake City that he seemed to be tiring. He could have returned home in time for Christmas. Instead, he decided to go around the world and headed west instead of east. During two months, Spencer and Camilla saw things they had only dreamed about and never thought they would see. Ever after, names like Singapore, Kuala Lumpur, Saigon, Bangkok, Rangoon, Calcutta, Delhi, Karachi, and Beirut conjured up images of places they had seen in person. They were especially impressed with Egypt and the Holy Land, where they visited the major historic sites. Elder Kimball questioned the authenticity of some of them but felt the Garden Tomb in Jerusalem was authentic. Stops in Greece, Italy, Spain, and Portugal completed their world tour.

For several years Elder Kimball's international travels were centered largely in South America. In addition to the trip in 1959, he made eight lengthy tours there in the 1960s, holding numerous meetings with missionaries and members and training local leaders in the skills necessary for stakehood. His efforts were rewarded when on May 1, 1966, he organized a stake in São Paulo, Brazil, the first stake in South America. Six months later he organized a stake in Buenos Aires, Argentina; and on November 12, 1967, he organized an additional stake in Montevideo, Uruguay. Meanwhile, other missions were created in South America, fueling a growth in Church membership that would literally explode in the years ahead. Doubtless contributing to that future explosion were impressions planted in Elder Kimball's mind as he saw the sadness created when members of black ancestry were precluded from full Church blessings because of the Church policy on priesthood.

In 1968 Elder Kimball was released from his duties in South America and was given apostolic responsibility for the missions in Great Britain. He made several lengthy tours there, urging missionaries and members to work harder, more efficiently, and more purposefully. He also encouraged the members to remain in their own communities and to build up the Church locally.

After President David O. McKay died on January 18, 1970, Elder Kimball was set apart as the Acting President of the Twelve. Harold B. Lee, who was called as the first counselor to President Joseph Fielding Smith, was also the President of the Twelve. Elder Kimball was sustained as the Acting President of the Twelve at the April 1970 General Conference.

After recuperating from prostate surgery in October 1970, Elder Kimball toured extensively in the Pacific, holding meetings in Tonga, Samoa, Fiji, and Hawaii. Then in August 1971 he traveled to Manchester, England, where he joined with members of the First Presidency and the Twelve and other General Authorities in holding the first area general conference.

On returning from England, Elder Kimball suffered a recurrence of both his throat and heart problems. Deciding to try to stabilize the throat problem first, he underwent twenty-four cobalt treatments during November and December 1971. Then on April 12, 1972, he underwent open-heart surgery. The lead surgeon, Dr. Russell M. Nelson, said he had the spiritual impression at the time that Spencer W. Kimball ultimately would become President of the Church.

Following the death of President Joseph Fielding Smith on July 2, 1972, Elder Kimball was set apart as President of the Twelve. At the same time, Harold B. Lee was ordained and set apart as the eleventh President of the Church, with N. Eldon Tanner and Marion G. Romney as his counselors.

With his heart and throat problems temporarily under control, President Kimball was imbued with a great sense of enthusiasm as he directed the affairs of the Twelve. He wrote once as he went to the temple, "My heart is singing." He accompanied a group of Church leaders to Mexico City in August 1972 for the second area general conference, made a lengthy trip to the Orient for a series of important meetings, and attended the third area general conference in Munich, Germany, in August 1973.

President Kimball was stunned, as were members of the Church worldwide, when President Harold B. Lee passed away suddenly on December 26, 1973. Being four years older than President Lee, and seemingly in poorer health, he never expected to survive him. He seemed to be in a state of shock when he was ordained and set apart as the twelfth President of the Church on December 30. In the press conference that followed, he said he intended to carry out the policies and programs of his predecessors.

The prophetic mantle publicly fell upon President Kimball on April 4, 1974, as he addressed a Regional Representatives' seminar. There he called for a greater emphasis on missionary work, asked the members of the Church to lengthen their stride and leave the plateau of achievement they had lingered on too long, and urged a stronger effort in reactivation. He repeated and enlarged on this message at the Regional Representatives' seminar in October 1974. And in a major talk delivered in general conference, he touched on more than a dozen subjects, including a campaign to clean up homes and farms, a warning against polygamist cults, the Word of Wisdom, Sabbath shopping, card playing, food storage, the virtues of work, frugality, living within one's means, the evils of blasphemy and profanity, avoidance of pornography, the destructive effect of abortion and adultery, and a warning against the evil influences of satanic forces. These themes and others also were developed in the many area general conferences held afterward.

Illustrating what he meant by a lengthened stride, President Kimball announced there would be not one but seven area general conferences during the following year: in Scandinavia, São Paulo, Buenos Aires, Tokyo, Manila, Taipei, and Seoul. He explained that since the Church belonged to the people, he intended to take the conferences to members throughout the world, encouraging them to "stay where they are and build Zion." President Kimball continued to hold area general conferences in all parts of the world for another five years. In planning them, he insisted there be no gaps in the scheduling for extra rest. He had an interesting definition of the term *rest*. He said the word was not synonymous with relaxation but meant the feeling of joy and satisfaction that one receives from doing one's duty.

During President Kimball's tenure as the head of the Church, twenty-six temples were dedicated or rededicated. He emphasized the need for templegoers to be worthy. He also emphasized that temples were not only places of peace and quiet where patrons could find rest and renewal but that they were workplaces. He envisioned the time when work would be carried on in the temples day and night.

Significant organizational changes occurred while he presided. A needed decentralization took place when stake presidents were authorized to ordain bishops and patriarchs. Auxiliary general conferences were discontinued and area, regional, and stake gatherings emphasized. In October 1975 the First Quorum of Seventy was reinstituted when three members in addition to the seven presidents were called. In addition, high priests were called to the Seventy, resolving questions of whether this aspect of organization, which had existed since the early days of the Church, was appropriate in modern times. Later, all Assistants to the Twelve were transferred to the Seventy. Three executive councils were created and given responsibility to oversee certain duties at headquarters and the work in areas throughout the world. Area presidencies were put in place, answerable to the executive councils and, through them, to the Twelve and the First Presidency.

Also, fifty-eight solemn assemblies were organized and carried out under President Kimball's direction. In these special meetings instructions were given to local priesthood leaders about crucial issues facing the Church.

President Kimball's most significant and enduring contribution to the work was the revelation on priesthood he received and which was announced on June 9, 1978. This made the priesthood and its blessings available to all worthy male members of the Church. The announcement was preceded by months of fervent prayers offered by the prophet in the temple and with his brethren. On May 4, following a council meeting, Elder LeGrand Richards told the Brethren that during the meeting he had seen a personage, whom he thought to be President Wilford Woodruff, dressed in white and sitting in the room. "I thought at the time," Elder Richards said, "The reason I was privileged to see him was probably that I was the only one there who had ever seen President Woodruff while he was upon the earth." (Lucile C. Tate, *LeGrand Richards: Beloved Apostle* [Salt Lake City: Bookcraft, 1982], p. 292.) President Woodruff had wrestled with the problem of plural marriage nearly a hundred years earlier, and that matter was resolved through revelation, as the priesthood question would also be resolved.

Culminating this process, the First Presidency and the Twelve met in the upper room of the temple, and a powerful, confirming spirit came to the Brethren as they prayed together. All the General Authorities accepted and sustained the revelation, as did the members of the Church assembled in a general conference. Latter-day Saints around the world greeted the revelation with joyous approval.

Shortly after the revelation on priesthood was announced, President Kimball dedicated the Monument to Women in Nauvoo. The prophet was most supportive of the aims of women. While recognizing that childbearing and childrearing are a woman's most important duty, he urged them to become educated and to develop their innate talents to the maximum extent.

In September 1979 President Kimball underwent surgery for a subdural hematoma, and he later underwent two other such operations. He also suffered from cataracts, ear problems, hernias, and back pains. These disabilities impeded the performance of his duties but did not disrupt them. He continued to direct the work, mostly by delegation through his counselors. When his counselors, N. Eldon Tanner and Marion G. Romney, developed physical problems, he called Elder Gordon B. Hinckley to the First Presidency in July 1981. At the death of President Tanner in November 1982, Brother Romney became President Kimball's First Counselor and Brother Hinckley became Second Counselor. As President Romney's health waned, President Hinckley directed the ongoing affairs of the Church through delegation from the prophet. He never exceeded his delegated authority and always obtained President Kimball's approval and direction before actions out of the ordinary were taken.

President Kimball passed away quietly on November 5, 1985. The eulogies at his funeral appropriately lauded his character and achievements. Nothing was said, however, or could have been said, to memorialize him better than the example he set of constant, concerned and unwearied work in the cause to which he had dedicated his life.

NOTE

This chapter is based on Francis M. Gibbons's book *Spencer W. Kimball: Resolute Disciple, Prophet of God* (Salt Lake City: Deseret Book Company, 1995) and the sources cited therein.

CHAPTER THIRTEEN

EZRA TAFT BENSON

Ezra Taft Benson, the thirteenth President of The Church of Jesus Christ of Latter-day Saints, already had a famous name when he was born on August 4, 1899. The name also belonged to the baby's great-grandfather Ezra Taft Benson, who served as a member of the Quorum of the Twelve Apostles from July 16, 1846, to September 3, 1869. Later in life, Ezra Taft Benson always used his full name to distinguish himself from his ancestor, who customarily was called Ezra T. Benson.

Ezra T. was the descendant of a long line of American farmers, beginning with John Benson, who arrived in Boston from London in 1638. He became a member of the Mormon Church on July 19, 1840, being baptized with his wife, Pamelia Andrus Benson, in the Mississippi River at Quincy, Illinois. The Bensons joined the exodus when the Mormons were driven from Nauvoo in February 1846. During the trek across Iowa, Ezra T.'s plural wife Adeline, the sister of Pamelia, gave birth to a son named George Taft

Benson while lying in a wagon box at Garden Grove. This baby became the grandfather of President Ezra Taft Benson.

Ezra T. was ordained an Apostle at Council Bluffs, Iowa, on July 16, 1846, was the captain of the second company of ten in Brigham Young's 1847 pioneer company, helped build Salt Lake City for a decade, and in 1857 was called to lead the Mormon settlements in the Cache Valley in northern Utah and southern Idaho. There the Benson family multiplied and thrived. Ezra T.'s six wives gave birth to thirty-eight sons and daughters. George T., the baby born in Garden Grove, Iowa, became an expert farmer and served as bishop of the Whitney, Idaho, ward for more than twenty years. His son George T. Jr. followed his father into farming, married Sarah Dunkley, and fathered eleven children, the oldest of whom was Ezra Taft Benson. This son came to be called "T" by family and friends alike.

That Ezra survived his birth was considered a miracle by the family. Because he weighed eleven pounds, he was delivered by instruments. Bloody and seemingly lifeless, the baby was laid aside while the doctor cared for the mother. Seeing the emergency, the two grandmothers took the baby into an adjoining room and alternately bathed him in cold and warm water. He began to cry lustily, either in protest or loud gratitude.

From infancy Ezra was introduced to the family routines of worship and work. Prayers were a daily ritual. Fasting was taught as a tool of charity and a builder of spirituality. Attendance at all Church meetings in the little Whitney Ward was mandated, though not forced. In time the boy was introduced to the scriptures, especially the Book of Mormon. He was taught to emulate chief characters in it, like Nephi. The book became a lifelong companion, even an obsession, of Ezra Taft Benson. It also became the lodestar of his prophetic ministry.

Farm chores came to young Ezra almost as soon as he could walk. He graduated from feeding the chickens, to hoeing, weeding, planting, harvesting, and milking. Unlike most farm boys, he not only did the work but also liked it—indeed, he loved it. In all of his growing-up years, he never aspired to be anything but a farmer like his ancestors.

New responsibilities came to twelve-year-old Ezra when his father was called to serve a full-time mission to the northern states. A man was hired to work the row-crop acreage on shares, and responsibility for the dairy herd and the pasturage fell on Ezra. To provide a nest egg for his family, the father sold part of his farm. The example of sacrifice for the Church this reflected had a lasting influence on the eleven Benson children, all of whom filled missions.

After completing grade school in Whitney, Ezra enrolled at the Oneida Stake Academy in Preston. His classes were weighted toward topics that would be helpful in farming. He excelled academically and in athletics. He also made many new acquaintances, including that of Harold B. Lee, called Hal by classmates. These two future Presidents of The Church of Jesus Christ of Latter-day Saints were born in the Cache Valley only five months and several miles apart.

While in his teens Ezra began a lifelong association with Scouting when he became Scoutmaster in the Whitney Ward. A memorable troop outing was a hike across the mountain to Bear Lake, celebrated as a reward for winning a singing competition. Because of a dare, the Scouts sported crew cuts for the trek while their leader was shaved bald. The camaraderie this created lasted throughout life. As an adult, Ezra became an outstanding leader of the Boy Scouts of America, receiving some of its most distinguished awards.

After the United States entered World War I, Ezra left Oneida to train with a military group at Utah State Agricultural College (now Utah State University) in Logan, Utah. He contracted influenza there during the 1918 epidemic. Bunk mates on either side of him died of the flu.

Ezra believed his life was miraculously saved because of priesthood blessings and because he heeded spiritual promptings to leave camp a day early.

Having graduated from Oneida, Ezra enrolled at Utah State Agricultural College. While on a visit to arrange for the school year, he saw a beautiful coed driving a sporty little car. He told friends this was the girl he would marry. They scoffed because Flora Amussen, a member of a wealthy family, was one of the most popular and talented students on campus. This did not deter Ezra, who later began to date Flora. The relationship was interrupted when he received a mission call to serve in Great Britain. When Elder Benson left Salt Lake City for the mission field in July 1921, Flora rode with him to Ogden so they could visit alone. It is inferred that while they were not officially engaged, they had an "understanding."

Arriving at mission headquarters in Liverpool, England, Elder Benson was assigned by his mission president, Orson F. Whitney, to labor at Carlisle in the Newcastle District. President Whitney, after whom Whitney, Idaho, was named, exerted a profound influence upon Ezra Taft Benson. He later performed Ezra's temple marriage to Flora. The Apostle's testimony of having seen the Savior in vision electrified and motivated Elder Benson.

Missionary work in the Newcastle District was impeded by bitter anti-Mormon literature and by a lurid film titled *Trapped by Mormons*. It portrayed missionaries as degenerates who wanted to lure women to Utah for immoral purposes. Despite the opposition to the Church this material generated, Elder Benson and his companion worked diligently and effectively.

Later Elder Benson was transferred to Sunderland to serve as conference clerk and president of the Sunderland Branch. And when David O. McKay succeeded Elder Whitney as the mission president, Ezra was appointed conference president. Under President McKay's leadership,

Elder Benson taught the concept "every member a missionary" and urged the Saints not to migrate to America but to remain in England to build up the Church locally. He was much loved by the British Saints, who fondly called him "our Benson."

After his release, Ezra toured for a month in Europe with a companion. In Lausanne, Switzerland, where his uncle Serge Ballif was mission president, he was reminded of his Swiss ancestry. Ezra's great-grandfather had been a prominent Swiss cleric before his conversion to Mormonism.

In Salt Lake City on the way home, Ezra received a blessing from the Church Patriarch, who promised him he would live to "a goodly age" and that his name would be held in honorable remembrance throughout time.

Ezra studied for a semester at the college in Logan and then transferred to Brigham Young University in Provo. Meanwhile, he resumed dating Flora. Apparently wanting to build her spiritual strength through service and also to avoid a premature marriage that might thwart Ezra's education plans, Flora sought to fill a mission and was called to Hawaii. While the "understanding" between them remained intact, it was agreed that Ezra would be free to socialize during Flora's absence, as she had done during his absence.

Although he carried a heavy academic load at BYU, Ezra excelled at his studies while engaging in a full round of social activities. Graduating with honors in the spring of 1926, he was voted Most Popular Man on campus and the one most likely to succeed. He also received a scholarship to pursue a master's degree at Iowa State College in Ames, Iowa. When Flora was released from her mission in June, they began dating in earnest. They announced their engagement on July 12 and were married in the Salt Lake Temple on September 10, 1926, by Elder Orson F. Whitney.

After a wedding breakfast in the President's Suite of the

Hotel Utah, the newlyweds left for Ames in their Model T Ford, packed to the limit with their belongings. The twelve hundred–mile trip took eight days. Ezra completed the work for a master's degree in a year, graduating with honors. He specialized in agricultural economics and marketing while taking all the basic courses in farm management. The Bensons returned to Whitney in July 1927.

For twenty-two months, Ezra and Flora labored to make the Benson farm a showplace. Ezra applied all his technical knowledge in making the farm operation efficient and productive while Flora spruced up the home with flair and imagination. In the interim their first child, Reed Amussen Benson, was born on January 2, 1928.

It was hard for Ezra to give up his dream of operating a successful farm. But because of his distinguished academic background, he accepted an appointment as agricultural agent for Franklin County. The family moved to Preston in the spring of 1929. Meanwhile, the second child, Mark Amussen Benson, was born on May 2.

Ezra brought new insights and techniques to Franklin County farmers. He instructed them individually and held seminars in modern farming practices. He also taught them marketing strategies and the value of cooperatives, helping to organize the Franklin County Grain Growers' Association. His achievements attracted the attention of professionals at the University of Idaho who persuaded him to become the agriculture economist and specialist for the state of Idaho. This position enabled him to extend his influence and share his expertise statewide. It also entailed moving his family to Boise.

Ezra continued to give individual and group instruction, traveling throughout the state to teach modern farm techniques and to help solve local problems. He published a bulletin to keep farmers up-to-date. He also became executive secretary of the Idaho Cooperative Council, an umbrella organization that helped foster and train local cooperatives like Franklin County's Grain Growers' Association.

While he disagreed with the council's underlying philosophy, Ezra initially instructed farmers on how to obtain subsidies under the federal Agriculture Adjustment Act by curtailing production. However, when the government began directing farmers to kill baby pigs to restrict production, Ezra balked and spoke out against it. His action stirred up such loud political controversy that he was forced to conform.

Several months after being sustained as first counselor in the Boise Stake presidency, Ezra received from the Giannini Foundation for Agricultural Economics a fellowship grant that enabled him to do graduate work at the University of California at Berkeley. He moved his family—which now included the two sons and a daughter, Barbara—to Berkeley, where they remained nine months. Ezra's intensive studies focused on farm cooperatives and marketing techniques. His crowded schedule became heavier when he was called to the high council, even though he had not been released from the Boise Stake presidency.

Daughter Beverly was born in September 1937, a few months after the family returned from Berkeley. On November 27, 1938, Ezra was sustained as president of the Boise Stake. With so many moves in such a short time, Flora and the children looked forward to settling down permanently in their attractive Boise home, amid friends and associates. It was not to be. In January 1939, after clearing with the General Authorities of the Church, Ezra accepted the position of executive secretary of the National Council of Farm Cooperatives (NCFC). This required a move to Washington, D.C. Following his release as stake president on March 26, 1939, and a round of farewell testimonials, he traveled to Washington alone. Flora and the children joined him after school ended.

The NCFC was an umbrella organization that provided

a voice in Washington for four thousand agricultural cooperatives throughout the country. These, in turn, represented a million and a half farmers. With the aid of a staff and members of NCFC standing committees, Ezra was spokesman for the interests of these many cooperatives and their members. This work involved participation in congressional hearings and negotiations with the Department of Agriculture and with other associations having interests in common with the NCFC.

The Bensons planned and built a new home in the Edgemoor district of Bethesda, Maryland. There the standards of an exemplary Latter-day Saint home were perpetuated with family prayer, family home evening, scripture study, and regular fasts. The family was augmented by the birth of Bonnie in March 1940. And three months later, Ezra was shocked when he was called as the first president of the Washington D.C. Stake.

Because he was new to the area, Ezra tried to dissuade Elders Rudger Clawson and Albert E. Bowen of the Twelve from calling him to the position of stake president. The effort failed. Once installed, he completed the organization; made broad delegations of authority and responsibility to his counselors, Sam Carpenter and Ernest Wilkinson; eliminated all unnecessary meetings; and focused on missionary work, the law of tithing, and training leaders.

The entry of the United States into World War II after the bombing of Pearl Harbor revolutionized American agriculture. Farm shortages rather than farm surpluses became the challenge. The problem was aggravated by the movement of many farm workers into the military. These changes impacted on Ezra Benson's work with the NCFC. He now lobbied for more critical resources and supplies to be made available to farmers, and he fought against price controls. He also became a member of several key committees dealing with American agriculture. The most prestigious one was the National Agricultural Advisory

Committee, which met regularly with President Franklin D. Roosevelt.

On June 21, 1943, Ezra and his son Reed left Washington for a trip west. They spent two weeks in California visiting NCFC members and local cooperatives. They returned via Utah, where Ezra made courtesy calls on some of the Brethren, and then Ezra took Reed to visit relatives in Whitney and Preston, Idaho. Returning to Salt Lake City on July 26, Ezra was told that President Grant wanted to see him before he left for the East that evening. The prophet was at a cabin up Emigration Canyon, and Ezra and Reed were driven there by one of President Grant's sons-in-law and then shown into President Grant's private room. The prophet called Ezra as the youngest member of the Twelve. The new Apostle was overwhelmed. After an hour's visit, during which he was counseled to remain with the NCFC as long as necessary to make a smooth transition, Elder Benson and Reed left for Washington by train.

Accompanied by Flora, Elder Benson returned to Salt Lake City for the October general conference, at which time he and Elder Spencer W. Kimball were sustained as members of the Twelve. They were ordained and set apart on October 7, 1943, by President Heber J. Grant. Because the prophet still showed some ill effects of a stroke he had suffered several years before, he remained seated for the ordination while the new Brethren kneeled in turn before him. It was the only time in the history of the Church when two men who later became Presidents of the Church were ordained and set apart on the same day.

Elder Benson continued to serve as president of the Washington D.C. Stake until March 5, 1944, when he was released at a stake conference presided over by Elder Kimball. About that time he was also released as executive secretary of the NCFC, although he continued to serve on its board of directors.

The Bensons purchased a home in the Yale Ward of the

Bonneville Stake in Salt Lake City. Beth, the sixth and last child, was born on August 12, 1944. Confident his family was secure among caring neighbors, Elder Benson settled into the apostolic routines of stake conferences, mission tours, and headquarters duties.

The end of World War II and the death of President Heber J. Grant in 1945 brought immense changes in those routines. George Albert Smith, President Grant's successor, called Ezra to minister to the needs of the European Saints who had been ravaged by the war. He and a traveling companion, Frederick W. Babbel, left Salt Lake City on January 29, 1946. Establishing headquarters in London, England, the Apostle made numerous trips around Europe and the British Isles during an eleven-month period. He was stunned by the devastation he found, especially in Germany. Allied bombing had literally pulverized its major cities, had killed tens of thousands of civilians, and had terrorized the survivors. He made arrangements to distribute welfare commodities shipped from the United States to needy Saints, strengthened lines of priesthood authority and responsibility, trained local leaders and missionaries, and brought comfort and hope to the members through his optimism and his stirring sermons.

The experience confirmed Ezra's hatred of dictatorships and increased the energy with which he fought Communism in the years ahead. It also strengthened his reliance on spiritual promptings, which often had guided him in what to say and what to do.

The impact of his European experiences was shown in a talk he gave to the American Institute of Cooperation in August 1947. He emphasized America's status as a land choice above all other lands; warned that peace was fragile and that dangers lurked ahead; deplored the tendency toward indifference; and admonished all Americans to be more faithful, prayerful, and loyal. With variations dictated by the makeup of his audience, Elder Benson delivered that same message at the Church's general conference in April 1948. He also published an article in the *Improvement Era* titled "Survival of the American Way of Life." And over the years, he developed similar themes in talks given to audiences both inside and outside the Church. These were delivered with a sense of urgency that revealed Elder Benson's concern and that caused many to follow his counsel.

Meanwhile his prominence, gained in the NCFC and in his outspoken talks about postwar perils faced by the United States, brought Elder Benson to the favorable attention of Republican politicians. During his presidential campaign in 1948, New York Governor Thomas E. Dewey sought Elder Benson's advice on farming and other matters. It seems likely that Ezra would have become U.S. secretary of agriculture in Dewey's administration had Dewey won the U.S. presidential nomination.

Elder Benson's prominence never diverted his attention permanently from the thing most important to him: his family. In December 1949, for instance, he and Flora made a special trip to New York to attend the performance of a missionary chorus that their son Mark directed. And several months later, after Reed had been released from service in the British Mission and Mark from the Eastern States Mission, Elder Benson went east with Barbara and Beverly and, joined there by his two sons, then traveled back across the country visiting places of historic interest.

After Dwight D. Eisenhower's election as U.S. president in November 1952, Elder Benson was asked if he could accept an appointment as secretary of agriculture in the new administration. The inquiry was a surprise to Elder Benson, who had not been consulted on that matter during the campaign. President David O. McKay authorized him to accept if the invitation came "in the proper spirit." Following an interview with President Eisenhower in New York City, Elder Benson accepted after being assured he would not be asked to promote any policy with which he disagreed.

Announcement of the appointment created a stir. Knowing of his work with the NCFC, farm organizations generally were favorable. Democratic congressmen were wary, knowing of the appointee's opposition to fixed price supports. Some were critical because of his religious affiliation. Most were noncommittal, willing to judge him on his performance.

Soon after taking office, Secretary Benson became embroiled in controversy when he restructured the USDA headquarters organization and began to lay out his views on farm subsidies. Although he was obligated to maintain fixed price supports until 1954 because of an Eisenhower campaign promise, he made it plain he intended to press for flexible supports after that. He was attacked in Congress and in the press. The furor increased when he refused to recommend subsidies for beef and eggs. Many Republican congressmen from farm states joined in the criticism. Pressure was put on President Eisenhower to dismiss him; there was fear that his presence in the cabinet would be a drag in the 1954 election campaign.

While he questioned the timing of some of Secretary Benson's public statements, President Eisenhower agreed with his views on agriculture subsidies and price supports. Ezra took heart when the president publicly supported the Agricultural Act of 1954, which contained a provision for flexible price supports. The secretary then spent five weeks on the road, drumming up support for the legislation. Critics, including many Republicans, thought the administration was courting disaster. Most observers believed the legislation would be defeated overwhelmingly. There was a sense of disbelief when it passed the Senate 49–44. "The principle of flexibility is established to replace rigidity," read the *Kiplinger Letter* for August 14, 1954. "To ram this through Congress took guts . . . in both Benson and

Eisenhower. Benson was David against Goliath [and] Eisenhower was his firm backer, contrary to much political advice. It was principle vs. politics, and much of the betting was on politics. Yet principle won."

Suddenly Secretary Benson became a political superstar. Many congressmen running for reelection sought his endorsement and were anxious that he come into their districts to campaign for them. He accommodated as many of them as his schedule would permit.

Typically, Ezra Benson attributed most of the success of this political victory to spiritual influences. Flora and the children had joined him in fasting and prayer that attitudes would be changed so as to bring about a result that would be in the best interests of the country as a whole. He felt those prayers had been answered.

As attitudes toward Secretary Benson changed, he and his family received much favorable media coverage. An Edward R. Murrow television show that featured the Bensons reportedly received a more favorable response than any of his other programs.

With the concept of flexible farm supports in place, Secretary Benson's major problem was farm surpluses. Government warehouses bulged with commodities acquired under Washington's farm subsidy programs. In reviewing the options available to help ease this problem, Ezra decided the best course was to try to increase exports. A useful tool was Public Law 480, passed in 1954, which authorized the sale of farm surpluses for foreign currencies and provided for bartering and donations to the poor. Other strategies included cooperative arrangements with trade and agricultural groups, participation in international trade fairs, and diplomatic efforts to lower trade barriers against U.S. farm products.

With the approval and encouragement of President Eisenhower, Secretary Benson decided to lead out in this effort. Designating himself "salesman at large," he began to conduct international tours to monitor and stimulate these programs. The first one was to the Caribbean and South America in February 1955. Later that year he spent eighteen days in Great Britain and Europe. At every stop he met with government and local agricultural leaders, endeavoring to break down barriers and to create friendships so as to provide openings for the introduction of U.S. farm products. He emphasized there would be no attempt merely to dump excess commodities but that his government would compete aggressively and fairly for its share of international markets. In time these efforts resulted in significant increases in U.S. farm exports. Later the "Food for Peace" program augmented the government's export strategy. Under it agricultural surpluses were selectively given to foreign nations to cement friendly relations. In 1960 alone, over sixty-two million people in ninety-two foreign countries received donations of surplus food under this program.

There were beneficial aspects of these trips unrelated to their main purpose. Flora and other members of the family usually accompanied Ezra, which fostered family unity and provided an unusual educational opportunity for them. He always tried to make contact with members of the Church in foreign lands; and he created lasting friendships with leaders around the world, as with Prime Minister Jawaharlal Nehru of India and Prime Minister David Ben-Gurion of Israel. He also gained important insights into local attitudes, for instance, when in Moscow he attended and spoke at a meeting in the Central Baptist Church. The warm reaction of the people to his message convinced Elder Benson that the Communist repression of religion had not worked and would never work.

Meanwhile, political turmoil at home swirled around him again. Opponents criticized Secretary Benson for making so many trips and for taking members of his family with him. There were periodic demands for his resignation, although they diminished temporarily after the sweeping Republican victory in 1956. But they revived with force after many Republican congressional seats were lost in 1958. Vice President Richard Nixon laid much of the blame for that upset on Secretary Benson, which accounted for much of the coolness that later developed between them. Secretary Benson took no part in the 1960 presidential race, closing out his career with international trips to Europe, South America, and the South Pacific. His service was memorialized when he was inducted into the Agriculture Hall of Fame at a ceremony conducted by the Sirloin and Saddle Club in Chicago, Illinois.

Elder Benson was convinced the Soviet Union was bent on world domination through subversion. Concerned about the drift of foreign affairs, he delivered a talk at the Church's semiannual general conference on September 30, 1961, titled "The American Heritage of Freedom." In it he pointed to Book of Mormon warnings about secret combinations; cited Joseph Smith's prophecy that the U.S. Constitution would hang by a thread, then be saved by the priesthood; and said the "Socialist, Communist Conspiracy" presented an ominous threat to the liberty of Americans. He urged Church members to become informed about the danger and to become active in trying to thwart it. During the following nine years, thirteen of his eighteen general conference talks dwelled on this theme or variations of it. He also wrote several books on the subject and referred often to literature published or recommended by the John Birch Society, a group devoted to the study and advocacy of constitutional principles. While Elder Benson never joined this group, his son Reed Benson was an official and an active promoter of it. This relationship caused some Church members to assume erroneously that Elder Benson was a member of the John Birch Society and that his approval of its literature constituted Church endorsement. This prompted the First Presidency to issue a statement denying that the Church endorsed the John Birch Society, while acknowledging the right of Church members to study its literature and to join if they wished.

President McKay also acknowledged Elder Benson's right to continue to speak out about Communism. However, the frequency and the fervor of his comments caused some leaders and members to question the propriety of his devoting so much time to the subject, which to them seemed foreign to his apostolic calling. Elder Benson ignored the criticism because the issue for him entailed nothing less than the eternal conflict between good and evil, a subject he deemed worthy of one who had been called as a special witness of Jesus Christ. It was a case of honest disagreement between men of goodwill.

The conflicts this caused were ended temporarily when Elder Benson was called to preside over the European Mission on October 18, 1963. The two years he spent in Europe on this occasion were marked by a skillful revamping of the mission organizations and procedures, a reemphasis on missionary work using the public media, and a renewal of faithfulness and commitment among members.

Soon after Elder Benson returned from Europe, the 1776 Committee urged him to become a candidate for U.S. president in 1968. President McKay told him to allow the committee to proceed but that he should not become actively involved. He complied, although he commenced to give many talks on the same subjects as before. When the efforts of the 1776 Committee stalled, Elder Benson was asked to become a presidential candidate for the Independent Party. And later, Governor George Wallace asked him to become his vice presidential candidate. Nothing came of these initiatives, which ended any thought of his becoming involved as a political candidate.

While Elder Benson continued to watch the political scene closely, his Church assignments claimed priority. In

August 1968 he was given responsibility to supervise the work in the Far East. Over the next two years he made several trips there. He was assisted by Elder Bruce R. McConkie of the First Council of Seventy. At first it was felt advisable that he not visit Vietnam because of his high political profile. Later he did make a trip there, holding meetings with servicemen. He was concerned about the government's policy of slow escalation of the war, hoping instead for a negotiated settlement. Afterward a book he wrote strongly criticized that policy. During his tenure in the Far East, Elder Benson oversaw the completion of the Church exhibit for Expo '70 in Osaka, Japan, and dedicated the land of Indonesia for the preaching of the gospel.

After the death of President David O. McKay in January 1970, Elder Benson moderated his public talks, avoiding the strong anticommunist rhetoric of previous years. This was because President Joseph Fielding Smith and his counselors, Harold B. Lee and N. Eldon Tanner, did not share his views about the preeminent importance of this issue. Thereafter, his conference talks developed more conventional gospel themes. During this period he also became involved in the supervision of the Church-owned farms in Florida, California, and New Zealand. And at headquarters he was appointed to the important Expenditures Committee and to the board of Bonneville International Inc., the umbrella corporation that controlled the Church-owned radio and television stations.

When President Harold B. Lee died unexpectedly in December 1973, Elder Benson became President of the Twelve, serving under President Spencer W. Kimball. In this position he directed the work of the Twelve and had some supervisory authority over the Assistants to the Twelve, the First Council of Seventy, and the Presiding Bishopric. His leadership style reflected the many years he had spent as a Church and government administrator. He took a special interest in those whom he directed, creating something akin to a family relationship. He also made broad delegations of authority. He did not like long meetings and disapproved of "dog and pony shows," presentations long on visuals but short on real substance. When he felt a discussion had run its course, he might suggest there was enough hay down and that it was time to do some baling. The ruling criterion he applied as to any proposed action was "What is best for the Kingdom?"

Added distinctions came to Elder Benson when the Ezra Taft Benson Agriculture and Food Institute was created at Brigham Young University and when he was appointed to the White House Forum for Domestic Policy and was given the Freedom Foundation Award. The satisfaction he received in being so honored paled in comparison to the joy he felt when President Kimball announced the revelation on priesthood in early June 1978. He rejoiced with his brethren of the Twelve that the Lord had spoken to resolve a complex problem the Church had faced for so long.

The following month, President Benson suffered a broken hip when a horse he was standing close to reared and fell on him. Only six months later he left for a tour of South America. He returned there not long afterward to create the first stake in Bolivia, at Santa Cruz. A month later he organized the one thousandth stake in the Church at Nauvoo, Illinois.

Despite the discomfort caused by the fractured hip, President Benson made four lengthy and tiring trips during the next year—two to South America, one to the Middle East, and one to Europe. Nagging problems with the hip dictated a hip replacement operation in October 1981. While convalescing and learning to walk with the artificial hip, he fell, fracturing his pelvis. While recovering from this accident, President Benson suffered a series of dizzy spells that were first diagnosed as a stroke. Later it was found they were caused by a circulatory problem, which was solved by implanting a pacemaker.

Meanwhile, changes were made in the First Presidency when Elder Gordon B. Hinckley was called as an additional counselor because of physical problems suffered by all three members of the First Presidency. Then when President Tanner died in November 1982, President Hinckley became Second Counselor. Since Presidents Spencer W. Kimball and Marion G. Romney had physical disabilities and were limited in what they could do, President Hinckley administered the daily affairs of the Church under delegations of authority from President Kimball. President Benson and the other members of the Twelve were very supportive of President Hinckley in this delicate situation as he led out in areas within the scope of his delegated authority while always seeking direction from President Kimball on matters beyond that scope. Feeling the need for counsel on certain matters pertaining to temple ordinances and disciplinary councils, President Hinckley invited President Benson to meet with him on a weekly basis to handle them. A close working rapport developed between them. This was reflected when, following the death of President Kimball on November 5, 1985, President Benson called President Hinckley as his First Counselor. Elder Thomas S. Monson was called as Second Counselor.

President Benson's first trip out of Utah following his ordination as the thirteenth President of the Church was to Washington, D.C., in early January 1986. There he divided the Annandale Virginia Stake and reorganized the presidency of the Washington Temple. During an address at the stake conference, he discussed the Book of Mormon at length. In the year that followed, he delivered twenty-eight major talks on this subject. He quoted the Prophet Joseph and emphasized that the book was a new witness for Jesus Christ, that it contained the fulness of the gospel, that it was the keystone of our religion, and that a person could get closer to God by reading it and following its teachings than in any other way. He also expressed the opinion that his ministry would be best remembered by his emphasis on the Book of Mormon, just as President Lorenzo Snow's ministry is best remembered because of his emphasis on the law of tithing.

During the first months of his ministry, President Benson also extended an invitation to all disaffected members to return to full fellowship, permitted worthy persons married to unendowed spouses to enter the temple to receive their endowments, discontinued stake seventies quorums, changed stake conferences to enable stake presidents to preside over one of the two conferences in their stakes each year, and dedicated a new temple in Denver, Colorado, while authorizing his counselors to dedicate temples in Buenos Aires, Argentina, and Lima, Peru.

The prophet's main discourse at the April 1987 general conference again admonished diligence in reading the Book of Mormon regularly. It also counseled prayerful study of the Doctrine and Covenants, which he called the capstone of our religion.

A few days after that conference, President Benson suffered a mild heart attack, which slowed him for several months. However, on February 27, 1988, he broke ground for the temple in San Diego, California. The major sermon he delivered at the April general conference a few weeks later dwelled on the pure love of Christ, the theme exemplified by the temple ordinances and suggested in the beautiful, heavenly appearance of the San Diego Temple. He said the pure love of Christ represented a "total commitment of our very being—physically, mentally, emotionally, and spiritually—to a love of the Lord. The breadth, depth, and height of this love of God extend into every facet of one's life. Our desires, be they spiritual or temporal, should be rooted in a love of the Lord. Our thoughts and affections should be centered on the Lord."

President Benson's sermons at the semiannual general conference six months later were the last ones he delivered in the Salt Lake Tabernacle. In them he called for a "massive flooding" of the earth with the Book of Mormon. He also bore "pure testimony and witness" of that which he knew to be true. In a litany of nineteen declarations that followed, each beginning with the words "I testify that," the prophet bore solemn testimony about, among other things, our pre-mortal existence; the way God leads his children through revelation; the birth, ministry, and sacrifice of the Savior; the Apostasy and Restoration; the Book of Mormon; the favored status of America; the role of living prophets; the conflict between good and evil; the need for the Saints to be actively engaged in the work; and the Final Judgment and cleansing that will take place. He ended with these words: "I testify to you that a fulness of joy can only come through the atonement of Jesus Christ and by obedience to all of the laws and ordinances of the gospel, which are found only in The Church of Jesus Christ of Latter-day Saints." It was a fitting climax to the thousands of sermons spoken by Ezra Taft Benson during the long life promised him in his patriarchal blessing.

Not long after that conference, President Benson suffered a stroke that prevented him from ever speaking again from the Tabernacle pulpit. He was able to communicate to his family and to his brethren in short, simple phrases and to give direction on any matters requiring his prophetic approval. While limited in his capacity to communicate with words, his benign countenance and loving gestures conveyed meanings beyond verbal expression. And the power of his testimony and his intellect continued to be shown when his words spoken and written earlier in life were repeated by others.

President Benson's beloved wife, Flora, died in August 1992. His own health continued to deteriorate, and he passed away quietly on May 30, 1994. He had lived a long, productive, and distinguished life, the outlines of which were traced by those who spoke at the funeral in the

Tabernacle. President Howard W. Hunter captured the essence of President Benson's years of apostolic leadership in his remarks. "He spoke to everyone and had concern for all," said President Hunter. "He gave wonderful, personalized counsel to the entire membership, whatever their personal circumstances. Those sermons will continue to sustain us and guide us as we reflect upon them."

President Benson was buried in the small cemetery in Whitney, Idaho, beside Flora. All along the route from Salt Lake City, people waited beside the highway or at overpasses to greet the funeral cortege—people of all ages, some waving flags and all with heads bared to show their respect to this son of the soil who had grown to become a prophet of God. His grave was near the place where he was born, surrounded by the fields he had tilled and by the relatives and friends whom he loved.

NOTE

This chapter is based on Francis M. Gibbons's book *Ezra Taft Benson: Statesman, Patriot, Prophet of God* (Salt Lake City: Deseret Book Company, in press) and authorities cited therein.

CHAPTER FOURTEEN

HOWARD W. HUNTER

Boyhood qualities of character often appear in the grown man in a magnified form. Such is the case with Howard William Hunter, the fourteenth President of The Church of Jesus Christ of Latter-day Saints. The poise and self-possession shown by the man in two dramatic incidents had their roots in the boy who was born and grew up in Boise, Idaho: first, when he fell in mid-sentence at the Salt Lake Tabernacle pulpit, then recovered and continued without missing a word or making an explanation; and second, when he stood, unmoved and silent, before an audience in Provo, Utah, as a man threatened him with what appeared to be a bomb and a detonator.

From the earliest days after his birth on November 14, 1907, this boy, the son of John William (called Will) and Nellie Rasmussen Hunter, was disposed to go his own way and to seek his own counsel. Taught early to pray and to have faith in God by a devoted Latter-day Saint mother, he yet honored and was obedient to his father, who was not a member of the Church and who would not allow him to be baptized at age eight. However, when he saw twelve-year-old Howard's keen disappointment at being unable to pass the sacrament with his friends in Boise's small branch, Will Hunter relented and allowed his son to be baptized. The ordinance took place on April 4, 1920. He was ordained a deacon on June 21. Howard's early dedication to the Church was shown when he was the first to make a pledge—twenty-five dollars—toward the construction of a new chapel. The amount was significant to one whose hourly wage was computed in pennies. Perhaps influenced by his obedient son, the father later joined the Church and was sealed to Nellie, after which the children, Howard and Dorothy, were sealed to them.

That the Latter-day Saints were a small minority in Boise, derided and maligned by some, had no negative effect on Howard. He lived within himself, fed by the security he found in his family and the Church. The parents encouraged scholarship. The encyclopedia and other books found at home were read with the children, as were many other books borrowed from the public library. A piano, which the children learned to play, encouraged musical interests and introduced a cultural quality into the family. Howard later learned to play several other instruments, which led him to a temporary career in music.

As he grew, Howard presided over a menagerie of pets—dogs, cats, and rabbits; collected birds' eggs, stamps and coins; helped cultivate a family garden and orchard; held a variety of jobs, among which were selling newspapers and working as a "cash boy" at a department store; and began to keep a diary. He also became absorbed in Scouting, receiving the second Eagle Scout Award given in Boise. We gain insight into the competitive fires that burned within this young man from a statement he made about the boy who was Boise's first Eagle Scout: "The race was on between Edwin Phipps of Troop 6 and me," wrote Howard, referring to their scramble for merit badges, a prelude to the Eagle award.

Howard's competitiveness was always accompanied by genuine friendliness and goodwill. He never seemed to be competing. He was always genial and kind, the sort of young man who tipped his hat to adults on the sidewalk and who, like a good Scout, surrendered his seat to the elderly on the streetcar.

In high school, academics had to compete for Howard's attention with ROTC, music, and after-hours employment. Eventually he was commissioned a major, the highest ROTC rank at his level. He learned to play the marimba, drums, saxophone, clarinet, trumpet, and violin, in addition to the piano; and he worked alternately as a golf caddy and in a pharmacy, an art store, and a hotel. His versatility in music led him, in his junior year of high school, to organize a band called Hunter's Croonaders, which played at dances and concerts throughout the area.

After Howard graduated from high school in June 1926, the band's success led to a job providing dance and concert music and accompaniment for silent movies aboard the SS *President Jackson* during a two-month luxury cruise to the Orient. Embarking from Seattle, Washington, on January 5, 1927, the five-man combo played not only aboard ship but also in several hotels at stops along the way. At ports of call in Yokohama and Kobe, Japan; Shanghai and Hong Kong, China; and Manila, the Philippines, the young Americans were exposed to foreign cultures and economies as they toured these ancient, exotic cities. While at Yokohama, Howard and two companions traveled to Tokyo, where by chance they saw the body of deceased emperor Yoshihito lying in state at a Buddhist temple near the royal palace. They also saw the emperor's oldest son, Hirohito, who succeeded him. There was unrest at Shanghai caused by conflicts between communist and nationalist troops outside the city. Within a few years, during World War II, the names of

Generalissimo Chiang Kai-shek (commander of the nationalist troops) and Hirohito would become household words throughout the United States.

Following his return from the Orient, Howard tried his hand at several things: selling shoes at Falks Department Store, working with a partner to open a supper club called the Plantation Roadhouse, and engaging in an advertising promotion that involved posting attractive placards featuring local businesses and containing announcements and time schedules.

Since none of these ventures held the prospect of a permanent career path, Howard, while mulling over his options, traveled to Los Angeles, California, in March 1928 for a short vacation. Attracted by the climate and by the energy and the optimism that seemed to infuse everything and everybody, he decided to stay permanently. He soon obtained employment at the Bank of Italy and began living with a great-uncle and great-aunt, Edward and Lyde Nowell. Howard became a member of the Huntington Park Ward and enrolled in night classes at the American Institute of Banking. When his parents and Dorothy moved to Los Angeles a few months later, he lived with them, transferring his membership to the Adams Ward.

In Los Angeles Howard became acquainted with an energetic and attractive group of young people who shared his religious values and his zest for life. He also came under the influence of an able Sunday School teacher, Peter A. Clayton, who opened his mind to an understanding of gospel principles. "I think of this period of my life as the time the truths of the gospel commenced to unfold," Howard later recalled. It also was a time when his mind began to open to the prospects of marriage. His social group included an attractive young woman named Clara May Jeffs, who was called Claire by her friends. Howard and Claire dated over a period of three years, intermittently at first, then exclusively. By the spring of 1931, they knew they wanted to be man and wife and began to plan for marriage. As Howard looked to the future, he decided that the erratic schedules and negative associations of a dance band musician (an activity he had continued to pursue as a sideline) were incompatible with a successful Latter-day Saint family. So on June 6, 1931, after playing his last engagement, he packed up his band instruments and never used them again, except occasionally in a family setting. He and Claire were sealed in the Salt Lake Temple four days later by Elder Richard R. Lyman of the Twelve.

Two incidents connected with the marriage revealed a certain flair for the unexpected that surfaced often during Howard's life. First, before going to Salt Lake City, he surprised Claire with a new black Chevrolet sport coupe with a rumble seat and red wheels and loaded with extras. He paid cash, approximately seven hundred dollars, plus his old Model A Ford. Second, when they returned to California, they moved temporarily into a pricey furnished apartment at the beach, where they enjoyed a honeymoon while working at their jobs, he at the bank and she at a department store. After the honeymoon, they moved into a small, economical, unfurnished apartment.

The first four years of marriage were strenuous. The effects of the Depression struck home when the bank Howard worked for at the time, the First Exchange State Bank, collapsed in January 1932. After a year of makeshift jobs that offered no permanency or hope for the future, the couple moved in with Claire's parents to save on rent. They remained there for three years. Father Jeffs died in 1933. The presence of the Hunters in the home was a comfort to the mother. In January 1934 Howard's prospects improved when he was employed in the title department of the Los Angeles County Flood Control District. When this employment exposed him to lawyers and to legal procedures and concepts, Howard decided to make the law his life's career. He soon enrolled in night courses at Southwestern

University. After a year he satisfied the entrance requirements, and in September 1935 he was admitted to the university's law school.

Meanwhile, joy and then sorrow visited the Hunters when their first child, Howard William Hunter Jr., was born on March 20, 1934, but died seven months later. The parents' grief was particularly acute for Claire, who did not have a helpful distraction as did Howard with his work and school responsibilities. So to help take her mind off the empty nest, she worked temporarily at Bullocks, an upscale department store.

Although the four years Howard spent in law school were strenuous, they were filled with hope for the future. His studies required focus, intelligence, and discipline so he could successfully compete with younger students who did not have family responsibilities and full-time employment as he did. He graduated cum laude in June 1939, third in his class. After passing the bar and being admitted to practice in early 1940, he rented an office from an established attorney and for a while divided his time between his practice and work with the county. In time he devoted himself exclusively to the law.

During this interval, major changes occurred in the Hunter family and in Howard's personal life. In May 1936 the second son, John Jacob Hunter, was born; in June 1938 the third son, Richard Allen Hunter, was born; and in August 1940 Howard was shocked to be called as the first bishop of the El Sereno Ward. He was ordained a high priest and a bishop by Elder Joseph F. Merrill of the Twelve.

Serving for six years, Bishop Hunter was known for his kindness, for his interest in the youth, and for his foresight in developing a building fund, even though war restrictions prevented construction at the time. After his release in November 1946, he was called as the president of the stake high priests quorum.

During the years that followed, Howard established

himself as a successful corporate lawyer, as an exemplary husband and father, and as an effective priesthood leader. His legal practice was weighted toward real property matters and counseling businesses. He served on the boards of directors of many companies. One of these, the Watson Land Company, controlled property interests that traced to a Mexican land grant. Howard served as a director of this company from the mid-1940s until the time of his death. In the 1950s he also was appointed to the board of the Beneficial Life Insurance Company headquartered in Salt Lake City. Howard seldom litigated in court. When he did, he was always well prepared, was poised and self-confident, and was usually successful. He was never abrasive or unpleasant, although he never yielded a point easily and was tenacious in protecting the interests of his clients.

As Howard's professional reputation increased, so did his personal wealth, accumulated not only from legal fees but from wise investments. In 1948 the Hunters purchased a new ranch-style house in Arcadia. There they created an exemplary Latter-day Saint home, marked by family prayer, love, and mutual respect. They held regular family home evenings, even though that program had not yet been re-adopted Churchwide. Howard and Claire encouraged their sons in music, academics, and sports and helped them become Eagle Scouts like their father.

In February 1950 Elders Stephen L Richards and Harold B. Lee of the Twelve called Howard W. Hunter as president of the Pasadena Stake. As stake president, he took part in many fund-raising and building projects, including a stake center, the Los Angeles Temple, and a welfare farm. As the regional council chairman, President Hunter spearheaded special regional MIA conferences held in Los Angeles that featured musical events and worship services in the Hollywood Bowl and dance festivals in school stadiums. The featured speaker at the 1954 conference was President David O. McKay. In 1955 President Stephen L

Richards was featured, as was President J. Reuben Clark in 1956.

During the nine and a half years Howard served as stake president, he and Claire hosted the General Authorities who came for stake conferences. They had a special room in their home reserved for the visitors. In this way, the Hunters became personally acquainted with most of the General Authorities.

President Hunter was a skilled executive who delegated broadly and who expected performance from his associates. He was always thoughtful of the feelings of others, avoiding negative comments, except as they were necessary to strengthen the work. Later, as a member of the Twelve, reporting on conference visits or mission tours, he was noted for avoiding critical comments and focusing instead on the positive things he observed. His attitudes reflected, in part, the impact on him of Napoleon Hill's writings, who dwelled on the power of thought to create wealth or to influence conduct. This seems to account for the small gadget inscribed with "Think" that was often seen on Howard Hunter's desk.

Howard was surprised following the morning session of general conference on October 9, 1959, when he was told that President David O. McKay wanted to see him. He was shocked and overwhelmed with emotion when the prophet told him the Lord had spoken and that he had been called to the Twelve. He was sustained the following day and ordained and set apart on Thursday, October 15. The whole experience had a dreamlike quality about it for Howard. Reality set in when he and Claire had to close out their affairs in California and move to Utah. It took almost two years to do this. In the interval, Elder Hunter traveled to Salt Lake City each week by train or air for the Thursday temple meetings. Soon after his ordination he also began to fill stake conference and other apostolic assignments. He was released as stake president in late November 1959.

Arriving in Salt Lake City in April 1961, the Hunters lived in rented facilities until their new home in the Oak Hills district was completed. They moved into it on July 22, 1963.

In the interval before moving to Salt Lake City, Howard and Claire traveled to the South Pacific to meet Richard, who had completed his mission in Australia. They then spent two months traveling around the world with their son. They had done the same with John when he completed his Australia mission in the autumn of 1958. The Hunters' global views were enriched when in late 1961 they traveled to the Middle East with Elder and Sister Spencer W. Kimball. The two Apostles and their wives spent several weeks tracing the paths of the ancient patriarchs and the Savior and his disciples. They traveled to Iraq, reminiscing about Abraham's life in Ur of the Chaldees. They visited Egypt, where they recalled the experiences of the Savior and his parents and of Abraham, Joseph, and the children of Israel in that ancient land. And they traveled the length and the breadth of the Holy Land, reading the sacred accounts of the Savior's birth, ministry, crucifixion, and resurrection at the places where the events occurred. Elder Hunter's life and the perceptions of his ministry were never the same after this experience. Before returning home from this trip, Elder Hunter toured in Great Britain and Europe, holding meetings in seven missions.

Elder Hunter's early travels to the Orient with the Croonaders, his two trips around the world with Claire and their sons, and his tour through the Middle East with Claire and the Kimballs gave him a global perspective of the Church and its mission. That perspective was broadened later as he traveled extensively in Mexico and Central America, in South America, in Africa, in the islands of the Pacific, in the Soviet Union, and in China and Japan. In all his travels, Elder Hunter showed unusual zest and enthusiasm. He liked to arrange his own itinerary, relying on his own knowledge of places and travel accommodations. And he enjoyed doing unusual things, such as when he led a BYU group riding on camels up Mount Sinai and when he spent a night in Carthage Jail with a group of mission presidents to enhance his understanding of what Joseph Smith and his companions suffered. Wherever he went, Elder Hunter kept foremost in mind his role as a special witness of Jesus Christ in all the world. In all places he bore sincere testimony of the divinity of the Savior, the truthfulness of the gospel, and the preeminence of The Church of Jesus Christ of Latter-day Saints among the world's religions.

The nature of his travels in Mexico and Central America changed markedly after his appointment as chairman of the advisory board of the New World Archaeological Foundation in 1961. For several years he made annual visits to archaeological sites in those areas, traveling into remote places by primitive means. He enjoyed getting out into the open and seeing the magnificent scenery and ancient structures and artifacts. He also was fascinated by correlations between scientific archaeological findings and the Book of Mormon.

Elder Hunter became president of the Genealogical Society in January 1964. During his tenure, vast changes in methods of storing and accessing genealogical data were made after the advent of electronic retrieval systems. He took special training in computer technology so that he was knowledgeable about the technical changes being made. He directed the World Conference on Records held in Salt Lake City in August 1969, marking the seventy-fifth anniversary of the Genealogical Society. The event enhanced the position of the Church as the dominant organization in genealogy in the world. Elder Hunter also conducted the ceremony dedicating the mountain storage vault, where many genealogical records are kept, in Little Cottonwood Canyon on June 22, 1966. The dedicatory prayer was offered by President Hugh B. Brown.

Following the death of President David O. McKay on January 18, 1970, President Joseph Fielding Smith was ordained and set apart as the tenth President of the Church. Soon after, Elder Hunter was surprised when he was appointed Church historian and recorder, succeeding President Smith, who had served in that position for several decades. It was a position for which he was eminently qualified by training, temperament, and interest. Elder Hunter had been a careful and precise diarist from the days of his youth in Boise. He respected the role of history in explaining the past and in providing a focus for the future. After a change in procedure regarding the role of the Twelve in headquarters assignments resulted in his release as Church historian and recorder in 1972, he continued to serve as an adviser to the Historical Department until 1978.

A wry sense of humor lurked beneath the surface of Elder Hunter's benign and dignified exterior. He once asked a stake president whether one of the Brethren senior to him in the apostleship would be present at a stake conference. When told no, he said, "Good, we'll do what we want to do." This was accompanied by a genial smile and a gentle chuckle. When the circumstances were appropriate, he enjoyed light repartee and a good story. But his humor was always kindly and never had a hard edge to it. In filling assignments, Elder Hunter was bold to act as he was prompted even if it seemed drastic. So it was in Mexico City that he once created fifteen stakes out of five. His judgment was vindicated when the new stakes thrived and when one of them had to be divided again in two years.

In January 1965 Elder Hunter was appointed president and chairman of the board of the Polynesian Cultural Center. Created fifteen months earlier to provide work opportunities for Polynesian students attending the Church college at Laie, Hawaii, the center was running a deficit at the time Elder Hunter was appointed. It soon began to be self-sustaining and then to produce good surpluses. During the eleven years he served, the center expanded its operations until it became one of the most popular attractions on the islands. Tourists thronged there to see the students dance, sing, and perform in their native costumes. The center not only provides work opportunities to help students gain an education, but it helps showcase Church spiritual and intellectual values, exemplified by the nearby temple and the college. When President David O. McKay broke ground for the college in Laie in February 1955, he predicted that "millions of people" would come there eventually "seeking to know what this town and its significance are." Laie attracts about a million visitors annually.

There was a cosmopolitan quality about Elder Hunter, seemingly a native endowment enriched by his global travels. This quality, which added to his negotiating and diplomatic skills, prompted the First Presidency to give him principal responsibilities in funding and developing the Orson Hyde Memorial Gardens on the Mount of Olives and in developing the Jerusalem Center for Near Eastern Studies, which also is on the Mount of Olives adjacent to Hebrew University's Mount Scopus campus. The Orson Hyde memorial commemorates the prayer Orson Hyde offered on the Mount of Olives in 1841, dedicating the land of Palestine for the gathering of Abraham's posterity. The Jerusalem Center houses living quarters and classrooms to accommodate Brigham Young University's study-abroad students and also has facilities for the Jerusalem Branch of the Church. Elder Hunter made numerous trips to Israel during the development of these two projects, meeting with government, religious, and business leaders as the diverse problems were worked out. He was aided by many able people who provided expertise in various fields. His empathy for both Jewish and Islamic groups and his understanding of their concerns helped bridge many problems. He attended and conducted the dedicatory services for the

Orson Hyde Memorial and participated in the dedication of the Jerusalem Center in May 1989.

When this center was dedicated, Ezra Taft Benson had been President of the Church since November 1985. He was the fifth prophet under whom Elder Hunter had served and would be the last. Howard had been a member of the Twelve for more than ten years when President David O. McKay died in January 1970. Special ties bound Howard Hunter to President McKay. The younger man had received his call to the apostleship through that prophet. Their world travels were equally extensive, and there was a similarity in the courtly quality that characterized their personal relationships. They were always poised and genial in meeting others, were careful in their personal grooming, and enjoyed a good chuckle. Despite President McKay's advanced age and ailments, Elder Hunter deeply mourned his passing, referring to him as "this great, sweet, kindly man."

At the time of President McKay's death, Elder Hunter had been for a decade under the immediate direction of Joseph Fielding Smith, who was President of the Twelve. Their shared interest in Church history brought them close, as did their penchant for care and precision in writing and speaking. Howard gave President Smith the same loyalty he had given to President McKay. That carried over to President Harold B. Lee, whose influence on Elder Hunter was pronounced from the time he called Howard as a stake president in 1950. And the love and special rapport that existed between Elder Hunter and President Spencer W. Kimball was a bond strengthened during their lengthy tour of the Holy Land and the Middle East. He loved all of these men, as he did President Ezra Taft Benson, and he sought to serve them and to emulate them. Following the ordination of President Benson as President of the Church, Elder Hunter was set apart as Acting President of the Twelve, because of the disabilities of Marion G. Romney, who was the quorum President.

Howard's love for the prophets was exceeded only by his love for his family. All his efforts were aimed ultimately toward creating a family unit that would exist eternally in a celestial setting. In concert with Claire, he spared no effort in laying the groundwork for that eventuality. Their home was a place of culture and refinement where love, reverential worship of God, scholarship, good music, and good conversation abounded. Howard's skill in law and business enabled him to accumulate enough wealth to help his sons obtain a good education and to become established. Both sons graduated from law school and acquired legal stature, John as a judge and Richard as a successful practicing attorney. These sons and their wives, Louine and Nan, are the parents of eighteen children, a progeny which, in time, may expand Howard and Claire Hunter's family to Abrahamic proportions. Howard and Claire cherished each of these special people, lavishing upon them all the love and attention of which they were capable. Meanwhile, both John and Richard became bishops in the Church and served in other priesthood callings.

Elder Hunter's love of family extended to those outside the immediate circle and embraced both the living and the dead. He was an avid genealogist who spent much time and money gathering family history data and additional effort in performing or securing the performance of temple work in behalf of deceased ancestors.

And Howard Hunter was a good householder and a good neighbor who was handy with tools in fixing things in his own home or in helping neighbors with their odd jobs. No honest task was too menial or too unimportant for him to give it his careful attention.

Except for the death of their first son and for John's brush with polio at age six, the Hunter family was free from any further trauma or serious illness until the early 1970s.

At that time, Claire began to suffer severe headaches and some loss of memory, resulting in a diagnosis of hardening of the arteries. Her condition did not yield to treatment or medication and became progressively worse. After several years of intermittent hospitalizations, tests, and treatments, she underwent shunt surgery in the hope of reducing the pain. It produced little change. As Claire became incapacitated, special care was provided for her at home by an aide who lived in the basement apartment. After Claire suffered cerebral hemorrhages in 1981 and 1982, it became necessary to transfer her to a nursing care facility where she could receive more constant and skilled attention. Juggling his heavy Church assignments, Elder Hunter visited her at least once and usually twice a day, talking to her quietly and soothingly. Although she could not respond in words, her facial expressions and mannerisms bespoke of the love she had for her husband. It is said she responded that way only to him. She died in October 1983 after more than ten years of dire, debilitating illness.

During the later years of Claire's illness, Elder Hunter also began to suffer physical problems. They began in February 1977, when he contracted the mumps. While his contracting this so-called children's illness induced much good-natured banter among the Brethren, it was no laughing matter when his recovery period included serious complications. Months later he underwent abdominal surgery for the removal of a benign tumor; and while recovering, he suffered a heart attack. As a result, Elder Hunter followed a disciplined regimen of walking, the benefits of which warded off serious illness for several years. When the heart problem flared up again in October 1986, quadruple-bypass surgery was required. Seemingly recovered, he and Richard traveled to Europe and the Middle East in January 1987. On returning, he began to suffer severe lower-back pains, diagnosed as the deterioration of a spinal disc. While assessing the need for back surgery, he was operated on for a bleeding ulcer in April. Having recovered from that, he underwent back surgery in June, the effect of which was to relegate him to a wheelchair. This made it necessary to deliver his October 1987 conference address while seated. Determined to walk again, he began a disciplined therapy program. He finally graduated to a walker, an accomplishment that was largely the result of faith and supreme mental toughness. It was during this period that Elder Hunter fell while speaking at the Tabernacle pulpit and yet was able to complete his address, his audience unaware that he had been injured during his fall.

After the death of President Marion G. Romney on May 20, 1988, Elder Hunter was set apart as President of the Twelve. He then began a series of lengthy international trips, including the May 1989 trip to the Holy Land to attend the dedication of the Jerusalem Center.

On Thursday, April 10, 1990, President Hunter made an announcement to the Twelve that was so typical of the unexpected twists his life had taken in the past. He told the Brethren he would be sealed that afternoon to Inis Stanton by President Gordon B. Hinckley. Only the couple, President Hinckley, and the two witnesses—President Thomas S. Monson and Inis's bishop—would be present. Inis was an acquaintance of President Hunter and Claire from the days when he lived in El Sereno, California. She had been married before and had lived in Salt Lake City since the early 1970s, working as a hostess in the Church Office Building. A poised, attractive, and friendly person, Inis became a perfect companion for President Hunter, filling, insofar as possible, a void that had existed since Claire's passing.

Inis was soon introduced to the nomadic lifestyle of an Apostle. During the first two years after their marriage, she accompanied him on trips to South America, Alaska, Hawaii, Central America, Japan, Korea, China, Africa, Jerusalem, and England. He enjoyed acquainting her with these countries and their peoples, in introducing her to the members of the Church, and in seeing her respond to challenges wherever they went. He was pleased with the skill and sensitivity she displayed in speaking to the Saints and in mingling with them.

Following the trip to England in May 1992, Inis underwent knee surgery, which temporarily curtailed their travels. As soon as she recovered, however, they were at it again when in September they traveled to Russia, the Ukraine, Armenia, and Austria. While in Vienna on September 12, 1992, President Hunter dedicated the country of Austria. Following the October general conference, the Hunters attended a regional conference in England and participated in the rededication of the London Temple. The following month they traveled to the Pacific.

After returning from the Pacific, President Hunter suffered internal bleeding. He was hospitalized for two weeks and spent the remainder of the year convalescing and handling routine matters at headquarters. Following the incident at the BYU Marriott Center in Provo in February 1993, when he was threatened by an assailant and yet remained calm and dignified, President Hunter, accompanied by Inis, traveled to Australia, Singapore, and Japan. In March they went to Brazil, and in April they attended the dedication of the San Diego Temple.

A few weeks later, President Hunter underwent what was expected to be routine gall bladder surgery. It became complicated, however, when he failed to regain consciousness. He remained in a deep sleep for twenty days, then revived. Some thought he would never recover. He not only recovered but, after a few months, was able to resume his apostolic duties.

President Ezra Taft Benson died on May 30, 1994. Six days later, on June 5, Howard W. Hunter was ordained and set apart as the fourteenth President of the Church. While his tenure was less than a year, it was significant. He presided over ceremonies in Nauvoo, Illinois, commemorating the 150th anniversary of the martyrdom of Joseph Smith and Hyrum Smith; traveled to Europe; created the two thousandth stake of the Church in Mexico City; dedicated temples in Orlando, Florida, and Bountiful, Utah; and spoke at other special gatherings. Most significant, however, was the spiritual tone he set, asking all to be more kind, more courteous, more patient, and more forgiving. He invited the members of the Church "to establish the temple of the Lord as the great symbol of their membership and the supernal setting for their most sacred covenants." He also expressed the hope that "every adult member would be worthy of and carry a current temple recommend, even if proximity to a temple does not allow immediate or frequent use."

Shortly after the dedication of the Bountiful Temple in January 1995, President Hunter was hospitalized with bone cancer. He passed away quietly on March 3, 1995, at age eighty-eight. Born in obscurity in Boise, Idaho, he lived to become the head of an international church, loved and admired by its more than nine million members. He was eulogized at ceremonies held in the Salt Lake Tabernacle and was laid to rest beside his beloved Claire.

NOTE

This chapter is based on Eleanor Knowles's book *Howard W. Hunter* (Salt Lake City: Deseret Book Company, 1994); the diaries of Francis M. Gibbons, 1970–94; *Howard W. Hunter, Prophet of God* (Salt Lake City: The Church of Jesus Christ of Latter-day Saints, 1994, videocassette); and articles in the *Ensign* and the *Church News* about President Hunter.

CHAPTER FIFTEEN

GORDON B. HINCKLEY

An understanding of President Gordon Bitner Hinckley, the fifteenth President of The Church of Jesus Christ of Latter-day Saints, is helped by knowing of his ancestry, which extends into early American history. One ancestor, Stephen Hopkins, was aboard the *Mayflower* on its maiden voyage. Stephen's family, a wife and three children, was the largest among the company. A fourth child, fittingly named Oceanus Hopkins, was born at sea. The father was one of twelve "Masters" who signed the Mayflower Compact, men who were considered to be the aristocrats of the company.

Thomas Hinckley, another early American ancestor, was governor of the Plymouth Colony from 1681 to 1692. He was the last governor of the Old Colony, which was later absorbed into the Massachusetts Bay Colony under its royal charter. Along with his administrative abilities, Governor Hinckley was said to have been "addicted to writing poetry," implying good language skills. The governor's grandson Thomas Prince, pastor of the Old South Church in Boston, was obsessed with collecting early Plymouth documents, which he compiled in a manuscript titled "Ms History of the Plantation of Plimouth." The Prince manuscript later disappeared from Old South, perhaps during the Revolutionary War. It resurfaced in 1844 when it was discovered in the library of Fulham Palace on the outskirts of London.

Both Stephen Hopkins and Thomas Hinckley were of English descent, the former having been born in Wotton-under-Edge, Gloucestershire; and the latter having descended from Samuel Hinckley, who arrived in America in April 1635 from Harrietsham, Kent.

The Hinckley presence in The Church of Jesus Christ of Latter-day Saints traces to Ira Nathaniel Hinckley, born October 30, 1828, whose family was converted in Ontario, Canada, by John E. Page and an Elder Sherwood. Orphaned while young, Ira moved with the Judd family to Nauvoo in 1843, where he learned the blacksmith trade and became imbued with a testimony as he heard Joseph and Hyrum Smith and other Church leaders speak. In Utah, after the Saints' exodus from Missouri, he lived first in Salt Lake City and then in Coalville, where he was a builder. President Brigham Young, needing a man of "sound practical judgment and experience," called Ira to build Cove Fort in Millard County, Utah, where he and his family lived for several years. Later he was called as president of the Millard Stake and so moved to Fillmore. He presided for twenty-five years and was then called as stake patriarch. He was a man of few words, wise, thoughtful, and persistent.

Ira's son, Bryant Stringham Hinckley, Gordon B. Hinckley's father, was born on July 9, 1867. A prominent educator, Church leader, and businessman, Bryant was an eloquent speaker and a lucid writer. For many years he was the principal of LDS Business College in Salt Lake City, while teaching both there and at LDS University. He also supervised the development and construction of the

Deseret Gymnasium, which he then managed for twenty-five years. He served as a counselor in the Liberty Stake presidency and then as president of the stake. For several years he was a member of the YMMIA General Board, and in the mid-1930s he presided over the Northern States Mission. Afterward, he worked closely with President Heber J. Grant, writing books, manuals, and articles; handling sensitive correspondence; and filling personal assignments received from the prophet.

Bryant Hinckley's first wife, Christine Johnson, died in July 1908, having given birth to ten children, two of whom died in infancy. Thirteen months later he married Ada Bitner, who was a member of the LDS Business College faculty. Ada, a "brilliant and lovely woman," had fourteen sisters and four brothers in two families, a fact that helped her assume the direction of the Hinckley household with confidence. She also bore five children, the oldest of whom, Gordon Bitner Hinckley, was born on June 23, 1910.

Gordon was a frail child. While a toddler of two he caught whooping cough, which was aggravated by the pall of smoke created by Salt Lake's coal-burning stoves. To alleviate his condition, the Hinckleys purchased five acres in East Millcreek, above the city smoke, where they built a summer home. With other nearby acquisitions, this residence grew to a thirty-five-acre farm. The family soon developed the routine of spending eight months each year at the city home and four months at the summer home. At the farm, Gordon learned to work, harvesting fruit from the orchard, planting, weeding and watering the garden, and tending the animals. But there also was time for play and for reflection on the miracle of the growth cycle from seed to fruit. He also became intensely aware of the magnitude and the orderliness of God's heavenly creations as he was able to see the night sky clearly, unobstructed by smoke or undimmed by city lights.

The city home had a library whose walls were lined

with books. It was furnished with a large oak table, comfortable chairs, and a good lamp. The ambience of this room and the studious habits of the parents provided strong impetus toward scholarship. Gordon was always drawn to this library where he was first introduced to the great literature of the world. Yet as a boy, he had what he later called a "trenchant dislike" for school. Such was his aversion that he rebelled against enrolling at the Hamilton School at age six. He started there at age seven and was soon advanced to his proper grade. In time he adjusted well to school routines, completed seven grades at Hamilton and grades eight and nine at Roosevelt, and graduated from the Church-operated LDS high school in Salt Lake City and later from the University of Utah.

The Hinckleys' city home was in the First Ward, which embraced several blocks north of Liberty Park between Sixth and Ninth East. It included fifteen hundred members and had five deacons quorums. Instruction in priesthood meetings and Sunday School, along with numerous activities, dances, plays, and athletics, broadened Gordon's knowledge and interests. His social skills developed, and his spiritual senses were sharpened. Once at a priesthood meeting, Gordon received a profound spiritual witness of the truthfulness of the restored Church as the brethren sang a favorite hymn, "Praise to the Man." The self-possession and eloquence of a young neighbor, Marjorie Pay, as she gave a reading in Primary, made a lasting impression. Their youthful acquaintance would later evolve into courtship and marriage.

Repeatedly Bryant S. Hinckley urged his children to "be somebody." It was a call to personal excellence. The notable achievements of his descendants suggest the admonition had no small impact. As Gordon entered the University of Utah, he aimed toward a career in journalism. He took every writing course available to him at the university. He also became absorbed in English literature, avidly reading the classics. His minor was in ancient languages, Latin and

Greek. He earned his way through the university by working nights at the Deseret Gym as an electrical and plumbing maintenance man. There he learned to use good tools—"And I love them," he has said, a love that has been shown throughout his life, wherever he has lived.

Influences in the home, a natural bent, and his university training have endowed Gordon B. Hinckley with rare language skills. These have been an important factor in his life's work. He respects words and their meanings, and he uses them selectively and sparingly. His preference runs to short words that clearly convey meaning to the ordinary reader or listener. Long training in the proper usage of the written word has spilled over into President Hinckley's speaking so that a transcript of extemporaneous remarks usually reveals the same disciplined structure as his writings.

After graduation, Gordon and a friend briefly harbored the idea of spending a year in the South Pacific, writing about life in the islands as Robert Louis Stevenson had done. This fantasy quickly gave way to plans to attend graduate school at Columbia; and these plans soon yielded to the urging of Bishop John C. Duncan that Gordon fill a mission.

The call was to the European Mission. It came during the depths of the Depression when money was scarce. A small savings account his mother had left, money he had saved, and his father's and brother's backing provided the necessary financing. In June 1933 he entered the Missionary Home, which stood north of the Beehive House on State Street in Salt Lake City. When Elder David O. McKay, then a member of the Twelve, spoke to the missionaries, he asked them to write a paper on what it means to be a missionary. Later Elder McKay invited Gordon to his office and told him his was the best paper on the subject he had ever read. As we shall see, the incident had implications for the future.

Gordon was set apart by Elder George Albert Smith of

the Twelve. Before he left Salt Lake City, Gordon's father handed him a small card with the inscription "Be not afraid, only believe" (Mark 5:36). This admonition, and another one received from his father in the field, had a marked influence on him during his mission and afterward.

En route to the East Coast, Elder Hinckley stopped in Chicago, where the World's Fair was in progress. Embarking in New York City on the SS *Manhattan* of the U.S. Lines, he crossed the Atlantic to Plymouth, England. He was assigned to labor in Preston, Lancashire, where the first Latter-day Saint baptisms in England had been performed in the River Ribble in 1837.

The historic significance of Preston could not diminish Elder Hinckley's feeling of loneliness as he traveled there, nor his sense of failure after he had labored there for several weeks. Discouraged and ill, he wrote home saying his mission seemed a waste of time and money and suggesting he ought to return to Salt Lake City. His father's unexpected answer had a bracing effect. It simply told Gordon to forget himself and to go to work. And the next morning as he studied Mark 8:35 with his companion, Elder Hinckley resolved to tough it out. It was a turning point in his mission and his life.

After five months in Lancashire, Elder Hinckley was called to the mission office in London to serve as assistant to the European Mission president, Elder Joseph F. Merrill of the Twelve. He spent the remainder of his mission there. It was a crucial period of growth for the future prophet. His writing skills flowered as he wrote for the mission publications. He learned to speak extemporaneously with poise and precision despite the heckling crowds he addressed in Hyde Park. And his deftness in diplomacy and discretion was sharpened. This last quality shone when President Merrill assigned him to confer with a publisher whose firm had republished as fact a repugnant anti-Mormon book. Told at first the editor would not see him, Elder Hinckley persisted until he obtained an interview. His explanations were so persuasive that the executive recalled the books at considerable expense in order to insert a statement in them that the work was fictional. Equally important, a friendship grew between this man and Elder Hinckley, resulting in an exchange of Christmas greetings over many years. It was Gordon Hinckley's reputation for tact and persuasiveness that caused President Merrill to ask him to meet with the First Presidency on his return home to explain problems in the missions of Europe.

When his mission was completed, Elder Hinckley and two companions traveled through Europe. They rode the trains third-class at night and walked to see the sights during the day. Returning to America on the SS *Manhattan,* Gordon purchased a new car in Detroit for his father, a Plymouth that cost $740. Weary when he arrived in Salt Lake City in 1935 and weighing only 126 pounds, he said he had no desire "ever to travel again." Indeed, he felt that a promise in his patriarchal blessing, "the nations of the earth shall hear thy voice," had been fulfilled.

At the request of the former publisher of the *Deseret News,* Gordon interviewed with the manager of the paper, seeking employment. He was told quite bluntly there was no opening and that if there were one, others more qualified than he were available to fill it. Far from being dejected, the thought occurred as he left the office that one day he would direct the *Deseret News.* Whether the impression was revelatory or merely a reflection of Gordon B. Hinckley's innate character, it proved to be correct when he later became the chairman of the board of Deseret News Publishing Company.

Meanwhile, he was granted an interview with the First Presidency to outline Elder Merrill's concerns. He was told he had fifteen minutes. He was there more than an hour answering questions. The next day President David O. McKay, then a counselor to President Heber J. Grant, doubtless remembering the theme he had written while in the Missionary Home, invited Gordon to his office. Out of this came an invitation for Elder Hinckley to write for the Church and to serve as executive secretary of the Radio, Publicity, and Mission Literature Committee. Thus began what at this writing is sixty years of continuous service at Church headquarters, broken only by an interval during World War II when he was employed by the Denver & Rio Grande Railroad.

The Radio, Publicity, and Mission Literature Committee, chaired by Stephen L Richards of the Quorum of the Twelve Apostles, was composed of six members of the Twelve. Under the overall direction of the committee, Gordon Hinckley "pioneered the making of visual and audio materials for use in the missions and handled the radio work for the Church." Over the years, this work entailed writing hundreds of scripts for radio, filmstrips, and motion pictures, as well as pamphlets and other written materials for use in the missions. He also instructed groups in the Missionary Home about radio and publicity strategies.

At first Gordon was paid $65 a month, which was supplemented by $35 a month received for teaching seminary an hour each weekday. Later his earnings increased to $150 a month, not a bad salary during those days of Depression. With this slender income Gordon and Marjorie were married on April 29, 1937. The ceremony was performed in the Salt Lake Temple by Elder Stephen L Richards. They fixed up the summer home in East Millcreek, where they lived while Bryant S. Hinckley presided in the Northern States Mission. Meanwhile, Gordon was called to the Sunday School General Board. In this role he wrote manuals and traveled extensively throughout the Church.

At the end of World War II, Elder Stephen L Richards persuaded Gordon to leave his promising employment with the railroad and to return to work with the Radio, Publicity, and Mission Literature Committee. Soon after

Gordon was called as second counselor in the East Millcreek Stake presidency. Two years later he became the first counselor, and in 1956 he was called as the stake president by Elders Harold B. Lee and George Q. Morris.

After Stephen L Richards was sustained as First Counselor to President David O. McKay in April 1951, he invited Gordon to assist him in supervising the Missionary Department. The association had a lasting effect on Brother Hinckley. President Richards, a skillful attorney and law professor, was reputed to be among the most brilliant of the graduates of the University of Chicago law school. When he began to direct the missionary work, the Korean War had created many thorny problems arising from missionary quotas imposed by local draft boards. As President Richards sought to involve his assistant in solving them, Gordon protested because he lacked legal training. President Richards assured him this was not an impediment but an advantage, because a lawyer might try to solve the problems through litigation, something he wished to avoid. He said he would provide any necessary legal counsel and that what was needed was someone with negotiating skills who could work around problems with finesse. This was the strategy Gordon Hinckley used as he sought to solve draft problems during the remainder of the Korean War. In reality it was an expression of innate qualities in his character, proved in practice and guided by a brilliant tactician almost without peer. Habits developed or confirmed during this period became an ingrained part of Gordon B. Hinckley's approach to problems during his tenure as a General Authority. His inclination is to compose differences and to avoid confrontations where that can be done consistent with principle.

In 1954 President David O. McKay called Brother Hinckley to find methods to present the temple ceremonies in various languages. This led to producing the temple ceremonies in fourteen languages using film. During the production period, Brother Hinckley spent much time in the assembly room on the fifth floor of the Salt Lake Temple where the first film of the temple ceremonies was prepared. He used one of the nearby rooms as an alternate office.

When the film was completed, he personally carried it to Switzerland, where it was first used in the Swiss Temple following its dedication in September 1955. Since then, President Hinckley has had an unequaled involvement in the dedication or rededication of temples around the world. Of the forty-seven temples now in use, he has dedicated or rededicated more than half.

On April 6, 1958, President Hinckley was sustained as an Assistant to the Twelve; and on October 5, 1961 he was ordained an Apostle and inducted into the Quorum of the Twelve Apostles. His skills and his long experience at Church headquarters enabled him to render significant service from the beginning. He played a key role in setting up the program for the first worldwide seminar for mission presidents in 1961, working with President Henry D. Moyle. In the summer of 1962, he and President Moyle toured twenty-one missions in Europe during a twenty-three-day period, holding day-long seminars with the missionaries. Meanwhile, as a member of the Missionary Executive Committee, he helped to work out a plan to divide missions into various areas to be directed by members of the Twelve. Elder Hinckley's first assignment under this plan was to supervise missions in Asia. He served there for eight years, traveling back and forth twenty-one times. Among other things, he organized the Korea Mission, opened missionary work in the Philippines, dedicated South Vietnam and Thailand, traveled through Vietnam during the war, secured permission to send the first missionaries to India, and participated in creating the Tokyo Stake in March 1970, the first stake in Asia.

He was then assigned to supervise missions in South America. There he created new stakes in Brazil and Peru and received authorization to create new stakes in Chile and Brazil. He also opened missions in Ecuador and Colombia. Later Elder Hinckley supervised missions in Germany, Switzerland, Austria, and Italy, as well as scattered groups in the Middle East and Africa.

Meanwhile, during the first decade of his service in the Twelve, Elder Hinckley filled numerous headquarters assignments, including membership on the BYU Board of Trustees, the Church Board of Education, the Church Information Committee, the Correlation Executive Committee, the Military Relations Committee, and the Missionary Executive Committee. He also served as chairman of the Priesthood Committee, chairman of the Children's Correlation Committee, and as an adviser to the Primary and the Sunday School. Moreover, during this same period, he became president of the *Deseret News* and served on the boards of the Newspaper Agency Corporation, the Beneficial Life Insurance Company, Zion's First National Bank, Utah Power & Light Company, radio station WNYW in New York, radio and television station KIRO in Seattle, Bonneville International Corporation, and the radio and television station KSL in Salt Lake City. As regards the last two, he also served as a member of the executive committee; and he served as committee chairman and chairman of the board for Bonneville International Corporation.

A highlight of Elder Hinckley's service under President Joseph Fielding Smith was attendance at the first area conference of the Church, held in Manchester, England, in August 1971. During the conference, he and President Spencer W. Kimball, then Acting President of the Twelve, traveled to nearby Preston to visit again the key historic sites connected with the first missionary effort there in 1837, which President Kimball's grandfather Heber C. Kimball had directed.

A year later, in September 1972, President Harold B. Lee, who had succeeded President Joseph Fielding Smith in July following President Smith's death, invited Elder Hinckley to accompany him to Europe and the Holy Land, his first overseas trip after becoming the President of the Church. A special bond tied this pair together. In 1936, when Harold B. Lee became managing director of Church welfare, he was assigned an office next to Gordon Hinckley on the second floor of the Church Administration Building. Gordon had commenced working with the Radio, Publicity, and Mission Literature Committee the year before. For five years afterward, they worked side by side as headquarters staff personnel until Brother Lee was called to the Twelve in 1941. In Jerusalem, following visits in London and Athens, President Lee became severely stressed from a lung congestion that caused violent coughing. After Elder Hinckley administered to him, the prophet expelled two blood clots, which gave him relief. President Lee considered the incident to be "a miracle in this land of even greater miracles."

Elder Hinckley also accompanied President Lee on his last overseas trip. In August 1973 the prophet invited Gordon and Marjorie to accompany him and his wife on an eight-day trip following the area conference in Munich, Germany. Meetings were held on the continent and in England, including meetings with members and missionaries and with workers at the London Temple. Four months later, President Lee died unexpectedly. Elder Hinckley was one of the principal speakers at his funeral, eulogizing the friend and companion whom he had welcomed to the Church Administration Building almost forty years before.

Elder Hinckley served as the first chairman of the Special Affairs Committee and as an adviser to the Department of Public Communications during most of the 1970s and until 1981, when he was called to the First Presidency. In these positions he played a key role in several Church initiatives affecting the public and having moral implications. Chief among these were the contest over the Equal

Rights Amendment (ERA) and the fights against pornography and liquor-by-the-drink legislation in Utah.

The Church opposition to the ERA was not founded on a denial of women's rights but on the conviction that both men and women were already guaranteed full civil rights under the Constitution and that passage of the amendment would create needless confusion and might lead to interpretations on abortion, homosexuality, and other issues pressed by radical feminists that would be contrary to the teachings of the Church.

The Church also feared that a failure to restrict pornography would increase problems such as immorality, sexual deviancy, and crime. Elder Hinckley and his committee worked aggressively on these issues with significant success. It is believed that the nationwide influence of the Church, exerted through the Special Affairs Committee, was a major factor leading to the defeat of the ERA.

Elder Hinckley was called as a third counselor to President Spencer W. Kimball in July 1981. Earlier there were incidents that suggested the prophet's confidence in Elder Hinckley and that foreshadowed his call to the First Presidency: Elder Hinckley accompanied President Kimball to Fayette, New York, for the events connected with the sesquicentennial celebration of the Church in April 1980. There Elder Hinckley read a proclamation to the world from the First Presidency and the Twelve. In March 1981 Elder Hinckley accompanied the prophet to Washington, D.C., for a personal interview with President Ronald Reagan. In May 1981 a statement crafted by Elder Hinckley and the Special Affairs Committee, opposing construction of the MX missile site in western Utah and eastern Nevada, was approved and signed by the First Presidency.

When Elder Hinckley was called to the First Presidency, all three of its members had serious physical problems, although their mentality was unimpaired: President Kimball, in addition to long-standing heart, throat, and other problems, had undergone two recent operations for subdural hematomas; President Tanner suffered from Parkinson's disease and was losing his sight; and President Romney was quite feeble and practically blind. Thus the responsibility to carry on the day-to-day work of the First Presidency fell largely on President Hinckley, acting under delegations of authority from the prophet. That responsibility increased markedly when President Tanner died on November 27, 1982, and President Hinckley became chairman of the Budget Committee, the Personnel Committee, and the Investment Committee. These added responsibilities had a crushing effect at first, causing weariness and a sense of oppression at the ever-mounting problems. The crisis came to a head in February 1983, when one morning, upon entering his office and seeing the large volume of paperwork on his desk, President Hinckley fell to his knees and implored God for strength and direction. In answer there came into his mind the words "Be still and know that I am God" (Doctrine and Covenants 101:16), and with that came a calm assurance that the problems would be solved in time and one at a time.

During the years President Hinckley served as a counselor to President Spencer W. Kimball, he walked a fine line. He was careful not to exceed the limits of his delegated authority. Yet he was unwilling to allow the Church to drift or stagnate. As a result, several major initiatives were undertaken that originated with him but were endorsed and authorized by President Kimball.

In March 1982, for instance, three executive councils were created and given policy jurisdiction over headquarters organizations falling under the captions of Missionary, Priesthood, and Temple and Genealogy Work. Also the ecclesiastical units throughout the world were divided into three groups, with each executive council having jurisdiction over one of them. Originally each council was composed of three members of the Twelve, two members of the

Presidency of the Seventy, and a member of the Presiding Bishopric, with a member of the First Presidency as chairman. Later, members of the Twelve were appointed chairmen. At this time the Coordinating Council was dissolved. This action simplified and improved headquarters administration and provided a direct-line access to specified General Authorities from the field. Any matter an executive council could not resolve was referred to the Twelve or to the Council of the First Presidency and the Twelve.

The international administration of the Church was further improved in August 1984 when the world was divided into thirteen areas, each to be presided over by an Area Presidency composed of three members of the Seventy. In time the directors of temporal affairs in the international areas were placed directly under the Area Presidencies.

These two key changes provided for greater integration and control of the administrative machinery of the Church while allowing for more latitude and independence in the field as the Area Presidencies were able to provide direct and consistent supervision on the ground. And the format was flexible so that as the Church grew, new areas were created by divisions.

As these changes were implemented and as the work moved forward, President Hinckley reported regularly to President Kimball, keeping him fully advised and seeking his direction on any matters beyond the scope of his delegated authority. And he regularly briefed the Twelve so that all were apprised of the status of affairs.

Beginning with the April general conference in 1983, President Hinckley called on President Ezra Taft Benson, president of the Quorum of the Twelve, to conduct some of the sessions and to carry a heavier speaking load. A few months later he also invited President Benson to meet with him weekly as he considered sensitive cases dealing with temple blessings and appeals from judgments of local disciplinary councils.

The effective manner in which the Church continued to progress, despite the disabilities of two members of the First Presidency, is a testament to the inspired nature of the Church organization, the apostolic unity among the First Presidency and the Twelve, and the skill and persistence of Gordon B. Hinckley.

These qualities were clearly evident as he handled a wide variety of duties with composure. For instance, in August 1982 he dedicated twelve of the restored homes in Nauvoo; a few weeks later he hosted President Ronald Reagan in visiting a Church cannery in Utah; on April 3, 1983, he rededicated the Assembly Hall on Temple Square; two days later he dedicated the N. Eldon Tanner Building on the BYU campus; and in September 1984 again hosted a visit to Salt Lake City by President Reagan. President Hinckley spoke at many funerals, including those of President Tanner and Elder Bruce R. McConkie, and was the featured speaker at special Church and civic gatherings. During the same period, he was often away from Salt Lake City dedicating or rededicating temples in various parts of the world; and in the spring of 1984 he held a series of solemn assemblies in which priesthood leaders were given special instruction. He continued to serve on the board of directors of many Church-owned or Church-controlled corporations, as well as on the boards of the Utah Power and Light Company and Zion's First National Bank.

This hectic routine ended with the death of President Spencer W. Kimball on November 5, 1985. Soon after, Elder Hinckley was called as First Counselor to President Ezra Taft Benson. Although he was eighty-six years old at the time, President Benson was in relatively good health and was able to lead out. And President Thomas S. Monson, the other counselor, was in excellent health and was a seasoned and able leader after having served for twenty-two years as a member of the Twelve. For a while this First Presidency functioned in a normal way with each member assuming his share of the duties. Later when President Benson's health began to wane, it became necessary for the counselors to pick up most of the presidential duties, which they performed under delegations of authority from the prophet. For President Hinckley, the burden of responsibility was lighter than before because President Monson was there to share the load.

During this period, a vicious campaign of vilification was waged against President Hinckley by a group of apostates and enemies of the Church. Their efforts were thwarted when a committee of the Twelve employed a distinguished nonmember attorney to study the charges. Using a team of investigators, the attorney found they were based on lies and misrepresentations. Yet the affair took its toll on President Hinckley and his family, who were stressed by the nature and the unfairness of the attacks. In retrospect, the incident appears to have been but another link in the chain of events qualifying Gordon B. Hinckley to occupy the prophetic office.

Following the death of President Ezra Taft Benson on May 30, 1994, President Hinckley was called as First Counselor to President Howard W. Hunter. This role was essentially the same as the one he served under President Benson. But it was one of much shorter duration, for President Hunter died on March 3, 1995. President Hinckley loved Howard W. Hunter. They sat side by side in the circle of Apostles for twenty years. "A majestic tree in the forest has fallen," said President Hinckley at the funeral, "leaving a place of emptiness. A great and quiet strength has departed from our midst."

In accord with custom, the Twelve gathered in the upper room of the temple on Sunday, March 12, to consider the reorganization of the First Presidency. There Gordon B. Hinckley was sustained and ordained as the fifteenth President of the Church. He selected Thomas S. Monson and James E. Faust as his counselors. The next morning the new prophet faced members of the media at a press conference in the Joseph Smith Memorial Building. He responded patiently and eloquently to many questions. He did not announce any new initiatives. He merely said he intended to build on the foundations laid by his predecessors. He said he would do this in a spirit of faith and optimism. "You can't, you don't, build out of pessimism or cynicism," he told the audience. His later words and his actions have confirmed this philosophy. He has traveled widely and has spoken often since then. Invariably he sounds a note of happiness and optimism. Occasionally his remarks contain nuances of a wry and uplifting sense of humor.

Except for these initial hints, it is too early to see the outlines of President Gordon B. Hinckley's prophetic ministry. However, one significant step has been taken already whose impact on the Church will be profound. Effective August 15, 1995, the office of Regional Representative of the Twelve was eliminated to be replaced by the office of Area Authority. The Area Authorities, who will serve for a period of years while continuing their normal occupations, will be line officers functioning under the direction of Area Presidencies. Already, some Area Authorities have been designated as members of Area Presidencies.

Whatever form President Hinckley's prophetic ministry ultimately takes, it certainly will reflect the qualities of faith, perseverance, and creativity that have marked his life thus far. And his myriad experiences during long years of service at Church headquarters, including the refining and challenging obstacles he has had to overcome along the way, will lend a quality of charitable understanding to the decisions he will be called upon to make.

Many of the fine qualities seen in the character of President Gordon B. Hinckley have been enhanced, if not molded, within his family circle. He and Sister Hinckley are the parents of five children: Kathleen, Richard, Virginia, Clark, and Jane. Well educated and happily married, they all are building strong Latter-day Saint families. Despite the aura of distinction surrounding their ancestry and the achievements of their husband and father, they have maintained attitudes free from conceit or vanity. Their gatherings are marked by the same jovial feelings that existed when President Hinckley was relatively unknown throughout the Church. The gentle humor and the love evident among them is illustrated by an incident arising from the trauma he faced while trying to pare down the size of his library in the move to a condominium. At the time his wife, Marjorie, was heard to say, "You would think he would be able to give up his eighth-grade algebra book, wouldn't you?" The incident may provide a metaphor for the future—a reluctance to part with things of the past combined with a willingness to make changes that circumstances require.

NOTE

This chapter is based on manuscripts covering the lives and families of Ira Nathaniel Hinckley, Bryant S. Hinckley, and Ada Bitner Hinckley; diaries of Francis M. Gibbons, 1970–95; miscellaneous articles in the *Ensign* and the *Church News;* and George F. Willison's book *Saints and Strangers* (New York: Reynal and Hitchcock, 1945).

INDEX

341

Kimball, Alice (wife of JFS). *See* Smith, Alice Kimball
Kimball, Andrew (son of SWK), 267, 270
Kimball, Andrew (father of SWK), 146, 261, 262, 266
Kimball, Camilla Eyring (wife of SWK), 265–69, 273–76. *See also* Kimball, Spencer Woolley
Kimball, Clare, 265
Kimball, Edward, 267, 270
Kimball, Gordon, 265
Kimball, Heber C.: joins Church, 34; serves mission to England, 12, 38; hears doctrine of plural marriage, 23; serves as counselor to BY, 45, 94; prophesies of HJG, 155; dies, 100; is grandfather of SWK, 261
Kimball, J. Golden, 177, 261, 264
Kimball, Josephine Cluff, 263, 266
Kimball, LeVan, 267, 270
Kimball, Mary Connelly, 266
Kimball, Olive Beth (daughter of SWK), 266
Kimball, Olive Woolley (mother of SWK), 261–63
Kimball, Spencer LeVan, 266
Kimball, Spencer Woolley (SWK), 12th President of Church: early life of, 146, 261–64; serves in Central States Mission, 224, 264; marries Camilla, 265; early employment of, 266–67; tours Europe, 268–69; serves as stake president, 246; applies welfare principles, 269–70; is called to the Twelve, 174, 189, 246, 270, 290; health problems of, 253, 272–75, 277,

281; works with Lamanites, 192, 272–73; tours Europe and South America, 273–77, 332; serves as President of the Twelve, 277; becomes President of the Church, 278, 299, 316; dedicates temples and makes organizational changes, 278–80; receives revelation of the priesthood, 280, 299; calls GBH as counselor, 334; death of, 281
Kimball, Vilate, 34
King, V., 138
Kington, Thomas, 39, 88
Kinney, John F., 51, 97
Kirtland Safety Society Bank, 12, 36, 61, 112
Kirtland Temple: dedication of, 11–12, 86; ordinances for, 23
Kirtland, Ohio, 9
Knight, John M., 241–42
Knight, Joseph, 8
Knight, Newell, 8
Komatsu, Adney Y., 205
Korean War, 330

L'Etoile du Deseret, 70
Lamanite Committee, 272
Lambson, Edna, 137
Lambson, Julina. *See* Smith, Julina Lambson
Lane, Reverend, 2–4
Law, William, 27, 65
Lee, Fern Tanner (wife of HBL), 241–42, 245, 247, 251, 254–55. *See also* Lee, Harold Bingham
Lee, Freda Joan Jensen (wife of HBL), 241, 255, 257, 259–60. *See also* Lee, Harold Bingham
Lee, Harold Bingham (HBL), 11th President of Church: early life of, 238–40, 284; serves in Western States

Smith, John, 225

Smith, Joseph (son of JFS Jr.), 225

Smith, Joseph F. (JFS), 6th President of Church: early life of, 132–33, 217; called to Hawaii mission, 134; marries, is called to the British mission, 135–36; on second mission to Hawaii, 118, 136–37; enters into plural marriage, 137, 216–17, 262; is called to the Twelve, 138; presides over European mission, 138–39; goes on historical mission to the East, 139–40; called as counselor to JT, 78, 105; in exile to Hawaii, 141–42; returns from exile, 83, 142; called as counselor to WW, 108, 143; after the Manifesto, 144; preaches tithing faithfulness, 145–46; sustained as President of the Church, 146; dedicates monument to JS, 146–47; tours northern Europe, 148; is falsely charged, 148–49; travels extensively, 150–53; has vision of spirit world, 153–54, 224; blesses HJG, 169; death of, 154, 180, 224

Smith, Joseph Fielding (JFS Jr.), 10th President of Church: early life of, 216–17; marries and is called to Great Britain mission, 218–19; works in Church Historian's Office, 220–21; writings of, 221; remarries and is called to the Twelve, 222; serves as secretary to JFS, 224; serves as Church Historian, 225; marries Jessie, 227; tours

Pacific, England, and Europe, 228–29; becomes President of Salt Lake Temple and then President of Twelve, 231; travels extensively, 232–34; serves as counselor to DOM, 215, 234; is sustained as President of the Church, 235, 256, 277, 298, 314, 316; makes organizational changes in Church, 235–36, 256–57; death of, 237, 257, 277

Smith, Joseph Richards, 139, 216, 219

Smith, Joseph, III, 24, 135, 140, 224

Smith, Joseph, Jr. (JS), 1st President of Church: early religious experiences of, 1–3; First Vision of, 3–4; is visited by Moroni, 4–5; works for Stowell, 5; retrieves gold plates, 5; translates gold plates, 6–7; is baptized and receives priesthood, 7; organizes Church, 8; meets BY, 34–35; receives revelations, 9–14; suffers persecution, 10–11; involved in failed Kirtland Bank, 12, 36, 61; calls JT to Twelve, 61; forms Zion's Camp, 15–16, 35, 85; explores Adam-ondi-Ahman, 16–17; charges against, 17–19, 24–25, 89; in Liberty Jail, 19–20, 37; establishes Nauvoo, 20; seeks redress in Washington, D.C., 21–22; creates city charter for Nauvoo, 22; introduces plural marriage, 23–24, 82; runs for President of U.S., 25–26, 64–65; conspired against from within Church,